D0909863

The Games War

A MOSCOW JOURNAL

also by Christopher Booker

THE NEOPHILIACS

GOODBYE LONDON
(with Candida Lycett-Green)

THE BOOKER QUIZ

THE SEVENTIES

CHRISTOPHER BOOKER

The Games War

A MOSCOW JOURNAL

FABER AND FABER
London & Boston

First published in 1981
by Faber and Faber Limited
3 Queen Square London WC1N 3AU
Printed in Great Britain by
Fakenham Press Limited
Fakenham, Norfolk
All rights reserved

British Library Cataloguing in Publication Data

Booker, Christopher
The games war.
1. Olympic games, Moscow, 1980
2. Sports and state
I. Title
796.4'8'09048   GV722   1980
ISBN 0–571–11755–4
ISBN 0–571–11763–5 Pbk

For Nicholas

The lack of bitter experience of people in the West
makes them incapable of imagining tragedy.

VLADIMIR BUKOVSKY,
BBC TV, 19 October 1980

Contents

Acknowledgements   *page* 13

Prologue   15

PART ONE
The Road to Moscow (1974–1980)

1. Mr Nixon's Legacy   21

2. Ring Round the Moon   30

PART TWO
The Looking-glass Olympics (16 July–4 August 1980)

3. Through the Looking-glass   45

4. First Impressions   55

5. Something Good in Everything You See   66

6. The Games Open—A Lesson in Crowd Control   74

7. Inside the Bubble   84

8. Settling Down   94

9. In the Compression Chamber   106

10. The Lie at the Heart of the Soviet Union   119

11. Comrade Popov's Thinking 'In the Correct
    Direction'   131

12. Blunts and Smudges   137

13. British Weekend at the Lenin Stadium   145

Contents

14. Visit to an Occupied Country *page* 157

15. A Little Mild Hysteria 171

16. Pilgrimage to Peredelkino 179

17. The Flame Goes Out 192

PART THREE
The Road From Moscow (August–December 1980)

18. From the Lenin Stadium to the Lenin Shipyard 207

19. Remember Kronstadt 217

20. The End of the Road 223

Index 229

Acknowledgements

A number of books have been particularly useful to me in attempting to unravel the mysteries of life in the Soviet Union. While I was in the USSR I was especially grateful to the superb *Blue Guide to Moscow and Leningrad* (Ernest Benn, 1980), edited by Evan and Margaret Mawdsley; and also to Hedrick Smith's masterly guide to the labyrinth of Soviet life, *The Russians* (Times Books, Sphere, 1976). For the chapter 'British Weekend at the Lenin Stadium' I drew heavily on *The Soviet Road to Olympus: Theory and Practice of Soviet Physical Culture and Sport* by N. Norman Shneidman (Routledge, Kegan Paul, 1979); and similarly, for the chapter 'Visit to an Occupied Country', on Andres Kung's *A Dream of Freedom: Four Decades of National Survival versus Russian Imperialism in Estonia, Latvia and Lithuania 1940–80* (Boreas Publishing House, 1980). I would like to thank the authors and publishers of all these books, both for permission to quote and for all I learned from them.

I am also most grateful for what I have drawn from the following books (and where appropriate would like to thank the publishers for permission to quote): *What I Saw in Russia* by Maurice Baring (Nelson, 1905); *Russia in the Shadows* by H. G. Wells (Hodder and Stoughton, 1920); *Through Bolshevik Russia* by Mrs Philip Snowden (Cassell, 1920); *The Practice and Theory of Bolshevism* by Bertrand Russell (George Allen and Unwin, 1920); *Ten Days That Shook The World* by John Reed (Communist Party of Great Britain, 1926, Penguin Books, 1966); *Memoirs of a British Agent* by R. H. Bruce Lockhart (Putnam, 1932); *Russia* by Bernard Pares (Penguin, 1940); *Nineteen Eighty-four* by George Orwell (Secker and Warburg, 1949); *Eastern Approaches* by Fitzroy Maclean (Jonathan Cape, 1949); *Dr Zhivago* by Boris Pasternak (translated by Max Hayward and Manya Harari, Collins and Harvill Press, 1958); *Journey into Russia* by Laurens van der Post (Hogarth Press, 1964); *Message from Moscow* by 'An Observer' (Jonathan Cape, 1969); *Lenin* by Robert

Acknowledgements

Conquest (Fontana Modern Master, 1972); *Letters to Soviet Leaders* by Alexander Solzhenitsyn (Collins, 1974); *To Build a Castle* by Vladimir Bukovsky (André Deutsch, 1978); *Sport in the USSR* by James Riordan (Collet's, 1979); Fodor's *1980 Guide to the Soviet Union* (1980); and *Journey for Our Time: The Journals of the Marquis de Custine* (originally published as *Letters from Russia*, 1843, republished in 1980 (in translation by Phyllis Penn Kohler) by George Prior Publishers).

Thanks are also due to those responsible for the various Soviet publications from which I have quoted, and to which attribution is made in the text where appropriate.

My special thanks are also due to a number of people without whom this book could never have been written and published: notably to John Bryant, Features Editor of the *Daily Mail*, and David English, Editor of the *Daily Mail*, without whom I would never have gone to Moscow in the first place. I was most grateful while in the Soviet Union for the presence of various of my colleagues, notably Ian Wooldridge, Frank Keating, Peter Hildreth, David Miller and Ian Jack who helped in more ways than they can know; also for Valeriy Golovin and others I have not named. I would like to thank James Bishop and Barbara Kingston for help with copying; also, for invaluable help in various ways, Masha Slonim, Christine Booker, Serena Booker and Bennie Gray; and, finally, for their love and patience, Valerie and Nicholas.

Prologue

When one has seen a thing which had hitherto been vaguely
familiar suddenly illuminated by a flood of light, making it real,
living and vivid, it is difficult to recall one's state of mind before
the inrush of the illuminating flood; and still more difficult to
discuss that thing with people who have not had the opportunity
of illumination . . . I find it extremely difficult to recall what I
thought Russia was like before I had been there; and I find
Russia difficult to describe to people who have not been there.
There is so much when one has been there that becomes so soon
a matter of course that it no longer strikes one, but which to the
newcomer is probably striking . . .

Maurice Baring, *What I Saw in Russia* (1905)

The Moscow Olympic Games in the summer of 1980 aroused more
controversy than any sporting event in history. For some, including
their organizers, they were intended to be the ultimate demonstration
that 'sport is above politics'. They ended up, for many, bearing out
Orwell's dictum that 'international sport is war without the shooting'.
For evermore the Moscow Olympics will inescapably be recalled as
the Games which took place 'in the year of Afghanistan and Poland'.

When I went out to Moscow to cover the Olympics I had no
intention of writing anything more than a series of newspaper articles.
But within days of arriving I found myself witnessing an event so
extraordinary on so many levels, that I felt I had to write a book about
it.

Others who were in Moscow may have had the same reaction. If so,
I look forward to reading what they have to say—because I should
warn that, as its semi-journal form might suggest, this is an intensely
personal view of what was going on.

Sports enthusiasts will certainly find many references to the sporting events, such as the celebrated duels in the Lenin Stadium between

Britain's two top middle-distance runners, Sebastian Coe and Steve Ovett. But this book is not centrally concerned with sport. I have tried to set the sporting content of the Moscow Games in a much wider context. Right from the start, the decision to stage an Olympic Games in the heart of the Communist world was bound to ensure that they would be like none of their predecessors. With the Soviet invasion of Afghanistan, that became doubly certain.

Although I had visited the Soviet Union before, I was in no way prepared for the overwhelming experience that I found being in Moscow during that historic fortnight to be. I found that it provoked the deepest reflections on the nature of Communism, of sport, of Russia, of truth and falsehood, on human nature itself, which continued to echo in my mind long after the experience itself was over.

When I returned to England, many people asked, 'What was it really like in Moscow?' I could only reply, 'It is almost impossible to describe.' But in this book I have tried. I hope it will read like a continuous story, which at times travels very far from the Olympics themselves—but, as is only appropriate, I begin with the strange tale of how it was that the 22nd Olympic Games came to be staged in Moscow in the first place . . .

PART ONE

The Road to Moscow

1974–1980

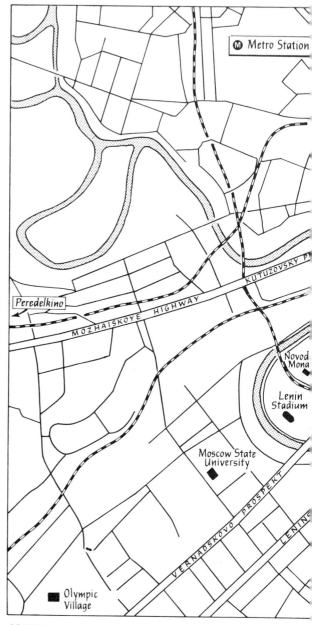

OLYMPIC MOSCOW

I

Mr Nixon's Legacy

The city of Moscow has seen many strange arrivals by foreigners in the sixty-odd years since the 1917 Revolution—but few can have been quite so bizarre as that which took place on 27 June 1974.

The grey, haggard figure who came to the door of the American air force jet when it taxied to a halt at Vnukovo Airport, twenty miles south-west of Moscow, was a different man from the smiling, confident Head of State who had last arrived there two years before. It was hardly surprising that Richard Nixon looked tired and strained. For eighteen months the shadows of Watergate had been lengthening over his Presidency to the point where it seemed he could not survive much longer. Increasingly, as he found himself trapped at home in a threatening twilight, he had sought consolation in playing out his role on the world stage. Here at least he could still imagine himself a great man, he could convince himself that he still had a contribution to make, particularly in pursuing that policy to which he devoted so much of his last two years in office, *détente* between East and West.

On his visit to the Soviet Union in those closing days of June and early July 1974, President Nixon enjoyed his last ghostly fling as a world leader. He was given a magnificent reception in Tsar Nicholas I's Great Kremlin Palace, beneath the gilded chandeliers of the white-and-gold Hall of St George, looking down over the Moscow River. He had talks with his old friend First Secretary Leonid Brezhnev at Brezhnev's palatial villa at Yalta on the Black Sea. Their discussions ran through all the familiar stock-in-trade of *détente*—arms limitation, grain sales, technical exchanges. There was not much Nixon could now do, but cross the t's and dot the i's on matters already agreed at a lower level.

But there was one other little matter which Mr Brezhnev was particularly anxious to discuss. It had already come up on the secret agenda when the two men had met the previous year in the United States. The date was soon approaching when the International

Olympic Committee was due to choose which city should have the honour of staging the 1980 Olympic Games. There were only two likely contenders, Los Angeles and Moscow. And Mr Brezhnev dearly wanted the choice to fall on Moscow.

To say that the Soviet leadership was desperately keen to secure the 1980 Olympics for Moscow is to put it mildly. There was almost no prize on the international stage they coveted more. Even in the West the Olympic Games were commonly referred to as 'the greatest show on earth'. But in the Soviet Union, in the twenty-odd years since Soviet competitors had made their sensational debut in the 1952 Olympics at Helsinki (when they immediately came equal top with the United States in the unofficial 'points table'), the Games had been deliberately built up to an importance few Westerners can imagine. For Mr Brezhnev and his ageing colleagues, to win the chance to stage the Olympics in Moscow would be a triumph. They had already been turned down once, back in 1970, when their application to play host to the 1976 Games had been rejected in favour of Montreal. But, as the Soviet leaders well knew, an Olympics in Moscow would be more than just another Games, more than just a sporting occasion. It would be a symbol, both to the world at large and to the multitude of peoples over whom those leaders held sway. It would be a chance to show off Moscow and the glorious achievements of Russian Socialism in a way that had not been possible in all the sixty years since the Revolution. It would be almost like a last act of legitimation, a belated coronation ceremony for the Soviet regime and all it stood for.

Although it was never, of course, mentioned in the communiqué at the end of their talks, Nixon gave Mr Brezhnev his private assurance that everything would be all right. Los Angeles could wait. There were ways and means of arranging these things. Moscow would get the Games.

Barely three weeks later, after he had flown back to Washington, President Nixon was faced with three articles of impeachment by the House of Representatives. On 5 August he finally admitted, in the face of new evidence from the tapes, that he had known about the Watergate cover-up, and on 8 August he resigned. But steps had already been taken to ensure that his last promise to Mr Brezhnev would be kept.*

* I have attempted to reconstruct the curious story of how Moscow came to be chosen as the site of the 1980 Olympics from a number of public and private sources. I suspect

In October that year, representatives of sixty-one countries on the International Olympic Committee met in Vienna to make their decision about the venue of the 1980 Games. They knew that the Soviet Union had been pulling out all the stops for Moscow. The lessons of the 1970 failure had been learned. Over the previous two years, millions of roubles had been spent on flying the world's leading sports officials and sporting journalists to the Soviet Union in a lavish public relations exercise, to enjoy Soviet hospitality and to inspect the country's superb new sporting facilities, such as the rowing canal built for the 1973 World Championships at Krylatskoye on the outskirts of Moscow, and claimed to be the best in the world.

Indeed, on the face of it, it might have seemed extraordinary that there should be any argument over the Soviet Union's right to play host to an Olympic Games. Ever since their debut in 1952, Soviet competitors had dominated the Olympics. Except in 1968, when they came second to the United States in Mexico City (and to Norway in that year's Winter Olympics), the Soviet Union had never failed to come top of the unofficial 'points table' published by the *Olympic Bulletin*—in other words, on eleven out of thirteen possible occasions.

Yet the fact remained that there were still doubts in many foreigners' minds as to whether Moscow could stage the Games properly. Many people had been particularly shocked by what had happened the year before in 1973, when Moscow had played host to the World Student Games. Journalists had been appalled by the inefficiency of telephone and telex services, the security checks, the delays in publishing results. Athletes had been appalled by the poor standard of their accommodation, the inedible food. Most shocking of all, however, had been the treatment of competitors from Israel (less than a year after the deaths of eleven Israeli athletes in the 'Black September' terrorist incident at the Munich Olympics). At the Luzhniki Stadium the Moscow crowd had openly booed, whistled and hooted as the Israeli team made its appearance. Whenever Israeli sportsmen had performed, the harassment had continued. At one football match in particular it was quite clear to Western observers that the anti-Israeli demonstration was officially organized, led by young Red Army soldiers in civilian clothes who had occupied ringside seats all round the stadium.

---

that a good many further details will emerge when Lord Killanin, Chairman of the International Olympic Committee from 1973–80, publishes his memoirs.

The Road to Moscow (1974–1980)

All this weighed in the minds of the Olympic Committee members as they met under their new Chairman, the sixty-year-old hereditary Irish peer and Old Etonian ex-journalist Lord Killanin. Nevertheless, they had to admit that they were impressed by the hugely thorough presentation made by the city of Moscow, more elaborate than any put forward by a claimant city before. Not only did the Russian organizers provide piles of paperwork, giving exhaustive details of the preparations that would be made to ensure that Moscow laid on the most lavish and efficient facilities ever seen at an Olympic Games; they even included scale models of the array of stadiums, arenas and courses in which the Games would be staged.

In contrast, the presentation made by the city of Los Angeles on the other side of the room seemed strangely muted and tatty. In the words of one delegate, 'They just didn't seem to be trying. They didn't show us much more than a few tourist brochures, some out-of-date photographs of the city and an album of snapshots of competitors at the last Los Angeles Games in 1932.'

In the light of the inescapable disparity between the two presentations, the verdict was a foregone conclusion. Just before 9.30 on the morning of 23 October 1974, the world's pressmen filed into the splendid mock-Gothic setting of the Vienna Rathaus. At precisely 9.37 Lord Killanin opened the proceedings by leaning into a microphone and announcing, 'Good morning. The city selected to hold the 22nd Olympiad is Moscow.' President Nixon's last promise to Mr Brezhnev had been kept.

The world's reaction to the choice of Moscow was almost universally favourable. The problems over the World Student Games were forgotten. In London *The Times* pronounced in measured tones: 'It is on balance good that Moscow has been chosen as the meeting place for the 1980 Summer Games.' The *Guardian* spoke even more warmly: 'The achievements of Soviet sportsmen are so great that Moscow should long since have received the right to organize the Olympics and the IOC should have taken such a decision earlier.' The *Daily Mirror*, in the more robust traditions of popular journalism, simply told its readers: 'IT'S CAVIAR AND VODKA FOR THE PEOPLE'S GAMES.'

But 1980 was still a long way off. A lot of water had to flow under the bridge before the world had once again to consider what taking the road to Moscow might actually involve.

The policy of *détente*, that mood of relaxation which had so changed the world's political climate in the early seventies, of course survived the fall of Richard Nixon. In November 1974 the new American President, Gerald Ford, flew to Vladivostok to agree with Mr Brezhnev on new plans for nuclear arms limitation. The following February, just two days after Margaret Thatcher had succeeded Edward Heath as leader of the Conservative Party, the British Prime Mir ster, Harold Wilson, flew to Moscow to offer the Russians an unprecedented trade deal, a billion pounds-worth of low interest credit to buy British goods. In July 1975, the eyes of the world were focussed on what seemed to be the crowning symbolic ceremony of the *détente* years—the link-up in space between an American Apollo spacecraft and a Soviet Soyuz. In Helsinki, the signing of the Final Act of the Conference on Security and Co-Operation in Europe similarly seemed to crown six years of continuous negotiation, over a whole range of matters from arms limitation to human rights.

After the traumatic years of Vietnam and Watergate, the West seemed weary of conflict, eager for a period of respite and co-operation. The extraordinary events of March and April 1975 when, in only a few weeks, Communist forces overran South Vietnam, Laos and Cambodia seemed a long way away—an almost inevitable outcome to those thirty frustrating years of struggle in Indo-China which had left, first France, then even America herself exhausted.

To the leaders of the Soviet Union, a year after the choice of Moscow to hold the Olympic Games, the world looked good. They could afford to shrug off as little more than a pinprick the award of a Nobel Peace Prize to Andrei Sakharov who, since their unceremonious expulsion of Alexander Solzhenitsyn to the West the previous year, was the only dissident of world stature left in Russia. Things were going their way.

The year 1976 opened with the lightning take-over of the mineral-rich former Portuguese colony of Angola by the Soviet-backed MPLA—the Russians' first real political stake in southern Africa. Mr Brezhnev marked the growing expansion of his country's military and naval might across the world by taking the title of Marshal of the Soviet Union, the first political leader to hold such military rank since Stalin. In November he got rid of another troublesome dissident, by trading Vladimir Bukovsky to the West in exchange for the veteran Chilean Communist Louis Corvalan, who was given a hero's welcome in Moscow. There was also, of course, the Montreal Olympic Games, overshadowed as no Olympics before by controversy, political and otherwise.

The keynote of the 1976 Olympics seemed to be chaos—from chaos over Montreal's preparations (there were even last minute doubts as to whether the Olympic Stadium would be completed in time) to chaos over who should be allowed to participate. Western countries raised scarcely a cheep of protest over the expulsion of Taiwan, in deference to the wishes of Communist China (even though there was no Chinese team in Montreal). Twenty-eight African nations walked out in protest against the fact that New Zealand had recently played rugby against South Africa (even though rugby was not an Olympic sport). There were rows over drugs, over professionalism, over commercial sponsorship (which had never been so much in evidence). A Russian fencer, Boris Onishchenko, was disqualified for cheating. It was altogether a Games which, for many people, left unpleasant memories. However, by the time the giant scoreboard in the stadium flashed up the words 'FAREWELL MONTREAL, TILL WE MEET IN MOSCOW', one country at least could take cheer from the way things had gone. Not only had the Soviet Union once again topped the points table with a record 125 medals, but for the first time the USA was not even runner-up, having been pushed into third place by East Germany. As all the world could see, Eastern bloc countries had taken seven out of the first ten places. Never had the triumphs of 'Socialist sport' shone more brightly.

In 1977, the hitherto unknown ex-Governor of Georgia, Jimmy Carter, was inaugurated as President of the United States. Leonid Brezhnev marked the introduction of a new Constitution for the USSR by stepping up to replace Nikolai Podgorny as President of the Soviet Union. Soviet-backed forces of the newly Marxist Ethiopian Republic pushed towards the Horn of Africa, threatening Russian control of both shores of the Red Sea, on the vital oil route between Europe and the Persian Gulf. But despite expressions of growing alarm in the West at just what the Soviet Government was up to (notably from the new leader of Britain's Conservative Party, Mrs Thatcher, who had already been dubbed 'the Iron Lady' by the Soviet press), it was not really until the following year that there came the first flicker of trouble to disturb the outward amity of *détente*.

Curiously enough, what aroused the Western governments was not the news in April 1978 of a Soviet-backed coup in the faraway little country of Afghanistan, and the seizure of power there by a Marxist government. The West remained markedly unmoved by this news. What did provoke intense Western interest, however, were the growing number of reports that the Soviet Government was once again moving harshly against dissidents, prominent among them Alexander Ginsburg, the distinguished physicist Professor Yuri Orlov and Dr An: oly Scharansky. Among their other offences in the eyes of Soviet authorities, these men had been involved in the groups which had been set up in various parts of the USSR since 1976 to monitor what they regarded as breaches of the human rights provisions of the 1975 Helsinki Agreement. But this time, Orlov, Scharansky, Ginsburg and their colleagues were not simply expelled, as other prominent dissidents had been in the earlier years of the decade: in the summer of 1978 they were brought to trial and sentenced to savage terms in prison and labour camps—and at last the West stirred out of its *détente* slumbers to protest. The British Foreign Secretary, David Owen, even went so far as to suggest in a television interview that, if the Soviet Government 'continues to suppress human rights', the Russians should not 'take it for granted' that the 1980 Olympics would be held in Moscow. Similar noises in the USA prompted NBC, the company which had negotiated exclusive American rights to televise the Moscow Games, to take out massive insurance on their huge investment. But within a month or two, the fuss died down. The Soviet Government could once again, as it were, relax. And when at the end of 1978 the USSR signed a 'Treaty of Friendship and Co-Operation' with the new Marxist government of Afghanistan, under which Moscow agreed to 'intervene' in Afghan affairs if and when she was invited, most people in the West took even less notice than they had of the *coup d'état* eight months before.

One official Soviet body which could not relax, however, was the Olympics-80 Organizing Committee at its headquarters in an old building in Gorky Street in the heart of Moscow. As 1979 began, after four years of intensive activity, they were just about to move into top gear—and they had already been able to report to the International Olympic Committee that they were further advanced in their preparations than any host-country had previously been at the same stage in the countdown to an Olympics.

It was not just the array of sporting arenas and other facilities that were being prepared in Moscow, Leningrad, Kiev, Minsk and Tallinn, the five 'Olympic cities': these were spectacular enough, even though several of the stadiums, including the centrepiece of them all, the Lenin Stadium at Luzhniki in Moscow itself, had been built for other purposes long before. The Soviet Organizing Committee had a host of other concerns. One of its members, G. P. Goncharov, head of the Propaganda Committee of the Communist Party of the Soviet Union, was superintending the preparation of unprecedented press and television facilities (including a new Television and Radio Centre at Ostankino), to ensure that the Olympics were given the widest and most efficient coverage in history. New highways were being built, a new international telephone exchange, new airport terminals at Sheremetyevo, Vnukovo and Tallinn, as the Soviet Union, and Moscow in particular, prepared for the biggest single influx of foreigners they had ever known—an estimated 300,000, including many from the West.

By September 1979, as exhortatory posters appeared all over Moscow proclaiming, 'We will turn Moscow into a model Communist city', the five Olympic cities were in a fever of preparation. A mass of huge new hotels were nearing completion—half a dozen in Moscow alone, including the massive 'Ismailovo Complex', which consisted of five thirty-two-storey tower blocks, with accommodation for 10,000 guests. Thousands of shabby buildings were being repaired and repainted. Churches which had been falling down for decades disappeared under thickets of scaffolding. Long-dingy cupolas were being regilded. The Muscovites and the inhabitants of the other cities had never seen anything like it. There were even rumours that when the 'Olympic Summer' finally arrived, the shops would be flooded with such an abundance of carefully hoarded food and consumer goods that it would briefly be like 'living in the West'.

But there were also the first indications that the Olympic Games might have a darker side for the Soviet people. On 11 September 1979, it was announced by the Communist Party Central Committee that the coming months would see a major campaign against 'hooliganism, crime, drunkenness and speculation'. In November, dissidents reported a new wave of arrests by the KGB, sweeping up among others the mathematician Tatiana Velikanova, and Father Gleb Yakunin, who had both played key parts in monitoring breaches of the Helsinki agreement on human rights. Prisoners in psychiatric hospitals, like Mykola Plakhotnyuk, a Ukrainian doctor, in confinement for 'anti-Soviet agitation and propaganda', were told that 'until the Olympic Games are over' their cases would not be reconsidered. In December, it was reported that the 'pre-Olympic *chistka*

28

(or 'clean-up')' was spreading out to include hundreds, if not thousands, of people who could not by any usual standards be described as 'dissidents'. All over Moscow, ordinary citizens standing in food queues who had been overheard making even the mildest complaint were being taken off to the nearest police station for 'spreading rumours and falsehoods about Soviet life', and warned that unless their behaviour over the next six months remained impeccable their *propiska*, or permit to remain in Moscow, would be revoked—a harsh punishment indeed, since to live in Moscow is itself one of the greatest privileges in the Soviet Union.

Even so, none of this seemed to stand in the way of the great forthcoming triumph. Already in the West, special articles and television series were beginning to appear—such as the twenty-six-part BBC series *Russia: Language and People*, made especially for the Olympics with the full co-operation of the Soviet authorities—giving Westerners a fairly glowing picture of life in the Soviet Union. But then, on 26 December, just as the West was sunk in the torpor of Christmas celebrations, it was reported that Soviet troops and tanks were pouring into Afghanistan, to prop up the crumbling Marxist regime. On 27 December, it was announced that the Afghan President, Hafizullah Amin, had been 'deposed and executed', and replaced by a Soviet puppet, Babrak Karmal. On the last day of the year—and of the decade of *détente*—representatives of six Western nations met at President Carter's behest in the Foreign Office in London to consider responses to the Afghan crisis. One item on their agenda was a possible boycott of the Soviet Olympics. The road to Moscow was suddenly about to get rough.

2

Ring Round the Moon

New Year's Eve 1979 was intensely cold in the village of Lamyatt in Somerset, where I live. Shortly before midnight I stepped out into the icy village street to see a breathtaking sight. The whole frost-shining landscape of stone cottages and cider orchards around was brilliantly lit by the moon—and round the moon was the brightest and most perfect nimbus of light I had ever seen. It put me in mind of Vaughan's lines

> I saw Eternity the other night,
> Like a great Ring of Pure and Endless Light,
> All calm as it was bright . . .

I called out my neighbours opposite to see this phenomenon and to drink in the New Year, and as the sound of distant church bells rang out across the fields, we mused on the huge ring of light above us and on the prospects for the coming decade. Although we knew that it was only 'suspended ice crystals refracting light in the upper atmosphere', the nimbus seemed like a portent.

We were by no means alone in our sense of foreboding that night. Somehow the end of the seventies and the beginning of the new, unknown decade saw a sea-change in people's feelings towards the future. Suddenly, in a way that had not been true for fifteen years or more, people found themselves talking of the possibilities of a new world war.

The most immediate cause of this new mood of apprehension, of course, was the sharp rise in international tension created by the invasion of Afghanistan. The news that 80,000 Soviet troops were fanning out through that remote country on the edge of the Himalayas, launching wave after wave of attacks with helicopters, tanks and all the sophistication of modern warfare on primitively armed tribesmen, sent as much of a wave of shock across the world as anything since the Red Army went in to Czechoslovakia in 1968 and before that Hungary in 1956. The Russians, it was observed, seemed to suffer from an unfortunate twelve-year itch to invade one of their neighbours—each time, as it happened, in the year of an Olympic Games. The only difference was that the Games were due to be held at the heart of the Soviet empire, in Moscow itself.

On 1 January, at a NATO meeting in Brussels, the West German Government formally proposed that, as part of its response to the Afghan invasion, the West should consider a concerted boycott of the Moscow Games. The following day Sir Denis Follows, Chairman of the British Olympic Association, expressed the feelings of many British athletes when he said, 'We would resist as strongly as we could any attempt by government to interfere with our participating . . . our view is simple, sport is above politics.' A week later an equally fervent counter-view was expressed in London by one of the best-known of the Russian dissidents, Alexander Ginsburg, who had been released from prison in 1979 and was now in exile, and who pointed out that in the Soviet Union politics and sport could not be separated. In his opinion and that of his fellow-dissidents, it would be 'a tremendous mistake' to allow the Olympics to be staged in Moscow. Several Islamic nations began to talk of withdrawal in support of their Afghan co-religionists. Several commercial sponsors in Britain and America announced that they would no longer be supporting their countries' entries. Canada suggested that the Games should return to Montreal. On 14 January, President Carter sent a special envoy to London to discuss with Mrs Thatcher the possibility of a boycott. The battle lines that in succeeding months were to become only too familiar were beginning to appear.

On the morning of 15 January I received a call from John Bryant, the Features Editor of the *Daily Mail*. Would I come up to London to write an article on the boycott for the next day's paper? There had apparently been much talk at that morning's editorial conference about the Berlin Olympics of 1936, and a pile of forty-four-year-old cuttings had been dug out of the library for me to read. Apparently there was also a heated argument raging over the Olympics in the *Mail* offices. On one side were the paper's political writers, headed by Editor David English, who were worked up over Afghanistan and strongly in favour of the boycott. On the other was the sports department, including the well-known columnist Ian Wooldridge, who took the view that sport and politics should be kept as far apart as possible, and were passionately opposed to the boycott. In the light of my views on the Soviet Union, I suspected that I had been called in to represent the 'political' side, and to sound an unequivocal clarion call to the *Mail* readers in favour of pulling out of the Games.

But as I drove that morning over the snow-covered hills of north Somerset to catch the train at Bath, I began to reflect that it was not quite so simple. In all this talk of a boycott, two issues were in danger of getting confused. On the one hand, there was the quite specific question of Afghanistan—and the trouble here was that, if the declared aim of the boycott was to pressure the Soviet Government into withdrawing its invading troops, there was not the slightest chance that it would succeed. Not a single Russian soldier would be withdrawn from Afghanistan in response to an Olympic boycott, and in that specific respect the gesture could only fail.

On the other hand, the real reason why so many people were suddenly in favour of a boycott seemed to be something rather more general: they had woken up to the possibility that the Olympics, as at Berlin in 1936, were going to be used as a huge propaganda exercise to glorify and whitewash a hypocritical, aggressive and inhuman totalitarian regime. The trouble with this argument was that it had been as valid in 1974, when the Games were awarded to Moscow, as it was now in 1980. Why had Western governments accepted the Moscow Games in the first place? If it was the aggressive nature of the Soviet Government that was being objected to, why had that objection not been raised at almost any time in the previous six years, during the most dramatic series of violent, Soviet-backed seizures of power since the years immediately after World War Two—in Vietnam, Laos, Angola, Mozambique, Ethiopia, South Yemen, not to mention of course Afghanistan itself in 1978?

In London the 'boycott row' had grown into the major sensation of the day. The evening newspaper placards proclaimed that an all-party group of sixty MPs had launched a 'Hands Off Afghanistan' campaign, to persuade the International Olympic Committee to switch the Games away from Moscow. As I arrived at the *Daily Mail* offices, Mrs Thatcher was telling a packed House of Commons that the British Government was going to do everything in its power to get the Olympics moved. 'We cannot just stand back and see the Russians do what they have done in Afghanistan, deplore it, and do nothing at all.' Shortly afterwards, Lord Killanin issued a statement on behalf of the

IOC saying that the Games would be held in 'Moscow or nowhere'.

I sat in the *Daily Mail* library and read the yellowing cuttings from 1936—and was fascinated to find an immediate echo. When Hitler had sent his troops into the demilitarized Rhineland in March 1936, one of the first responses of the Western allies, led by France, had been to consider a boycott of the Berlin Olympics later in the year. A fierce controversy had broken out, in Britain, America and half a dozen other countries, involving all the same arguments between those who thought that the Olympic Games should not be used to give aid and comfort to an aggressive totalitarian regime and those—including the British Olympic Association—who thought that sport was something entirely separate from politics. In the end, of course, the 1936 boycott campaign all but collapsed. Hitler and Dr Goebbels enjoyed their propaganda triumph, and as all the world knows it was left to the black American athlete Jesse Owens to provide the only real sting in the tail for the Nazis, by winning four gold medals and becoming the undoubted hero of the Games.

I wrote my article, concluding:

> My own view is that the present political momentum towards some kind of Western attempt to boycott the Moscow Olympics will prove unstoppable—but that as a propaganda gesture it will go off at half-cock, just as the Games themselves are likely to. The Western boycott will be widely interpreted as yet another petulant and ineffectual response to the most terrifying political fact in the world today—the ever-growing shadow of brute Soviet power.

It was scarcely the clarion call the *Mail* had been hoping for—but for me it was to have some highly unforeseen consequences.

At this point, three weeks after the invasion of Afghanistan, despite all the shouting, the boycott movement was still at a very embryonic stage. Only a handful of Arab countries, including Bahrain, Saudi Arabia and Morocco, had positively committed themselves to staying away from Moscow. Mrs Thatcher and the British Government may have been attempting to give a lead to nations rather more significant in sporting terms, but the fervour of their desire that a British team should not take part at Moscow was only matched by the determination of Sir Denis Follows and many British athletes that a British team would be going. On 17 January France declared that it would ignore

33

the boycott. West Germany remained undecided. Then, on 20 January, President Carter chose the NBC *Meet The Press* programme to announce that 'unless the Russians withdraw their troops within a month from Afghanistan, the Olympic Games should be moved from Moscow.' It was an ultimatum. At last the boycott campaign had become a serious matter.

If the West and the rest of the non-Communist world were divided over the Games, at least one group of people had known precisely where they stood right from the start—and they now seized the unexpected chance of growing Western doubts over the Olympics to state their position as forcefully as possible.

On 20 January, the day of President Carter's ultimatum, Vladimir Bukovsky, the thirty-eight-year-old former dissident, now in exile in England, wrote an article in the *News of the World*. His theme was the terrible shadow that was falling over people in the Soviet Union as a result of the approaching Olympics. 'So Moscow is to be a showcase for the achievements of Socialism . . . presented as an ideal capital, of an ideal state, governed by the ideal system.' But did people in the West know what such 'ideals' really involved?

Bukovsky described the wave of arrests which had been gathering momentum since the previous November, involving not just prominent dissidents, such as his 'old friends' Tatiana Velikanova and Father Gleb Yakunin, but even comparatively ordinary teenagers such as 'Sergei Ermelayev and Igor Polyakov, sentenced to three years for shouting a few critical words about the regime in a Moscow tube train'. Only a few days previously (on 15 January) the dwindling dissident community in Moscow had been particularly shocked by the arrest of the Orthodox priest Father Dmitri Dudko, who had inspired them with his fearless sermons and been the spiritual counsellor to many, including Solzhenitsyn.

Bukovsky pointed out that the Soviet Olympic Organizing Committee included not only G. P. Goncharov, the head of the Communist Party propaganda machine, but also a senior KGB official, Alexander Gresko, who had been expelled from Britain in 1971 for spying (not to mention Boris Onischenko, the fencer disqualified at Montreal for cheating). He spoke of the smiling little 'Misha Bear' Olympic souvenirs being turned out in the KGB's prisons and prison camps (another dissident just out of a labour camp,

Nikolai Sharygin, had recently revealed that many of the 2,835 official Olympic souvenirs were being made in this way). He wrote of the official plans to 'clean up' Moscow, to move out drunkards and the unemployed, to ensure that more than a million teenagers and children would not be present in the city during the weeks surrounding the Games. He concluded: 'Are not the sportsmen themselves—and their fans—ashamed to build their success on other people's sufferings?'

Two days later, on 22 January, the extent to which this shadow was growing was brought home to the outside world more dramatically than Bukovsky could have dared imagine. On his way to a meeting of the Academy of Sciences, Andrei Sakharov was arrested by the KGB in a Moscow street, stripped of all his state awards and titles, and sent off 250 miles from Moscow to 'internal exile' in a one-room flat in the city of Gorki, which was closed to Western journalists. Over the next few days, the Nobel prizewinner was subjected to a campaign of unprecedented vilification by the Soviet press, being variously described as 'a provocateur', 'a spiritual renegade', 'a slanderer', 'a pathologically inhumane fascist', 'a supporter of Nazi ideas' (unspecified) and as having 'engaged in black market dealings'. For twelve years, Dr Sakharov's towering eminence as a scientist had given him relative protection as he directed his thoughtful criticisms at the Soviet regime in letters, articles and interviews. Only with the approach of the Olympics had the authorities decided that his continued freedom was at last too high a price to pay for their desire to present Moscow to the world as 'an ideal capital of an ideal state'.

From all over the Soviet empire, in those closing days of January, a faint but unmistakable cry was heard. A Czech dissident group smuggled out a letter to the West claiming that 'the Olympic flag at the Berlin stadium was an insult to thousands. The same flag at a Moscow stadium will be an insult to millions.' From the Baltic states, on 29 January, another letter smuggled out by a group of Estonians, Latvians and Lithuanians protested against the choice of Tallinn, the capital of 'the occupied country of Estonia', as the venue for the Olympic yachting events. On 30 January, twelve Russians issued a pamphlet in *samizdat* ('self-publishing') arguing that the Olympic Games would only give 'support for the continuation of tyranny and oppression'.

But there was, of course, another side to this argument. On 24

The Road to Moscow (1974–1980)

January a Mr Spartak Beglov had written to *The Times* from 'Pushkin Square, Moscow' complaining that President Carter was 'violating the human rights of thousands of young American sportsmen to compete in the world's greatest athletic event'. It was all a matter of one's point of view.

In the West, the boycott campaign became tinged with farce. On 22 January Mrs Thatcher suggested, no doubt with memories of the 1948 Olympics at Wembley, that part of the 1980 Games might be staged in Britain. It was pointed out that the only athletic track in London remotely up to modern Olympic standard was Crystal Palace, with room for a mere 18,000 spectators. On 1 February, huge headlines greeted President Carter's appointment of Muhammad Ali as his 'special Olympic envoy' to make a tour of African countries putting the case in favour of a boycott to their leaders. Scarcely had the ex-world heavyweight boxing champion arrived in Nairobi for top-level talks with President Daniel Raap Moi than it became apparent that he had been 'insufficiently briefed' on the arguments for and against a boycott. Although Kenya, for its own reasons, agreed to pull out of Moscow, a baffled Ali told the world's press on 3 February: 'If I knew before I left the US everything I have now found out, I wouldn't be here.'

Through those early days of February uncertainty grew as President Carter's deadline neared. The Winter Olympics came and went—fairly disastrously—at Lake Placid in New York State. In unseasonably mild weather, the Americans had to summon up their most sophisticated technology to install tens of thousands of tons of artificial snow on brown slopes for the ski-ing events. It turned out that the 'Olympic Village' had been designed as a prison (and would be switched to that function as soon as the last skaters and tobogganists departed). There were widespread complaints from journalists and visitors at the chaotic arrangements and widespread local profiteering (the price of a Lake Placid hamburger had risen 1,000 per cent for the duration of the Games). After a two-day session of the International Olympic Committee, Lord Killanin issued on 12 February his longest and most agonized statement so far on the crisis facing the Olympic movement, concluding:

> The very existence of the Olympic Games, the Olympic
> movement and the organization of sport through the

36

international federations is at stake. All seventy-three members present at the 82nd Session of the International Olympic Committee are unanimous that the Games must be held in Moscow as planned.

A week later, on 20 February, President Carter's deadline expired. Predictably, not a single Soviet soldier had been withdrawn from Afghanistan, where the Russians seemed to be bogged down in an endless struggle with the hostile population. The US President had little option but to announce: 'Our decision is irrevocable. We will not participate.' But, as with the argument between Mrs Thatcher and the sportsmen of Britain, what the US Government desired and what the American athletes themselves wanted were not necessarily the same thing—and over the next two months of March and April, the main interest surrounding the international boycott campaign was centred on the battles between the sportsmen of America and Britain and their respective governments. In the USA the struggle was relatively straightforward, even though it was not finally resolved until 13 April, when the United States Olympic Committee voted by two-to-one in favour of the boycott. The leading non-Communist sporting nation in the world was definitely staying away from Moscow.

In Britain the situation continued to be more confused. The Government applied every kind of pressure on the sportsmen, from refusing special leave to any civil servants or servicemen picked to compete, to ordering the British Army not to hand over £12,000 it had raised from voluntary contributions to the Olympic Appeal fund (three days later, after a row in the House of Commons, it was forced to relent). Despite an opinion poll in the *Observer* on 16 March showing that the British public was in favour of British athletes going to Moscow by three-to-one, MPs voted by a large majority the following day in favour of staying away. Finally, on 25 March, the British Olympic Committee voted by eighteen to five that a British team would go to Moscow, even though Sir Denis Follows made it clear that 'there will be no pressure to compete on individual sportsmen', and the equestrian, fencing, yachting and swimming associations decided to defer their decisions. One by one in April these stragglers came down on one side of the fence or the other—the horsemen, yachtsmen and hockey players deciding not to go. The Fencing Federation elected to go, but most of Britain's best fencers then individually decided to withdraw. The swimmers did not come to their decision—in favour of going—until 15 May, just nine days before the final deadline for competitors, on 24 May.

Like most people in Britain I had been following the tortured ins-and-outs of these boycott manoeuvres with desultory interest. My thoughts in that spring of 1980 were on a great many things other than the Moscow Olympics. Then, out of the blue, sometime in March, I had another call from the *Daily Mail*. What would I think about going to Moscow to cover the Olympic Games? The offer came as a complete surprise to me, for as a critic and commentator I am the kind of journalist who does not normally stray further from his desk than the kitchen next door to make a cup of coffee. But I decided it was an offer I could not refuse.

By the time of the final deadline for entries on 24 May, it was apparent that the boycott had so far been at least a partial success, in so far as fifty-six countries had pulled out of the Games altogether (another nine were to drop out before the Games opened). But in sporting terms, it was inescapable that most of them would scarcely be missed, even though the number also included the United States, Japan, Canada and Kenya. One of the last to decide had been West Germany, which kept the world waiting until 15 May when its Olympic Committee finally voted in favour of staying away.

No country in the world had presented remotely so disorderly a spectacle in reaching its decision as Britain. Tempers had run high —particularly, it must be said, on the side of the pro-boycotters. Many of the contending athletes had received vicious and obscene letters (over an issue which few of them saw in anything more than the simplest personal terms). On 13 April Sir Denis Follows had some-what ill-advisedly claimed that 'it will take something of the mag-nitude of a war to stop the Olympics', and the pro-boycott press swooped the next morning to rub his nose in the fact that a war had already been going on for some months in a country called Afghanis-tan (the *Daily Mail*'s front-page carried the huge headline 'AMAZING STATEMENT BY BRITAIN'S OLYMPIC CHIEF—THE FOLLY OF FOLLOWS').

Farce never seemed far away, right up to the end. A discus thrower, Peter Tancred, earned himself warm commendation from the pro-boycott press by solemnly announcing that he refused to go to Moscow, only for the significance of his action to be somewhat deflated the next day when the British athletics team selection committee gave out that he would not have been picked anyway. The Bishop of Sherborne similarly announced that he had decided not to accompany the British team as their official chaplain, only for it to be discovered that no one had realized until now that the British team was to have a chaplain.

Mrs Thatcher consoled herself by claiming that 'without the Americans and the West Germans . . . the Games will not be worthy of the name Olympic. Medals won at Moscow will be of inferior worth, and the ceremonies a charade.'* Her Foreign Secretary Lord Carrington more candidly admitted on 17 June that the British Government's boycott campaign had been 'a failure'.

Elsewhere in the world, the Greeks attempted to ameliorate the prevailing confusion by helpfully suggesting a last-minute switch of the Olympics to Greece. From America there were tales of woe as the commercially interested parties who had been hoping to make vast fortunes out of the Games counted their losses. Dakin Toys of San Francisco announced that they had a million unsaleable 'Misha Bear Mascots' on their hands. Ocean Specialities of Los Angeles were left with 80,000 'Misha Frisbees'. NBC announced that they had lost 68 million dollars through the cancellation of US television coverage, although thanks to their foresight during the shortlived previous boycott scare of 1978, all but 6 million dollars was recoverable from insurers, including a 45-million-dollar claim against Lloyd's of London.

On 8 June, from his tiny flat in Gorki, subjected to a twenty-four hour watch and constant harassment by the KGB, Andrei Sakharov managed to smuggle to Moscow (via his courageous wife Yelena Bonner) a last plea to the world that 'the broadest possible boycott of the Olympics is necessary. Every spectator or athlete who comes to the Olympic Games is giving indirect support to Soviet military policies.' But such pleas were now falling only on deaf or decided ears. The Soviet Government was able to point to the fact that eighty-seven nations had accepted invitations to the Olympics, considerably more than were staying away. The full-scale campaign of suppression against dissidents continued right up to the last minute, including the

---

* An attitude which she was to maintain seven months later, when she failed to recommend any of Britain's five Moscow Gold-medal winners for a customary mention in the 1981 New Year's Honours List.

deportation of several more to the West, such as Vladimir Borisov, a Leningrad worker who since 1978 had been attempting to set up a tiny 'free trade union'. On 19 June the Soviet authorities were able to pull their greatest coup yet in the battle against the dissidents, when during the nine o'clock news on Moscow television they showed an apparently calm and healthy Father Dmitri Dudko recanting his 'mistakes' and pledging his loyalty to the regime. For the handful of publicly identified dissidents left at liberty in Moscow, and for countless thousands more, it was a terrible shock. One of the most loved and respected figures in Russia had inexplicably 'gone over to the other side'.*

The six-year-long preparations for the greatest international 'Festival of Peace' in Soviet history were nearing their climax. As July began, some 2 million people, including almost everyone between the ages of eight and twenty, began a mass exodus from Moscow, either for more than usually crowded summer camps, or just to get away. The Soviet press was full of warnings about the dangers of having dealings with the invasion of foreigners that was about to descend on the Olympic cities. They would certainly include 'thousands of spies', many of them trained by the CIA at two top-secret espionage centres in Lancashire and Derbyshire in England. A ring of road blocks went up round Moscow, to prevent anyone entering the city except those who held a special pass. One hundred and sixty-five streets in the

---

* In *The Times* on 29 July 1980, the experienced Soviet observer Peter Reddaway attempted to quantify the scale of the pre-Olympic purge, on the basis of a mass of information smuggled out of the Soviet Union from various sources. Altogether it seemed likely that 'several million citizens' had been subject to the attentions of the KGB in one way or another, involving 'systematic intimidation; interrogations; house searches; threats of arrest; dismissals from jobs; physical attacks by official thugs; 15-day imprisonments; and warnings and vilification in the local media. Only the few who have declined to be intimidated, and continued to lead their embattled groups, have been arrested. According to our far from complete data these now number—since January 1979—252.'

These specific cases broke down into ninety-six 'leaders of Christian dissent'; ninety-five 'representatives of national minorities' (notably Ukrainians, Estonians, Lithuanians, Jews and Crimean Tartars); and sixty-one individuals 'promoting basic human rights'. In addition 'dissidents' were to continue being forced into exile in the West, under threat of long terms of forced labour in camps, even while the Olympic Games were in progress, notably three leaders of a Leningrad 'feminist group' who had published protests against the Soviet invasion of Afghanistan, expressing praise for the courage of the Afghan resistance and 'the shame of Russian women at their Government's lies' over the invasion. 'In some cases the KGB's terms have been less drastic: it has been satisfied with dissenters agreeing to leave Moscow and stay away all summer.'

centre of Moscow were closed to any but Olympic or other authorized traffic. It finally seemed that nothing had been left to chance, and for the Soviet authorities that nothing could now stand in the way of an almost total triumph.

There was only one tiny cloud on the horizon, no bigger at first than a scattering of down-page paragraphs in the Western press. On 1 July, in neighbouring Poland, the Government had introduced a new system for selling meat, which as the Poles were not slow to observe meant in effect that meat prices had risen by up to 70 per cent. On 2 July, protest meetings against the price increases and even stoppages of work took place in several factories in Warsaw. On 4 July, the strikes spread outside the capital. By 15 July, dissident sources in Warsaw reported that the strikes had spread to Lublin, that a total of thirty-three factories were now 'out' in different parts of the country, and that railway workers had for a few hours managed to block railway lines to the Soviet Union—at least in part as a protest against the constant draining eastward of Poland's meagre food supplies.

But of course none of this was mentioned in the Soviet press. The great day was at last approaching—and for that the sun must shine in a Socialist sky that was wholly cloudless.

PART TWO

The Looking-glass Olympics

16 July–4 August 1980

Why go to the Soviet Union? First and foremost, because it is one of the few adventures left to travellers. Your understanding of this spacecraft, Earth, can never be complete, we feel, without a visit to the largest country in the world ... the Soviet social order, so different from ours, will provoke the imagination, if you are politically aware ... on a more mundane level, you may enjoy the skill of Soviet athletics.

Introduction to Fodor's *Soviet Union 1980*

3

Through the Looking-glass

The country they are coming to see does not exist.

Vladimir Borisov, *World In Action*—ITV—just
before the Olympics, July 1980

When I arrived at London Airport shortly after nine o'clock on the
morning of Wednesday 16 July, to check in for flight BA 708 to
Moscow, I felt a certain apprehension. The adventure I was about to
embark on was like nothing I had ever faced before.

I had been to the Soviet Union before, but only as a casual tourist,
and never to Moscow. I had never been present at anything remotely
resembling the colossal jamboree of a modern Olympic Games. In my
twenty years as a journalist, I had never covered a 'news event' of any
kind, not even a local flower show. What was it going to be like
working for two weeks alongside thousands of journalists, all much
more experienced at what they were doing than I? What was to be my
role in Moscow?

The briefing from John Bryant, the *Daily Mail*'s Features Editor,
had been suitably vague. 'Regard yourself as an artist,' he said. 'Just
record impressions of whatever catches your eye.' In other words, I
would not be expected to get exclusive interviews with Bulgarian
weightlifters. I was there for 'atmosphere', simply to try to convey in a
series of feature articles what it was like to be in Moscow during this
unique fortnight in its history.

One of my few qualifications for going to Moscow was that, perhaps
rather more than most of my colleagues (who were going there, after
all, to do a different job), I was aware that the country we were about
to visit was in reality even stranger than it might appear at first sight.
In one way or another, I had spent a good deal of my life reading some
of the thousands of books about Russia—not just the more famous
novels and histories, but in particular the eyewitness accounts of

those, both Western and Russian, who had lived and worked in Russia during the sixty extraordinary years since the Revolution. Having spent time with friends in Eastern Europe, I knew something from the inside of what it was like to live in a Communist country; how totally different it was from the impression which might be gained by the visitor who stays in hotels, goes on guided tours and sees only the carefully presented surface of such a society. Russia itself is not only, in Churchill's phrase, more of 'a riddle wrapped in a mystery inside an enigma' than it might appear, but the easiest mistake of all made by so many Westerners is not even to see it as a riddle at all: to take everything at face value, and to assume that the little they do see (even then with largely uncomprehending eyes) stands for everything which they do not see. Long before the coming of Communism, the hardest thing for the Westerner to penetrate had been the ancient Russian capacity to dress up unpleasant realities (even among themselves) behind a deceptively pleasant façade. *Pokazukha*, they call it, something 'done for show'. And, of course, the most famous phrase for this is 'the Potemkin Village', dating back to 1787, when Catherine the Great's favourite, Grigory Potemkin, wanted to impress her with the wealth of her newly annexed dominions in the Crimea. He arranged for a series of large, prosperous-looking fake villages to be erected of painted wood and canvas along the banks of the Volga, in order to persuade her as she sailed regally past that her new lands were much richer and more populous than they were.

If Catherine the Great was taken in, how much more have been most of those millions of visitors to the Soviet Union since the Revolution, who have been exposed to an infinitely more ingenious and extensive series of Potemkin Villages than anything the eighteenth century could dream up? The library shelves of the West are groaning under the evidence for this phenomenon, seen from every angle. On the one hand are the wide-eyed memoirs of those who were fooled, because unconsciously they wished to be, because they wanted to find in the Soviet Union a realization of the heaven on earth of their own fantasies: Sidney and Beatrice Webb paying tribute in their *Soviet Communism: A New Civilisation* (1935) to the wonderful work of the OGPU in organizing tens of thousands of 'criminals', eager to 'work off their debt to society' by helping with the heroic task of building the White Sea Canal; Julian Huxley reporting excitedly that even Comrade Stalin himself would sometimes take time off from the cares of state to go down to lend a hand at the Moscow goods yards at three in the morning (whereas we now know that Stalin never even stepped inside a factory after he had come to power in 1924); Bernard Shaw, Mrs Cecil Chesterton and hundreds of others, coming back to portray the Soviet Union as a land overflowing with *crèches*, power stations and happy, smiling workers—at a time when, behind the scenes, literally millions were starving to death as a result of the collectivization programme, and millions more were about to be sent off to labour camps or shot.

On the other hand, even more now than in that heyday of the Potemkin Village, we also have the testimonies of those who were not fooled, who experienced some of the appalling reality behind those imposing wood-and-canvas façades. We even have descriptions, from the other side, of how the trick was actually worked, such as Solzhenitsyn's savagely ironic account of the writer Gorky's visit to the Solovetsky Monasteries in 1930, on that same White Sea Canal which the Webbs eulogized, and where more than 100,000 prisoners died in a sub-zero Arctic hell on earth; or the famous conducted tour given in 1944 to Vice-President Henry Wallace and Owen Lattimore round the slave camps of Kolyma, when they were shown healthy, cheerful, warmly clad NKVD employees dressed up as swineherds and gold miners, and came away happily convinced that they had seen the 'unfortunates of society going through a model course of rehabilitation'.

Of course things have changed in the Soviet Union in the past forty years—but to give an idea of the lengths to which *pokazukha* can be taken even in our day, I recall just two tiny examples. The first was described by a Russian friend who used to go with her friends for a holiday each summer to a poor fishing village on the Baltic coast, near Riga. One year they were amazed to find the village shop stocked up with chickens, caviar, tinned food and all sorts of delicacies which would not normally be seen there in a thousand years. The explanation, it seemed, was that the Shah of Iran might shortly be making a visit to Riga. Although this village was some way up the coast, it was just possible that the Iranian royal party might drive through. As it happened, the Shah's visit never materialized, but for my friend and her Latvian neighbours it was a summer they would never forget.

The other story is told by Vladimir Bukovsky in his book *To Build a Castle*. He describes how once, knowing he was about to be arrested by the KGB, he took off from Moscow to accompany a team of geologists on a six-month trip through the wilds of Siberia. One day as they neared Lake Baikal, after weeks of driving on nothing but the crudest of dirt roads (if they found roads at all), they were amazed in the middle of nowhere to come across

> fifty miles of beautifully asphalted roadway, with all the little villages along it looking incredibly neat and tidy, and as gaily painted as Easter eggs. At the far end of the road, beside the lake, there were two luxurious modern bungalows, with avenues of trees and a golf course.

The explanation was simple. Back in 1960, President Eisenhower had been planning to visit the Soviet Union for talks with Mr Khruschev. On his itinerary had been a trip to inspect a hydro-electric scheme near Lake Baikal, of which the Soviets were at that time particularly proud. Just for this brief visit the tireless authorities had erected 'this little piece of America in the midst of the trackless Soviet wilderness'—though in the end the U-2 incident had intervened, and Ike never made it to Russia after all.

Why was all this sort of thing in my mind in those days of July before I set off for Moscow? Obviously because, as the five 'Olympic cities' prepared to receive their biggest-ever influx of foreigners, as the USSR prepared for the most concentrated bout of coverage by the world's press and television, all the evidence suggested that the Olympic Games were going to be the biggest Potemkin Village operation the Soviet Government had ever staged. For the curious reporter, it was an irresistible challenge. But how much would any of us see?

In the weeks before departure, I read or re-read as many accounts of journeys to Russia as I could lay my hands on. Fortunately, our travel arrangements had been taken care of by an inexhaustibly patient lady called Pat Besford, who was not only going to Moscow to write about swimming for the *Daily Telegraph* but had taken on the formidable task of looking after all the visa, hotel, and other arrangements for the entire British press party, several hundred strong.

On the Monday before departure I went to have lunch with a Russian friend who came out of the Soviet Union a few years ago. I found her in a tumbledown gamekeeper's cottage, in the middle of a forest, on a large estate belonging to her friend, an eccentric aristocrat, who was writing a kind of symbolist play about his life. As he stood there talking in a high, musical voice about his play, tall, bearded and smocked, like a cross between Prince Mishkin and one of Chekhov's characters, the whole scene seemed somehow as timelessly Russian as anything I would be likely to encounter in a few days' time. My friend gave me a few telephone numbers of friends and relatives in Moscow; told me of restaurants and an Orthodox church in Nezhdanovoye where I might hear particularly beautiful singing. She talked of Arbat, the district of Moscow full of small streets and large decaying houses, loved by generations of writers, artists and bohemians, and she played me a plangent song by the poet-singer Bulat Okudzhava, 'Oh Arbat, my Arbat, you are my fatherland, And I'll never wander enough over you!' I asked her which of the various books I hoped to take might be confiscated by the customs and she replied scornfully, 'Just give them a *Playboy*—they won't give you any trouble—they can sell it for twenty-five roubles.'

On Tuesday I visited Collet's, the left-wing bookshop in the Charing Cross Road—full of unsold copies of *Pravda*—and was delighted to find that for the first time since the famous Baedeker of 1914 there was at last a really decent new guide book to Russia—a Blue Guide to Moscow and Leningrad which was to prove invaluable.

My last call, as instructed by Pat Besford on one of her voluminous sheets of advice, was to get an 'adjustable bath plug', as it is of course well known that no bathroom in the Soviet Union ever affords such an article. Having tried eight shops round Camden Town in vain ('there's no call for them these days'), I was obscurely pleased to find that the only shop in north London stocking what I wanted was the Co-op, a tiny triumph for Socialist enterprise.

And so it was that on that Wednesday morning armed with my plug and a short-wave radio to keep in touch with the BBC World Service, I finally arrived at London Airport.

It was an ill-assorted group waiting in the departure lounge. A BBC camera crew humping huge pieces of equipment and piles of film they were reluctant to risk on the airport X-ray security checks; several fit-looking young men wearing British Olympic Association blazers, who turned out to be the modern pentathlon team; and one or two less identifiable figures on their own, clutching portable typewriters and piles of news magazines, who I took to be fellow-journalists.

I never felt my lack of experience more than at that moment. These were members of a group which, in my highly compartmentalized profession, I had never met—the sporting journalists. They spent all their time doing this kind of thing, moving from airport to airport across the world. They probably worked telex machines in their sleep.

As it happened, my first encounter could not have borne out my preconception more vividly. A red-faced Irishman stuck out his hand to me and introduced himself as Terry O'Connor, one of the most experienced of my *Daily Mail* colleagues, a veteran of a thousand major sporting events from Olympic Games to world heavyweight fights. He had been in England only a day since flying in from a month with the British Lions rugby tour of South Africa, which had coincided with riots and shootings. O'Connor introduced me to another unshaven, bleary-eyed colleague, also just back from South Africa, Frank Keating of the *Guardian*.

The flight was uneventful. I was sitting face-to-face with the pentathlon team, wondering why they seemed to turn away whenever I looked at them (I later found that, as members of the British Army, they had been given strict instructions to have nothing to do with the press under any circumstances). O'Connor across the aisle forced me to vie with him in generosity over the double scotches (he needed them more than I did). Keating slept almost the whole way at the back of the plane.

Suddenly we were coming down through the clouds and there below us was Russia—vast stretches of forest, lakes and grassy spaces stretching to the horizon, with scarcely a building in sight. Schoolboy statistics floated through my mind—that the Soviet Union occupies a sixth of the world's land surface, that Moscow is nearer to San Francisco than it is to Vladivostok, that 38 per cent of the USSR is occupied by trees.

As we came lower, I saw far below us a group of tower blocks, as tiny as toys, seemingly in the middle of the countryside, but then it turned out that they were on the very edge of Moscow. There are no miles of sprawling suburbia, phasing countryside gradually into town. The city advances tower block by tower block into the fields (although elsewhere the outskirts of Moscow are still marked by hundreds of little wooden 'summer houses' or 'poor man's *dachas*', each with its little plot of garden).

The lavishly functional terminal at Sheremetyevo, in rich dark brick and glass, had been specially built for the Olympics by the West Germans. We passed through the Customs with little more than a casual glance from the officials (I had not brought any *Playboys*, but the handful of 'forbidden' literature in my case—Hedrick Smith's *The Russians*, a copy of Sakharov's latest lengthy statement from Gorki—remained unexamined).

Outside, a bus was waiting to take us to our hotel, the Rossiya, right next to Red Square in the centre of Moscow—where the world's press was quartered—and almost immediately we were off on the forty-minute drive into the city.

As we passed clumps of birch trees and half-finished tower blocks, a strange sense of exhilaration began to seize me—one I always feel when I enter an Eastern European country. It is hard to explain. Partly it is the sheer strangeness of everything; partly that it is in some ways like travelling back into the past; but more than anything perhaps it is the feeling that life here is somehow *serious*, reduced to grand simplicities, in a way that it is not in the West. The first posters appeared by the roadside—almost all Olympic messages—'TOWARDS PEACE ON EARTH!', 'PEACE AND FRIENDSHIP', 'MOSCOW WEL-COMES OLYMPIC VISITORS', 'O SPORT YOU ARE PEACE' (this one, a quotation from Le Coubertin, founder of the modern Olympics, must have pleased the Soviets no end), together with the inevitable smiling Misha Bears.

The buildings grew more densely packed. The half-finished tower blocks gave way to massive eight- or nine-storey older structures, dating from the great rebuilding of Moscow in the Stalin era; below them shops, like all such in the Communist world simply labelled with the type of goods on sale—Shoes, Fruit, Chemist, Food, even just Products.

We passed through a first vast square, Mayakovsky Square, scene of the great poetry readings of the late fifties and early sixties, named after the wild, unhappy Bolshevik poet from Georgia who committed suicide in 1930.

I was surprised how many other buildings had, here and there, survived the rebuilding of central Moscow—the occasional little two-storey, green-and-white plaster house, an imposing classical portico, a small, onion-domed church. We came down Gorky Street, a great ten-lane highway running down into the very centre of Moscow, lined with more massive buildings. Until forty years ago it had been a notoriously narrow street (again I remember from a childhood encyclopaedia a picture from the thirties showing one of the street's older buildings being moved back 160 feet on rollers, to enable Stalin's planners to turn Gorky Street into a fitting boulevard for the new Communist capital).

We emerged on to another tree-lined boulevard next to the Moscow River, snaking through the centre of the city, much narrower than the Thames at Westminster—and there above it, on a low bluff, were the high red walls, the shining golden cupolas and the green and white palaces of the Kremlin, each of its squat spires topped by a red star.

To the far side of the Kremlin rose the fantastic barley sugar sticks and bulbous domes of St Basil's Cathedral, all newly painted in swirls of blue and white, green and red, like nothing so much as a cluster of tethered Montgolfier hot-air balloons.

Across the river stood the five dreadnought-like smokestacks of an ancient power station, looking as if it had been carefully preserved from Tsarist days as a Revolutionary monument, its roofline bearing in white letters the famous 1920 Leninist slogan 'COMMUNISM EQUALS SOVIET POWER PLUS THE ELECTRIFICATION OF THE WHOLE COUNTRY'. Further downstream towered a strange, 'wedding cake' skyscraper, several hundred feet high.

Next to St Basil's, facing the river, stood a huge modern pile, with a tower block behind. It was the Rossiya, a kilometre all the way round, one of the largest hotels in the world—our home for the next three weeks.

The bus stopped on a wide apron of asphalt at the far end. On the pavement outside the hotel was a mass of journalists and cameramen who had arrived before us, each distinguished by a light blue identity card, with photograph, hanging round his neck on a thick white string. We headed for a side door, where there was already a queue waiting to be checked in by half a dozen eagle-eyed militia men (policemen). An old hand in front said that we would have to use this door every time we entered the hotel and that it could take up to half an hour to get in. In fact it only took some ten minutes before we were having to show our papers, and walking in through a pair of X-ray security screens (made by an American firm, each labelled FRISKEM).

We emerged into a huge, marble-floored, chandeliered foyer, surrounded by reception desks and souvenir counters, and dominated by an enormous television-projection screen. After checking in, we took the lift up to the seventh floor, where the entire British press corps was accommodated in what amounted to only a comparatively small corner of this vast building. Through plate-glass windows as we walked the two hundred yards or more from the lift to our rooms, we could see the stacks of the Leninist power station with its uplifting message across the river. We collected our keys at a 'corridor desk', run by the inevitable 'floor lady' who presides night and day over every floor of a Russian hotel (in the Rossiya there were several to each floor) and is a combination of watchdog, concierge, keeper of keys and provider of drinking water (from special squat metal siphons, kept in large, elderly refrigerators by her desk). In this case, as was to remain true night and day for the next three weeks, our 'floor lady' was accompanied by an unsmiling policeman in an ill-fitting light grey suit.

At last I was in my room, No. 272: a single bed, a table, a desk, a huge colour television set, plastic light fittings, a window looking down on the hotel's central courtyard, full of little fir trees, and an empty concrete basin for a fountain. It was just like a room in any modern, provincial Trust House Forte hotel in Britain, except for the simple, black-and-white drawing of a little onion-domed country church standing in a wintry Russian landscape which hung on the wall.

The bath had a plug.

A few minutes after my arrival, the door of No. 291 opposite opened and I was delighted to find that my nearest neighbour was Ian Wooldridge, fearless *Daily Mail* columnist, who had already been in Moscow for some time. Here for me was a 'living legend', for although he was only in his late forties, I had been reading his columns since he was a contributor to the *News Chronicle* in my schooldays. A dapper figure, in a lightweight suit, he gave me a warm welcome. A man of enormous nervous energy and enthusiasms, for whom everything was always 'sensational', 'hilarious', 'wonderful', 'disastrous', he was to be a great asset in the days which lay ahead.

We went down to one of the hotel's nine restaurants for dinner. In the lift I met an American journalist fuming because his room had just been 'gone over' as he claimed, and his tape recorder smashed. The restaurant was a long, high-ceilinged room, with regulation Soviet chandeliers, a grand piano sitting forlornly on a dais in the middle. The menu, as often in Soviet hotels, was lengthy, but only a third or so of the entries (the ones with prices marked) were actually available.

There was caviar (black) and caviar (red), there was baked sturgeon and boiled sturgeon, borscht, steaks, Chicken Kiev. There was even something called 'Boiled Zander', which turned out to be the Siberian pike-perch.

Unlike most of the Western journalists in Moscow, Wooldridge, like myself, spoke a little phrase-book Russian (an unusually important asset in a country where even the street signs are incomprehensible unless you can at least read the Cyrillic alphabet). He had learned it on National Service in the early fifties, and had spent most of his time listening in for Soviet submarines near the Kiel Canal. Hence his somewhat rusty Russian tended to concentrate on such useful phrases as 'Coming up to ten metres, captain' and 'Forward torpedo tubes loaded, comrade'.

When I arrived back in my room after dinner I called John Bryant in London. 'John', I said, 'I am bowled over by this country. I am certainly not going to file anything for at least a couple of days, until I have recovered my bearings.'

Although I didn't know it yet, in some ways it was going to take more like three months.

4

First Impressions

What can compare to the Kremlin which, having ringed itself
with crenellated walls, and adorned itself with the golden domes
of the cathedrals, sits on a high hill like the crown of sovereignty
on the brow of an awesome ruler? . . . no, neither the Kremlin,
nor its crenellated walls, nor its dark passages, nor the splendid
palaces can be described. They must be seen, they must be seen.
One must feel all they say to the heart and the imagination.

Mikhail Lermontov (1833)

Thursday 17 July
On my first day I did little more than take a walk round the centre of
this astonishing city. I had read many accounts of Moscow, but from
none had I really got a picture of what it was like. Above all, nothing
had prepared me for the sheer power of the place—the massive yellow
and grey buildings, the great, open boulevards, the huge squares. I
overheard two Americans coming out of the Press Centre, obviously
as surprised by their first impression as I was: 'In its own way it hits
you even more than Manhattan.'

Like most people, I arrived with that shorthand jumble of mental
images one has of any great city one has never visited: Red Square,
Lenin's Tomb, the Kremlin, the famous 'department store' GUM,
the marbled halls of the Metro, the white spire of Moscow University.
One of the first surprises was to find how close together most of these
things are, not more than half a mile from the Rossiya. The Kremlin,
up on its hill, closed off behind its forbidding walls, lies right at the
heart of the city, giving it an undisputed centre in a way that is true of
no other great city in the world. From this grimly beautiful, mysterious, ancient citadel, the city fans out almost exactly like a spider's
web, in a series of concentric rings. Immediately below the Kremlin
walls, to the north and east, are a succession of three vast squares—the
Square of the Fiftieth Anniversary of October, Revolution Square and

55

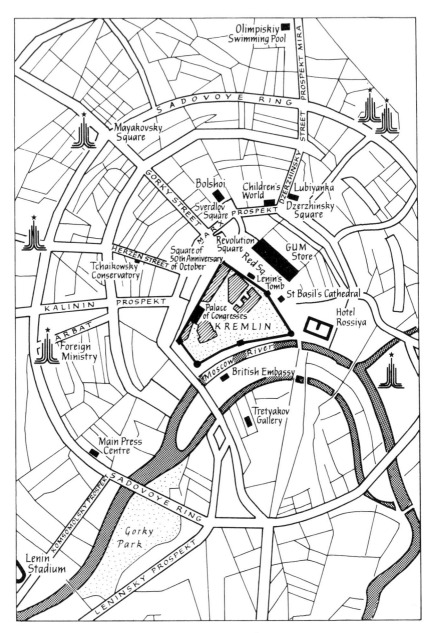

CENTRAL MOSCOW, THE KREMLIN 'AT THE HEART OF THE
SPIDER'S WEB'

Red Square (with GUM running down the far side of it). From here majestic boulevards, eighty to a hundred yards wide, radiate out like mighty spikes—Kalinin Prospekt, Gorky Street, Marx Prospekt. A mile-and-a-half or so out from the Kremlin the central area of the city is encircled by the Sadovoye Koltso, or 'Garden Ring', built in the nineteenth century as a great tree-lined boulevard, though most of the trees have long since vanished in the road-widening programme of the Stalin and Khruschev eras. To the south-west of the centre, another fine district of the city, with many older buildings, stretches out along a long ox-bow loop of the Moscow River towards the tree-covered Lenin Hills (from where, as Tolstoy described in *War and Peace*, Napoleon first looked down on the 'monuments of barbarism and despotism' of the city laid out below him, like an Oriental beauty' that he was about to ravish). Here today rises the mighty 790-foot tower of the Moscow State University building—and all around, extending to the horizon, with its 8 million inhabitants, lies one of the four or five largest cities in the world.

The first priority, after breakfast, was to go down to the Main Press Centre to be officially accredited. This was essential as, from now on, without one of the little plastic identity cards round our necks night and day we would be 'non-persons'—not allowed to enter or leave the hotel, or even to remain in the Soviet Union (like others, I was several times to wake up in the morning to find I had slept wearing mine all night).

A continuous stream of special press buses left from outside the Rossiya every few minutes for 'Olympic destinations' all over the city—indeed the bus service was one of the most obvious, immediate signs of the extraordinary efficiency with which these Games had been organized by our Soviet hosts. The route to the Main Press Centre down to the south-west on the Sadovoye Koltso ring road took us below the walls of the Kremlin along the Moscow River, past a vista on the opposite bank of trees, factories, modern office blocks, building sites, a distant funfair. The Press Centre was an imposing six-storey building, specially built for the Games rather in the 'South Bank bunker' style of huge, *beton brut* concrete slabs (as in the Queen Elizabeth Hall). The accreditation section was a seething mass of journalists from all over the world, being patiently shepherded by a group of friendly young Russians, speaking English, Spanish, French and German in attractive, soft Russian accents.

With my identity card, I was given a key to my 'box' in the main hall, where I found a rubber Misha (compliments of the Soviet Organizing Committee) and a mass of Olympic literature (the box was to be daily replenished with more handouts and results sheets). The Press Centre was superbly equipped, with restaurants and bars, telex and telephone rooms, a twenty-four-hour translation service. There seemed to be nothing the organizers had not laid on.

The regular bus route back to the Rossiya was different from the outward journey, leading through the older section of town round Kropotkin Street. On the way we passed a stall that seemed almost absurdly loaded down with fruit and vegetables. There was a queue of several dozen people carrying *avochas* (a word meaning 'just in case')—the string bags which Russians carry around 'just in case' they happen to come across a consignment of oranges or shoes or light bulbs or anything else during their day. I was to pass that fruit stall many times in the next fortnight. It was never less than well-stocked. There was always a queue.

I began my first walk around the centre of the city from the Rossiya. Literally in the shadow of the hotel, on the north side, looking almost like toys beneath its overhanging bulk, was a row of very old Moscow buildings, dating from the seventeenth and eighteenth centuries—a couple of little onion-domed churches built of brick, old wood and stone houses which looked as if they had not only been carefully repainted and restored, but even rebuilt. One of them, the so-called English House (*Angliskoye Podovor'ye*) was in fact the building put up for English merchants to stay in when they had first come on trading missions to Muscovy in the reign of Queen Elizabeth I.

I wandered into one of the churches—it was bare and empty, and the white walls were covered in photographs of waving corn, hydro-electric schemes and cement works. It was an exhibition, though of a kind scarcely calculated to bring a rush of tourists. I said to the old man half-asleep on the door, 'There are no visitors to your exhibition.' 'There will be delegations,' he replied.

In many ways I was prepared for the street level 'feel' of Moscow by my familiarity with Leningrad and other Eastern European cities: the drabness; the strange quietness of people as they walk along (you hardly ever hear voices raised); the notice boards carrying *Pravda*, *Izvestia*, *Trud*, with few people ever bothering to stop to read them (there is after all no reason to—for anyone who really wants these papers, they are freely available on news stands); the shop windows, with their pathetic displays of shoddy goods—a solitary transistor radio, a heap of tins. One of the commonest shop signs is simply *Remont* ('repair'); even within a few hundred yards of the Rossiya there were a dozen *Remont* shops, for bags, watches, shoes, radios, umbrellas—anything that can possibly fall apart and usually does, but still has to be cherished and hung on to.

One thing markedly not in evidence, however, was the usual exhortatory political posters, replaced by the now equally ubiquitous Olympic slogans—'TOWARDS PEACE ON EARTH', 'DRUZHBI MIR' ('Peace and Friendship'). Only here and there did a sign in more permanent form remain, like the metal letters across the top of a nine-storey building, 'GLORY TO THE COMMUNIST PARTY OF THE SOVIET UNION'.

I came through an alley, out into a vast square, Sverdlova Ploschad. This is named after Lenin's 'Old Bolshevik' comrade Yakov Sverdlov, the first President of the Soviet Union, who had led the cry for 'merciless mass terror' following the assassination attempt on Lenin's life in 1918, and died himself the following year at the age of only thirty-four (which was just as well for him—if he had survived, he would probably, like most of his comrades, have been murdered by Stalin twenty years later, and would never have had a square named after him).*

In the middle of the great expanse stood a granite statue of Marx, and beyond it, several hundred yards away across the square, the imposing cream-and-white pillared portico of the Bolshoi Theatre (little-known fact—the Bolshoi Company was started by an English showman named Maddox, in 1776). On the east side of the square was another building I particularly wanted to visit—the famous Metropole Hotel, with its art nouveau interiors (also, it happened, the work of an Englishman—the architect W. F. Walcott—around the turn of the century). Through the swing doors, said to be the only ones in Russia, I was very firmly stopped by a row of policemen inside, who told me that I would not be allowed to enter even if my best friend was staying there (this impenetrable security screen, I was to discover, applied to many of the Olympic hotels).

* In the West he is perhaps better known for having given his name to a class of heavy cruiser; but his most important memorial is the city of Sverdlovsk, formerly Ekaterinburg, where the Tsar and his family were murdered in 1918.

The Looking-glass Olympics (16 July–4 August 1980)

From Sverdlov Ploschad I walked a few hundred yards up the great boulevard of Marx Prospekt to another large square, Dzerzhinskogo Ploschad, named after Felix Dzerzhinsky, the Polish aristocrat who in December 1917 founded the Cheka, the Extraordinary Commission against Counter-Revolution, Speculation and Sabotage which has been such a central feature of Soviet life ever since, in its successive manifestations as the GPU, the OGPU, the NKVD, the MVD, the MGB and finally, today, the KGB. (How strange, the passing thought came to me, to be in a city in which so many squares and streets are named after psychopaths.) Dzerzhinsky Square is dominated by two large yellow buildings on its north side, which are the headquarters of the KGB and better known as the Lubyanka. I had read that 'the Lubyanka looks just like any other Moscow office building' (indeed one half of it did begin life in Tsarist times as the headquarters of an insurance company). But this is not true. With its blank, barred windows and its massive rusticated-stone base, this building in which so many untold thousands of people have been interrogated, imprisoned, tortured or shot in the past sixty years, has an unbelievably sinister air—an impression aided by the large numbers of unpleasant-faced men, in plain clothes and unarmed for the Olympics, who stood around it.

Back down Marx Prospekt, the bottom end of Gorky Street was overshadowed by the twenty-four-storey curtain-walled Intourist Hotel, a typically sixties skyscraper, with a few tatty flags hanging outside it. I walked up the steepish hill of Gorky Street, through one of the monumental archways leading off it—and I was into my first residential back streets, faded yellow nineteenth- and early twentieth-century apartment buildings, dark courtyards with lime trees. I walked down winding Nezhdanovoye past the little seventeenth-century Church of the Resurrection, with its regilded cupola, the grim-looking House of Composers and several of those little 'parks' or open spaces familiar in Eastern European cities— bedraggled patches of grass, full of hedge mustard and clover, birch trees, a few seats or a child's swing. Round a corner I came across a curiosity—a little red-sandstone Gothic 'English' church, St Andrew's, erected in 1894, according to a plaque, by a merchant from Glasgow (today used as a recording studio). A few hundred yards further on lay the Arbat, a charming old district, with pleasant, nineteenth-century houses, cafés and old churches. But today the Arbat is overshadowed, indeed sliced through, by the most spectacular modern development in Moscow—the great, eight-lane Kalinin Prospekt, lined by a cluster of nine skyscrapers, the so-called New Arbat, towering over a vast complex of shops, restaurants and cinemas. Dating from the mid-sixties, it was reminiscent of what happened to many British cities at the same time, and I thought of Solzhenitsyn's words in his *Letter to Soviet Leaders* (1974):

> We have dirtied ... and disfigured the heart of Russia, our beloved Moscow. What crazed, unfilial hand bulldozed the boulevards ... what evil, alien axe broke up the tree-lined Sadovoye Koltso and replaced them with a poisoned zone of asphalt and petrol? The irreplaceable face of the city and all the ancient city plan have been obliterated, and imitations of the West have been slung up, like the New Arbat; the city has been so squeezed, stretched and pushed upwards, that life has become intolerable...

It was now pouring with rain, and as I walked back across the vast square known as Fiftieth Anniversary of October, I could see looming up in the grey drizzle beyond, the towers of the Kremlin. Over a gateway hung a huge picture of Mr Brezhnev, bearing the words 'THE USSR WILL CONTINUE TO SUPPORT THE OLYMPIC MOVEMENT AS BEFORE—L. I. Brezhnev' (in English) and 'THE OLYMPIC GAMES REFLECT MANKIND'S UNCONQUERABLE ASPIRATIONS TOWARDS PEACE AND PROGRESS'. The rain was now coming down so heavily that I thankfully sought refuge in the welcoming portals of the Lenin Museum.

This is a huge building and I did not even see half of it. There were moments when, from faded copies of *Pravda* and *Izvestia*, or blown-up photographs of huge crowds in Red Square or Petrograd in 1917, it was possible to catch some faint echo of the heady atmosphere of those days which had brought to Russia this extraordinary thing—the Dictatorship of the Proletariat: the chaos, the wild hopes, the fierce will of Lenin himself as the one man (or one of the few) who alone knew in those days of collapse and misery and confusion precisely what must be done. One of the strangest exhibits, standing alone at the end of a long corridor, is the car Lenin used after the Revolution—a gleaming, perfectly restored Rolls Royce 'Silver Ghost Alpine Eagle' tourer, looted from the garage of some aristocrat or rich merchant. As a large East German delegation came racing by, their Soviet guide did not even mention the Rolls, indeed she seemed only too keen to hurry them past it (though one or two stragglers gave it bemused looks). I rather suspect that this curio from the great days of the Revolution has become something of a 'contradiction' in these more enlightened times, and may soon quietly disappear.

Other rooms exemplified little more than the stupefying pall of boredom which has fallen over Lenin's country since those stirring days: models of space rockets, sputniks, dams. In one room devoted to all the thousands of editions of Lenin's works published since 1917, an attendant was eager to switch on a huge globe which slowly revolves, with lights on every country which has published a complete edition of Lenin—including Britain and Madagascar.

The only moment of light relief came when I was examining an exact-scale model of the apartments in the Kremlin which Lenin occupied with his wife Krupskaya after 1917. An elderly lady attendant came over to point out each room in turn and explain what it was used for—Lenin's bedroom, Krupskaya's bedroom, Lenin's library and so forth, each reproduced down to the tiniest detail, even including the objects on the desks which stood in every single room (so that the Great Man never needed to cease working). I could not help observing amid this riot of verisimilitude that nowhere in sight could one see the slightest trace of a bathroom or lavatory. 'Why is there no toilet?' I asked. 'Surely Comrade Lenin had one?' She was most embarrassed, and pretended not to understand the question. I could not help thinking that, when that model was built, someone (or rather some committee) must quite solemnly and deliberately have taken the decision not to include Lenin's toilet arrangements. Demigods must remain above the earth.

The rain had diminished somewhat as I came back out into Revolution Square. I walked past the great red brick walls of the Kremlin and into Gosudarstvenny Universal'nyy Magazin, the 'State Department Store', better known as GUM. Any associations with Selfridges or Marks and Spencer should be dispelled—in Western terms GUM bears little resemblance to the familiar department store. It was in fact built between 1889 and 1893 as a typical late nineteenth-century arcaded market, to house the mass of market stalls which once stood on the edge of Red Square next door (there had been another market building, in the classical style, before it, put up after the Fire of 1812).

Inside, with its seething mass of shoppers criss-crossing the three floors of galleries joined by bridges, below a dirty glass and cast-iron roof, it looked like nothing so much as a cross between a rather tatty shopping arcade and a scene from Fritz Lang's *Metropolis*. The galleries are lined with little shops, selling anything from fur hats (hugely expensive) to saucepans. It was in a terrible state of repair. Water was dripping down from cracks in the glass roof. One end of the market had been closed off with scaffolding and piles of builders' materials. It looked as if nothing had been done to the place since it was taken over by the state in 1918.

Finally I came out of GUM into Red Square. This vast cobbled expanse was much larger than I had ever imagined. It is nearly half a mile long, and 73,000 square metres in area. Down one side runs the grey façade of GUM. On its own at the southern end, like some large grotesque toy, stands the strange Russo-Oriental fantasia of St Basil's Cathedral, built by Ivan the Terrible, perhaps the most famous building in Russia. The far side of the square is dominated by the battlements of the Kremlin, with a little row of silver-grey fir trees in front, looking as if it is perpetual winter and they have just had a dusting of snow. In front of them, the squat, four-tier reddish-black granite Lenin mausoleum, its recessed door guarded night and day by two immaculate guards in the blue epaulettes of the KGB, with gleaming fixed bayonets. At two minutes to each hour, struck by the famous clock in the Spassky Tower to the left, two new guards emerge from the Kremlin wall and come goose-stepping along in slow motion to relieve their comrades.

One of the strangest things about Moscow is that almost every street, every square, every district has been renamed after a revolutionary motif or hero (or at least ideologically harmless pre-Revolutionary national figures, such as Kutuzov, Turgenev, Pushkin—there is no Tolstoy Square or Dostoievsky Street). Yet the one place in the city which Westerners assume must have been the first to be claimed for their own by the Communists—Red Square—was virtually the only thing which they did not have to rename. In the seventeenth century this then busy market place beneath the Kremlin walls and Ivan's cathedral was called 'Krasnaya Ploschad', meaning 'Beautiful Square'. But as Communist luck would have it, 'Krasnaya' in Russian means not only 'beautiful' but also 'red'. 'Red Square' it has remained.

The Looking-glass Olympics (16 July–4 August 1980)

I would defy anyone not to be impressed by Moscow. In the nineteenth century awestruck visitors had spoken of their first distant glimpse, as they crossed the interminable plains, of the city of 'forty times forty churches', a thousand domes and cupolas, each with a cross, shining in the sun. In the earlier decades of the twentieth century, they had spoken of the contrasts—the imposing palaces of the aristocracy, the foetid squalor of the back lanes, the little wooden shacks, the beggars in rags. Under Stalin, from the thirties onwards, there had been a concerted plan to rebuild Moscow as a suitable capital for the Communist world. Some of the plans had been grandiose beyond belief (though one of these, Leonidov's visionary project to erect a huge replica of a factory chimney, fifty storeys high, on Red Square, dated from the twenties). Of the hundreds of churches which had been demolished, the most imposing of all had been the huge, 394-foot-high domed Cathedral of Christ the Redeemer, down on the river to the south-west of the Kremlin. In 1934 this was blown up, to prepare a site for a building of even greater size, the Palace of the Soviets, which was to stand more than 1,000 feet high, with a 330-foot statue of Lenin on top. But it had then been discovered that the foundations were too wet, so the site was turned into a vast open air swimming pool, with room for 20,000 swimmers a day.

Stalin's rebuilding transformed the face of central Moscow, sweeping away countless older buildings, including almost all the little wooden houses, replacing them with huge, gaunt apartment blocks and offices, lining the great new boulevards. But the most dramatic of all Stalin's innovations, one I had not been prepared for, was the construction right at the end of his reign of the seven great so-called 'Stalinist-Gothic' skyscrapers, which stand round the centre of the city in a ring. Everyone of course knows of one of these—the Moscow State University building on the Lenin Hills. But there are six others, slightly smaller—one the Foreign Affairs Ministry, one an economic ministry, three hotels, and an apartment building just down the river from the Rossiya (where various privileged artists have lived, including Ulanova and the writer Paustovsky).

It is not surprising that the Soviet Olympic Organizing Committee chose an idealized pictogram of these skyscrapers as the logo for the 1980 Games. Even now, when a good many towers of more familiar sixties' design have risen alongside them, they are still the most striking and distinctive feature of the Moscow skyline. Their impact in the late forties and fifties when they were first built, and were by far the tallest buildings in the city, must have been staggering. But I could not help reflecting that at the very moment when Stalin's architects began putting them up, George Orwell in *Nineteen Eighty-four* was imagining his totalitarian London of the future—of which the most conspicuous landmarks were a ring of four huge 900-foot towers.

To sum up: some cities may be described as beautiful, some as being full of life, some as having great charm. This austere city, I felt as I walked about it, is about power—power which all derives ultimately from the Kremlin at the heart of the spider's web. It is a city in which all roads lead back to that strange, grim citadel on its hill.

5

Something Good in Everything You See

People at home who spend so much time imagining Russia—one
cannot imagine it.

Edmund Wilson, *Journals* (1935)

Friday 18 July

A day of puzzles. Certainly this place is full of them. Nothing as yet
very serious or fundamental, but simply a matter of not knowing quite
what to make of anything one sees. As a tiny example, there is this
lavish, if not enormously appetizing breakfast we are confronted with
in the mornings. Why is it that everything—the undrinkable cherry
and orange juice, the butter, the milk, the little tinfoil cartons of
jam—is labelled 'Made in Finland'? It looks as if the whole 'breakfast
experience' here in the Rossiya has been bought as a package deal from
Helsinki. It is true that in England one would not think twice about
being served in a hotel with French butter, or even Polish jam. But the
Soviet Union is supposed to be hard up for foreign currency. Is
Finland really better equipped to supply orange juice than sun-
drenched Armenia? Are the farms of the largest country in the world
not capable of providing butter for our breakfast?

The day began with a small disappointment. Ian Wooldridge told
me that he was off to an International Olympic Committee press
conference at the 'House of Trade Unions', at which Lord Killanin
was to bow out (although he remains President until the end of the
Games) and his successor was to be named. But apparently there was
only one ticket for each newspaper. It was not so much the press
conference I was sorry to miss as a sight of the great 'Hall of Columns'
where it was to be held. Among the many historic scenes this former
Club of the Nobility has witnessed in the past sixty years was Stalin's
lying-in-state in 1953, when literally millions of people poured into
Moscow to pay homage, the Red Army had to cordon off the whole of

the city centre with tanks and hundreds died in the crush. Another major event in the 'Hall of Columns' was the great show trial of leading Bolsheviks, including Nikolai Bukharin and Yagoda, the former head of the NKVD in 1938. I shall never forget in my schooldays reading Fitzroy Maclean's vivid eyewitness description of those scenes in *Eastern Approaches*, as day after day Stalin's former colleagues pleaded guilty to an amazing catalogue of treachery, sabotage and attempted assassination, while a little window occasionally opened above the hall, and spectators could see a familiar, moustachioed figure looking impassively down at his victims. Everyone assumed that the prisoners had been tortured or drugged (they probably had). But then came a twist when Bukharin, the cleverest intellectual of all the Bolsheviks, made a brilliant, lucid speech tearing the prosecutor Vyshinsky's evidence to shreds. Yet he still, at the end, admitted his guilt on the main charge of having questioned Stalin's infallibility in the glorious task of building Communism, and was taken off to the Lubyanka to be shot in the back of the neck like the others.

I would have enjoyed the incongruous sight of Lord Killanin making his farewell speech to the world's press in such a setting. The most trenchant passage, I gather, was a horrific-sounding warning against attempts to manufacture 'the artificial person', but it turned out this was nothing political, only a reference to the use of drugs in modern sport.

I decided instead to visit the Kremlin. Only one gate into the citadel was reported to be open, on the north-west corner, and there was the inevitable long queue, largely made up of groups from Eastern Europe. When I reached the front, a stony-faced young woman with 'Control' on her arm pushed me aside and beckoned to the group behind me. I tried to have a word with one of her assistants, politely asking in best British manner, how did one get into the Kremlin? After several minutes, a girl in a red scarf snapped, 'Only delegations.' I suddenly got a very tiny flavour of what it must feel like to be on the other side of the barrier in this country—not a privileged British visitor, to be welcomed with smiles, but one of the anonymous others; not a member of a delegation.

I went off to the Tretyakov, the famous gallery of Russian art. The Gallery, standing in a tree-shaded back street, just south of the river, is an extraordinary red-and-cream plaster building, a style that might be called Art Nouveau Russo-Romanesque. I was pleased to find that a large part of the Gallery had been cleared for a special Olympic exhibition, 'The History of Moscow in Painting'—for one of the things I had increasingly been haunted by was the question: 'What was Moscow like *before* the Revolution? How has this city changed?' Here perhaps might be an answer.

The first room of the exhibition (which worked backwards in time from the present) was somewhat unpromisingly dominated by a huge canvas entitled 'Our Way To Communism', showing a smiling Mr Brezhnev applauding himself in front of a vast Party meeting, while thousands of delegates gave him a standing ovation. What this had to do with the history of Moscow was not entirely clear, but other pictures round the walls, in that peculiar style known as 'Socialist Realism' (not to be confused with 'social realism'), showed factories, blast furnaces, cranes and tower blocks under construction, with such titles as 'Moscow Is Being Built'.

Lest the tower blocks and bulldozers should pall, light relief was provided after a couple of rooms with another huge, idealized, full-length representation of a stern-faced 'L. I. Brezhnev', and also a portrait of Lenin. A picture by Yury Pimenov, 'New Moscow 1937', caught the feeling of an earlier period, when idealism was slightly less jaded and more imaginative: the spectator is looking over the shoulder of a pretty young girl, driving an open, thirties-style roadster (a red carnation stuck playfully into the corner of the windscreen), as she heads into the traffic of a Moscow boulevard, with the inevitable huge Stalinist buildings rising behind.

We were now back to the period just after the Revolution—early parades in a snow-covered Red Square—and then suddenly a picture of enormous, if not strictly artistic, power. Called simply 'Bolshevik', painted by Kustodiev in 1920, it showed a kind of bird's eye view of vast crowds surging through the narrow streets of a city, and towering above them, like Gulliver in Lilliput, the colossal, staring-eyed figure of a bearded 'worker-peasant', carrying a red banner streaming behind him in the wind, his face set in a mask of heroic, mad antagonism as he trampled churches and palaces beneath his gigantic boots.

Now the pictures became more interesting still, as we travelled back into that mysterious Russia before the Revolution. One striking thing, of course, was the dramatic change in artistic style—suddenly one began to see pale reflections of many better-known Western painters, a Russian Utrillo, a Russian Monet, a Russian Corot. But most interesting of all were the glimpses of pre-Revolutionary life: an aristocratic party picnicking by the lake of a country estate, as in a scene from Turgenev; a festival day at a country fair near Moscow, with every kind of jollity in progress—laughing peasants standing around in colourful folk costumes, a soldier playing the accordion while another danced the *gopak*; a night scene of a glittering Tsarist ball in St George's Hall in the Kremlin, with party-goers strolling out on to the balcony to look down over the river; a picture of Red Square in the days when it was still covered with market stalls, which summoned up Maurice Baring's description from *What I Saw in Russia* (1905):

> It is Palm Sunday and the customary fair is being held on Red Place in front of the Kremlin, and as it has been a lovely day the crowd of strollers is immense. This fair is one of the most amusing sights to be seen in Russia. Two lines of booths occupy the space which stretches opposite the walls of the Kremlin. At the booths you can buy almost anything—birds, tortoises, goldfish, grass snakes, linoleum, carpets, toys, knives, musical instruments, books, music, cakes, lace, ikons, Easter eggs, carved woodwork, etc. There are besides these a number of semi-official stalls where kvass is sold to drink, and a great quantity of itinerant vendors sell balloons, things that squeak, penny whistles, trumpets and chenille monkeys.

I spent another hour walking round the rest of the Gallery, looking at the incomparable collection of icons which has been gathered here from hundreds of Russian churches since the Revolution, and at some of the fine pictures by nineteenth-century Russian painters—notably Valentin Serov's haunting study of a young girl ('The Girl with Peaches') and Vasily Polenov's charming 'Courtyard in Moscow' of 1878, showing a child playing in a sunlit, almost countrified garden near where the skyscrapers of the Novy Arbat now stand. And then I decided it was time to take the famous Moscow metro.

It must be said that the Moscow metro system (begun in 1935 by Kaganovich and a then-unknown but rising forty-one-year-old Communist Party *apparatchik* named N. S. Khruschev) is enormously impressive to a Western visitor. The reasons why are familiar: the lack of advertising of any kind; the wide, imposing halls and subways, decorated with chandeliers, marble, paintings and *bas reliefs* depicting such themes as 'Pushkin Reading Poetry in the Ukraine'; the speed and cleanliness of the trains (which for the Olympics were fitted with special recordings, announcing the name of the next station and even 'Mind the doors' in English).

I travelled out to Proletarskaya and emerged in a place which reminded me of a working-class suburb of Prague. All around were tatty, nine- or twelve-storey blocks of fifties' concrete flats. Balconies were broken. Washing was hanging out of windows. A church was boarded up. It was a scene of desolation. In front of me was a patch of 'open space', an area of long grass covered by scrub and small trees, with a muddy path running across it. In the middle 'construction' was going on—a strip of concrete which looked like a road, except that it was going from nowhere to nowhere. On the edge of the concrete, five workers were sitting, three men and two girls, looking intensely bored. Behind them on the mud, a large bulldozer and a mechanical digger stood idle, their engines running full blast.

Before I left London, I had asked a number of people what they thought I should be looking for in Moscow. One of them replied, 'Find out where the meat stops.' We had been discussing the efforts the authorities would undoubtedly be making to disguise the shortage of meat in the Soviet Union (as far back as the previous March a Czech friend had told me that meat of all kinds had suddenly and inexplicably run short in Prague, and rumours had swept the city that it was all being carried off to the Soviet Union to be hoarded for the Olympics). So I set off to as remote a part of Moscow from the Olympics as possible, the kind of place where foreign visitors might be least expected to travel, the Ryazanskiy Prospekt.

This main road out of Moscow in the direction of Ryazan, the city where Solzhenitsyn lived for years, was long, straight, potholed by the occasional huge trucks which seemed to be its most regular form of traffic, lined with straggly trees and more anonymous blocks of flats stretching to the horizon. I walked for about ten minutes through housing estates until I came to a row of shops, including a supermarket. It was fairly empty, except for a long queue by the fresh vegetable counter. There were plenty of lumps of rather unappetizing-looking meat in a freezer, not arousing unusual interest. I looked around this sad place, with its drab piles of tins, margarine in grey packets (no butter), the women waiting in queues with resigned, expressionless faces and felt like a nosy intruder.

On the way back to the metro, I called in at a bar for some lunch.

Some of the other customers were eating plates of prawns and potato flakes (a cross between chips and crisps). I asked for one of these and some beer. As I began eating, a girl in her late thirties sat down opposite me and began to read a thick magazine of articles and short stories. We began a faltering but fairly hilarious conversation, about nothing much more than where we each lived, and what we did for a living (she was a book-illustrator). The record player was playing Abba singing 'I believe in angels, something good in everything you see'. My book-illustrator friend insisted on paying for my lunch, as a gesture of friendship to an English visitor to her city.

The big moment was nearing at last. The following day, Saturday, was to see the opening ceremony of the 22nd Olympic Games, and I thought it was time I paid a visit to the Olympic Village. The press bus from the Rossiya did not take the normal route, and as we curved round through empty, wet streets near the bottom of Gorky Street, it was clear why. Crowds eight or ten deep were lining the pavements all the way up the hill, held back by a line of militia men, waiting for the Olympic flame to arrive at the end of its 3,000-mile journey across Greece, Bulgaria, Romania and the Soviet Union.

We travelled down the Komsomolskiy Prospekt, a huge boulevard stretching out south-west from the centre, towards the Lenin Hills. The University skyscraper loomed ahead of us and then suddenly, down to the right, by the Moscow River, under great banks of arc-lights carried on four huge concrete towers, was the vast grey bowl of the Lenin Stadium. A few miles beyond stood the Olympic Village, eighteen sixteen-storey slab blocks, surrounded by high wire fencing.

I remembered my shock when I had first seen a picture of this so-called 'Village' in an English newspaper back in January. Anything less like a village and more like a bleak housing estate on the outskirts of Glasgow, it would have been hard to imagine. Only a few days earlier, before I left England, I had heard Dick Palmer, the *chef de mission* of the British team, saying on television, 'By any standards this is a good village,' and I had prepared to have fun conjuring up pictures of thatched cottages, ducks on the pond and KGB men playing cricket on the village green.

But now here was the reality, depressing beyond belief in the pouring rain. The gaunt tower blocks, the wire fences, patrolling

militia men*—a few forlorn figures in tracksuits, including several
Africans, jogging round a rainswept practice track, presumably wondering what on earth they were doing in this cold, wet, dark, godfor-
saken place.

But as I looked out to the horizon, with similar clusters of tower
blocks stretching away in all directions, I recalled that, even though
these sixteen-storey blocks did not look too much like a 'Village' in
anybody's language, the 'Olympic Village' at Montreal had been even
higher, rising to twenty-two storeys. The athletes had not enjoyed a
true 'village' in the traditional sense of little houses or bungalows at
any Olympic Games since Tokyo in 1964.

Then there was the memory of a remark made to me by my Russian
friend before I left England. 'When you see those tower blocks,' she
said, 'remember that Russians don't necessarily have the same feelings about tower blocks as people in Britain do. They are desperate for
somewhere to live, and compared with most housing in Moscow, that
Olympic Village is probably built to a good standard. As soon as the
Games are over, people will be dying to get into them.'

The bus returned past the Lenin Stadium. The arc-lights were now
blazing down with full brightness in the gathering gloom of the
evening. When I got back to the Rossiya, the foyer was full of
people—journalists, receptionists, militia men—all gathered round
the telescreen, watching the Olympic flame being carried through the
streets by a lone runner to the Town Hall, where it was to be guarded
(in a room from the balcony of which Lenin had made a historic
speech on his arrival from Petrograd during the Revolution) until the

---

* Another puzzle in the Soviet Union, which takes some time to sort out, is the
distinction between the various branches of the security forces. In this narrative I use
'militia men' and 'policemen' fairly indiscriminately—but the irony is that in a country
widely described as a 'police state' there is technically no such thing as a 'policeman'.
After the Revolution the word 'police' was supposed to be so contaminated by its
association with Tsarist oppression, that what we would call the 'police' were renamed
the 'militia'. This body comes under the Ministry of the Interior, and is responsible for
such things as traffic control, catching ordinary criminals and making sure no one litters
the streets. It is quite separate from the KGB, the 'secret police', responsible for state
security, who come under their own ministry and are normally in plain-clothes. In
addition, confusion may arise between the 'militia' and the Red Army, since in khaki
members of both look like soldiers, and when I use the word 'soldiers' in this narrative I
may on occasion be referring to 'militia men', or as we would call them 'policemen'. Got
it sorted out?

opening ceremony the following afternoon. The air of expectation was mounting.

Radio Moscow that evening was full of the arrival in Moscow, as an honoured guest, of Yasser Arafat, leader of the Palestinian Liberation Organization. The BBC World Service was reporting that in Poland, the army had been moved in to get supplies into Lublin, and that the Polish Government appeared to be offering 'limited concessions' to the strikers. The final count of competing nations in the Olympic Games was eighty-one—out of a possible total of 146.

On the way out of the Main Press Centre, after dinner, Ian Wooldridge, Ian Jack of the *Sunday Times* and I met two very drunk Russians. They introduced themselves as members of the Soviet Olympic Organizing Committee. 'You are journalists?' said the senior one conspiratorially. 'I tell you what. You call me up in the morning and we will put together very good story. Very good story.'

'What is your name?' we asked. 'Leonid Orlov,' he replied. 'Ah,' we said, scribbling it down, 'Leonid, as in Brezhnev?' 'Orlov,' he repeated. 'Got it,' I said, 'as in Yuri Orlov, your well-known dissident.' 'Yes,' he said, very drunk indeed, 'call me in the morning. We can put together very good story.'

Mr Orlov was not available when we rang him in the morning. But tomorrow was indeed to see a 'very good story'.

6

The Games Open—A Lesson in Crowd Control

The Olympic movement and the Games are above all the triumph of the ideals of peace. As the Soviet Union puts into practice the Leninist principles of peaceful co-existence, she never fails to support social forces and movements which strengthen mutual understanding and peace between peoples. This is why Moscow invites the Olympic Games.

Moscow's Red Carpet Welcome for 1980 Olympics
(official handbook)

Saturday 19 July

Today, at last, after six years of preparation, the Moscow Olympics opened in a three-hour spectacle which, everyone agreed, put into the shade any other opening ceremony in the eighty-four-year history of the modern Games. But what a strange day it turned out to be!

Sitting in my room in the Rossiya after breakfast, I decided it was time I made a few telephone calls. I had come out from London with a list of Moscow numbers, given me by friends, but I had little luck. Everyone seemed to be either out of Moscow, or otherwise unobtainable. The only contacts I succeeded in making were with David Satter, resident Moscow correspondent of the *Financial Times*, and a Russian couple whose niece I knew in London. When I got through to their number, the wife answered and said they would be delighted if I would come over this evening for dinner. Unfortunately her English was not too good, and rather than risk giving me the complicated instructions for reaching their flat herself, she suggested that I should ring back at two o'clock that afternoon, when her husband would be at home.

This I agreed to do, and I then set off by metro to see David Satter, who, like many Western correspondents, diplomats and other foreign residents, lived in one of the official ghettos for foreigners out on Kutuzovsky Prospekt, on the west side of the city.

When I came up from the subway, I was confronted by a street as impressive as any I had seen so far. Kutuzovsky Prospekt, some eighty to a hundred yards wide, is lined with massive fifties' apartment blocks which only look smaller than they are because of the colossal width of the road they are standing along. As with many main roads in Russian cities, a central strip of this road is marked off for official traffic only, known as the 'Chaika Lane' (after the type of car used by officials just below the very top, rather curiously called 'Chaika' or 'seagull'). Among all my memories from my previous visit to the Soviet Union, there was one which had remained in my mind more vividly than any. On a grey, bitterly cold February day, I had just been leaving the Peter and Paul Fortress in Leningrad when, ahead of me, I heard sounds of commotion—police whistles, shouting, cars braking. As I came out on to a vast, straight road, stretching to the horizon, I saw dozens of armed policemen almost literally bundling every car off the road. The same thing was happening as far as the eye could see. Then, right in the distance, moving at enormous speed, appeared a procession of vehicles, tearing down the 'Chaika Lane': motor-cycle police outriders, with sirens blaring, a couple of police jeeps, and then three enormous black limousines, with curtains drawn round the back windows so that we could not see the occupants within, followed by more outriders. Within seconds, the apparition had vanished.

I had later asked someone familiar with Soviet life what all this had been about, and he explained that it was a not unusual way for senior officials to travel around. In this case, the official in question had probably been Tolstikov, the then much-feared Leningrad Regional Party Secretary. But what had most indelibly impressed me about the spectacle was the unceremonious speed, almost the violence, with which that road had been cleared and the dull, accepting stares of the ordinary citizens as those unknown officials, shrouded from public gaze, had sped past.

Nothing so dramatic was happening on the Kutuzovsky Prospekt that morning as I surfaced from the metro, but this vast boulevard is doubtless no stranger to such scenes. For in Block No. 26 President Brezhnev himself has a closely guarded apartment, with Yuri Andropov, the head of the KGB, occupying the flat above him, and the Minister of the Interior the floor below.

The Looking-glass Olympics (16 July–4 August 1980)

Although we had never met, David Satter could not have been more welcoming. He was already dispensing coffee to three other Olympic correspondents, including an American television man who, having just arrived, was wondering how he could get his hands on some dissidents to interview. Satter coped with the stream of queries with the utmost patience, and offered me a free run of his elaborate filing system ('information isn't always easy to come by in this town'). I asked him one or two questions about the 'Potemkin Village' aspects of the Soviets' Olympic preparations. He said he had just sent a long dispatch on this to the *Financial Times*, and if I wanted to read it, since time was getting on, why didn't I come back after the opening ceremony? He then offered me a lift back to the Rossiya.

As we drove back across central Moscow the streets and squares were almost empty of traffic, the pavements deserted—except that everywhere we looked there seemed to be large numbers of men in uniform. There was a definite tension in the air. What was happening?

When I arrived at the Rossiya, it was almost two o'clock—time for me to ring back the couple with whom I was going to have dinner that night. I got through, and the wife answered. I told her who I was, and she gabbled something in panicky tones in Russian. I couldn't understand what she was saying, and when I asked whether her husband was there, she put the telephone down. I was worried. I was sure it had been the right number, but, just in case, I tried again; as soon as I spoke, the telephone was put back on the hook.

According to one of the many handouts with which we had been showered by the Soviet Olympic Organizing Committee, the USSR Research Institute for Hydrometeorological Information had given exhaustive study to 'the results of weather observations made over many years' and had concluded that 'it is precisely at the end of July and the beginning of August that meteorology and climatology studies promise two weeks of the fine weather essential for the Games.'

In fact during the previous three afternoons it had bucketed down with rain. Saturday had opened with Moscow under cloud, and it was still overcast.

As our bus travelled through the grey, deserted streets (except that there were now even more uniformed men in evidence than there had been half an hour before) it was an eerie journey. We drove on westward, beneath banners proclaiming 'PEACE AND FRIENDSHIP',

76

The Games Open—A Lesson in Crowd Control

'SPORT, PEACE, PROGRESS'. We passed the golden domes of the Novodevichy Monastery, where countless famous Russians are buried, including Khruschev, Chekhov, Gogol, Mayakovsky, Eisenstein, Prokoviev—and there at last, coming into view a few hundred yards beyond, was the colossal bulk of the Lenin Stadium, with its four great towers of arc-lights above.

On the far side of the river, up on a hill covered with fir trees, the Moscow University skyscraper dominated the skyline. Martial music was sounding from loudspeakers. Crowds were streaming in from all directions. It was already a powerful scene, and as I climbed sixty-odd steps and came out of a tunnel high up in the stadium itself its force was redoubled.

The vast Lenin Stadium, built originally for the World Student Games in 1957, must be one of the most impressive in the world. As I climbed to my seat, above the banks of press desks, fitted with TV monitor screens and telephones, one of my colleagues said 'This makes Wembley look a pretty tatty little place, doesn't it?'

Above each end of the packed stadium, which has a seating capacity of 103,000, was a giant electronic screen. Between them, blazoned in large Cyrillic and Roman letters round the top of the stadium, was the Olympic slogan 'Citius, Altius, Fortius' ('Faster, Higher, Stronger'). On the far side from us, below the great concrete bowl that was waiting to receive the Olympic flame, 5,000 Red Army gymnasts sat in a block from top to bottom of the stadium, carrying coloured boards that were to keep up a dazzling kaleidoscope of patterns throughout the afternoon—the so-called 'Artistic Background'—beginning, as we arrived, with the 'tower block' symbol of the Games in red and white. Round the entire perimeter of the track, as is customary at major Soviet sporting events, sat an uninterrupted line of soldiers, dressed for the occasion in blue tracksuits.

With less than half an hour to go, the exhaustive studies of the USSR Research Institute of Hydrometeorological Information proved not to have been in vain. The sun came out from behind grey clouds, bathing the stadium in light.

At precisely 3.59 pm, a recording of the famous Kremlin chimes, playing the Internationale, rang out across the arena. Trumpeters sounded a fanfare. We could see from the TV monitors that Mr Brezhnev was taking his seat alongside Lord Killanin and members of the Politburo in a projecting marble 'box' below us to the left. And at 4.04 precisely, as indicated in the programme, from the great doors at

77

the left-hand end of the stadium, the competing teams began march-ing out for the opening parade.

Now all the attention of most of the thousands of pressmen around me was centred on how the teams from the 'non-Socialist world' might or might not register disapproval for the Soviet invasion of Afghanis-tan. Apart from the sixty-five countries which had stayed away altogether, it was known that many teams would not as usual parade behind their national flags, but only behind the Olympic standard of five blue rings on a white background—while some teams would not take part in the parade at all.

The parade was a continuous hubbub around me as journalists tried to work out which team was which, and how the scene was being presented by the official Soviet television pictures. Each team came out preceded by a girl in a red dress, carrying the name-board of the country, then a flag-carrier. When the team from Afghanistan came out early in the parade it was greeted by one of the biggest roars of the afternoon from the Soviet crowd. Its numbers had been sadly depleted by 'defections', and even worse by the killing of most of the hockey team in an ambush some weeks before, on their way back from playing practice games in the Soviet Union (this was 'punishment for their collaboration' according to the Afghan guerrillas responsible).

Further roars were given to each of the Socialist countries, in particular the huge teams from Cuba, East Germany and Hungary. The Tanzanians broke into a ragged goose-step as they passed Presi-dent Brezhnev's box. From time to time, in place of a team, only the girl with the name-board and a solitary flag-carrier would come out—as when the grey-haired figure of Dick Palmer, representing Britain, wandered round holding an Olympic flag and smiling to the crowd. But the Soviet television audience saw little of this, as the pictures beamed out from the stadium were carefully cropped to show only the name-boards of the offending countries, while the commen-tator allowed himself a passing mention of this 'strange conduct by a few nations', so 'contrary to the traditions of the Olympic movement'.

Finally, to the loudest and longest roar of all, on came the largest team in the competition, that of the Soviet Union itself, nearly 500 strong, in immaculate blue blazers. The effects of the boycott showed in the unusually short time the parade had taken (less than an hour) and in the vast areas of green which remained empty when the teams lined up in the middle of the stadium. But at last the great moment had arrived.

The Games Open—A Lesson in Crowd Control

Three small figures came down from the official box to a platform looking out over the serried ranks of competitors—Ignati Novikov, Deputy-Chairman of the USSR Council of Ministers and Chairman of the Soviet Organizing Committee, President Brezhnev and Lord Killanin. It was strange to see the white-haired figure of the Old Etonian hereditary aristocrat standing between the two Communist *apparatchiks*, as they made their perfunctory little speeches. In trying to keep the Olympic movement 'above' politics, Lord Killanin trod a narrow tightrope. He emphasized that the Games had been 'allocated purely on the ability of the host city to organize them'. He thanked the participating athletes and officials for the 'independence' they had shown, 'despite many pressures placed upon them'. Mr Brezhnev's remarks, read out in a flat voice, declaring the Games open, consisted of only thirty-one words. And then, as preparations were made to hoist the Olympic flag, came one of the most curious incidents of the whole ceremony.

To a particularly jarring arrangement of Beethoven's 'Ode To Joy' from the Ninth Symphony, twenty-two soldier gymnasts came on to the track, blank-faced, in blue blazers and white trousers, and began a slow goose-step towards the flagpole. Each was holding one arm aloft with something white clutched tightly in his hand. When they came nearer, we saw that the white objects were twenty-two doves, in honour of the 22nd Olympiad. As the Olympic flag rose to the top of the flagpole, and the band began playing the interminable Olympic anthem, the soldiers released their birds—which, according to a handout, had been taught by two years of intensive training to perform a graceful circuit of the stadium, and then set off in tight formation to the West. Twenty-one doves performed this manoeuvre with machine-like precision, but despite the two years' practice, one 'dissident' bird insisted on leaving the rest, flying round in the opposite direction, and eventually perching on the stadium roof.

More rituals took place, including the handing-over of another Olympic flag from Montreal to Moscow, and then at 5.10 came an announcement. On the giant telescreens there flashed up pictures of two Soviet cosmonauts, at that moment allegedly looking down on the earth from somewhere over Ceylon, and a message from the spacemen crackled over the loudspeakers: 'The youth of the Soviet Union is greeting you, participants of the Olympiad . . . mankind desperately needs durable and reliable peace.'

The screens changed, to show a lone runner approaching the

stadium, carrying aloft the Olympic flame. All the spectators craned to see him enter. I looked across at the great bowl opposite, to see where the steps were up which he would have to run—and there weren't any! How on earth was he going to get up there? As he ran round the track, to waves of cheering, and approached the far side, a remarkable thing happened: across the 'Artistic Background' a white line began to form, as the soldiers held a row of shields above their heads. The runner ran up over this 'human bridge', miraculously opening up before him, until he reached the top. There was a momentary pause, as he stood there in the sunshine; and then, from the giant bowl, the flame billowed upwards. With the most unexpected masterstroke so far, the 22nd Olympiad was under way.

A cantata, 'Ode to Sport', was sung by massed choirs, thousands more doves were released, the competitors took the Olympic oath, the Soviet national anthem was played again, the thousands of competitors filed out of the arena—and the second, even more spectacular part of the Olympic opening ceremony began.

No one present, certainly none of the journalists alongside me, had ever seen anything like what unfolded before us over the next hour. In honour of the ancient Greek founders of the Games, the spectacle opened with a Ben Hur-like procession of Greek chariots, surrounded by hundreds of pink-clad Greek maidens. The arena then filled again and again with wave upon wave of performers (16,000 in all). There were dancers in the colourful costumes of the fifteen nations making up the Union of Soviet Socialist Republics—Estonians and Lithuanians, Georgians and Armenians, Ukrainians and Uzbeks. There were dancing gymnasts dressed as Misha Bears. There were jugglers, acrobats and other circus performers. To a succession of compositions, with titles like 'The Sun' and 'Dance Suite: People's Friendship', based on tunes by Borodin, or written by Soviet composers such as Rodion Schedrin,* they formed and re-formed in a continuous kaleidoscope of colours and shapes—one moment making up the five Olympic rings, the next forming a succession of 'towers', each built up of several hundred performers standing on each other's shoulders, up to nine deep. It was an astonishing display of mass physical cohesion which with the music, the continuous cheering (even from the

---

* Since the deaths in the seventies of Shostakovitch and Khatchaturian, Schedrin (who is married to the leading Bolshoi ballet dancer Maya Plisetskaya) has become the *doyen* of Soviet composers. He is scarcely in the same league as his predecessors, however, and has been ridiculed for his blatant plagiarism of other composers.

journalists), the exploding, swaying, expanding and contracting patterns of colour laid out below us, was quite mesmerizing.

About a quarter of an hour before the end of the display, I had to leave to keep my appointment with David Satter on Kutuzovsky Prospekt across the city. As I came down the steps, I was dizzy from the spectacle I had just left. Music was still blaring from the loud-speakers. There were a lot of policemen around. At one point I had to push my way through a milling crowd of folk-costumed dancers who had already finished their performance inside. It was strange to see them close up. From a distance they had looked just like 'real folk dancers' from anywhere in the world. Now it was obvious that they had been heavily made up for the cameras. Many were smoking. Their 'traditional' costumes, which from afar had looked like brocaded satins, velvets and silks, turned out to be cheap, modern affairs, made of artificial fibres. Apart from the high cheekbones and narrow eyes of the Uzbeks and Kirghiz, they reminded me of nothing so much as a crowd of extras from some costume spectacular, standing round a canteen at the BBC Television Centre.

A few yards further on, in a heavily guarded cordoned-off space behind the official box, were about twenty huge, black, white-curtained Zil limousines, used by Mr Brezhnev and the members of the Politburo. Inside the stadium Frank Keating and one or two others had told me with awe how they had seen these arriving, roaring in down the 'Chaika Lane' of a nearby avenue, with their mass of motor-cycle outriders.

Walking in the same direction around me were several groups of Russians, talking in low voices. Behind us, the music from the loud-speakers had already begun to fade into the distance. We turned the corner, to be greeted by one of the most astonishing sights I have ever seen.

On each side of the road ahead of us, making a lane only a few yards wide, stood thousands of soldiers, literally shoulder to shoulder. Each of them was staring ahead of him with a fixed, grim expression—and behind them, in groups, stood hundreds more.

As we began to walk that gauntlet of stares, the most eerie thing of all was the complete silence. No one was uttering a word. The only sound was the shuffling footsteps of the Russians around me, as we walked on towards the metro station.

Occasionally I looked into the faces of the soldiers as I passed them. They looked back unwaveringly, straight between the eyes. They were not armed—but, I thought, they did not need to be. Whatever message such an extraordinary show of strength was intended to convey was coming across quite clearly enough without a little detail like that.

We turned another corner, and ahead of me was a tall man in a yellow anorak, who looked rather English, being photographed against the serried walls of soldiers by a girl. As I passed, I heard them talking English. When I reached the entrance of the metro station, I waited until they caught up, and said, 'I'm glad you've got that on record.' He turned out to be a British journalist, working for a North American publishing group. He said that he had lived in Moscow for some years, and that in all his time there he had never seen anything like it.*

The strange air of tension hanging over central Moscow that afternoon seemed to persist throughout my journey. As I was walking up the stairs at the metro station the other end, I heard behind me a sudden explosion of noise—the kind of yell a Chinese kung-fu expert is supposed to give as he jumps on his opponent. I looked round, and two policemen were throwing themselves on a man whom they pinned up against a wall. Although I turned round for a good look, none of the dozens of people around me appeared to take the slightest notice. They just walked on.

It was a relief to arrive at David Satter's office. He gave me various notes and old articles to read. As we drove back to the Rossiya, I asked him whether he had any advice. He said, 'Don't make the mistake so many people do when they come here, of looking at the Russians as if they were animals in a zoo.' We drove along the Moscow River embankment below the walls of the Kremlin. A Union Jack was hanging from a flagpole outside an imposing recessed mansion on the far bank. It was the British Embassy.

---

* Though I was later to find an interesting echo of this experience in Hedrick Smith's *The Russians*: 'My own first exposure to the system's obsession with control of the masses was unforgettable. It came after an international soccer match with the Irish team . . . coming out of the stadium with 100,000 other fans, I saw the streets lined with armed soldiers standing shoulder to shoulder in a wall of khaki. They formed a channel through which the crowd had to flow towards subways and bus lines. Along another street, the foot soldiers were reinforced by mounted cavalry, also lined up side by side. The array of power was numbing.' Note that on this occasion (as is usual) the soldiers were armed.

The Games Open—A Lesson in Crowd Control

Only later did I discover how unusual a sight that Union Jack had been. Apparently Stalin had got fed up with looking out of his office window in the Kremlin and seeing this 'imperialist' flag hanging across the river. The British Ambassador had received a request that it should no longer be flown. Today, for the opening of the Olympics, was the first time in thirty years that the Union Jack had been raised there.

Later that evening I strolled out to sit on a granite balustrade overlooking the river. I had been quite shaken by the day. It had begun so well, with the prospect of dinner with a friendly Russian family—and then the panicky jabbering in Russian when I had rung them back. Those incredible displays of mass-precision in the stadium had, of course, been stupendously impressive, but there was something unreal and muffled about the opening ceremony, about this whole city. And what of those thousands of soldiers outside the metro station? Why had they been there? Obviously they had not been intended for the benefit of Western visitors, most of whom would have been rushed back to their hotels in special buses, through specially cleared streets. So who were the people that show of force had been intended to intimidate?

I had the feeling that something quite creepy had been going on in Moscow that day. On the one hand there had been the superbly stage-managed spectacle, the dancing, the music, the show. On the other was this dark, mysterious underside. It was only later that we learned that, during the three hours of the ceremony, Sheremetyevo Airport and all the air-space round Moscow had suddenly, without warning, been closed to all aircraft except those from 'friendly' Socialist countries (as Ian Wooldridge put it, 'What were they expecting—dissidents swooping in on hang-gliders, showering the arena with leaflets bearing a personal message from Bernard Levin?'); and that anything upwards of 200,000 troops and militia men had been deployed round Moscow that afternoon in one of the biggest security operations the city had seen since the death of Stalin.

7

Inside the Bubble

You can feel the Olympic mood everywhere in Moscow . . . you
won't find a person here who regards the Olympics as a burden,
for everyone feels directly involved and is happy to contribute
his share . . . this in my view contrasts sharply with the previous
Olympics.

> Arpad Csanadi, Hungarian member of
> International Olympic Committee, quoted in
> *Olympic Panorama*, a quarterly published by the
> Olympiad-80 Organizing Committee

All will have a chance of . . . enjoying an extensive cultural
programme, including visits to museums, exhibitions and places
of historic interest. They will see plays, films and the Soviet
people at work, at home and at rest. They will visit clubs,
schools, kindergartens. They will see for themselves how peace
on earth is cherished by the Soviet people.

> *The Soviet Contribution to the Olympics*, Novosti
> Press Agency Publishing House (1979)

Sunday 20 July

Today the sport begins. After breakfast, my hundreds of colleagues
fan out to all corners of Moscow, to watch handball, volleyball,
basketball, cycling, rowing and swimming in the dazzling array of
new and renovated arenas which have been prepared for the Games.
The mass of official handouts lay constant stress on the huge feat of
organization which has lain behind the provision of the finest facilities
ever laid on for an Olympics, the unprecedented scale, complexity and
minute-by-minute precision of the sporting schedule, etc. As the
official handbook *Moscow's Red Carpet Welcome* puts it:

> As long as two years before the start of the Olympics, it was
> known that a competitor in free pistol shooting would at 11.30

am on 20 July become the first champion and number one prizewinner of the Moscow Olympic Games. Such a categorical statement was made after studying the hourly timetable of Olympic events which the sports programmes department had worked out on the basis of the daily schedule.

I cannot yet take part in all this excitement as I have to spend most of today sitting in my room in the Rossiya, writing my first long despatch for the *Daily Mail*. As I pace up and down, looking out at the poor little stunted fir trees in the Rossiya's huge courtyard, drinking innumerable cups of Nescafé made with hot water supplied by my 'floor lady' from her 'electric samovar' (electric kettle), there is only really one theme for my opening article, and that is the extraordinary two-sided nature of what is going on here in Moscow.

On the one hand, we are living inside what I have already come to think of almost instinctively as 'the bubble'. It cannot be denied that this is very impressive, superbly organized and, at least by normal Soviet standards, amazingly easy to live in. Here we are, tucked up in one corner of this enormous hotel (so big that we never have to enter three-quarters of it, and anyway we are channelled into 'our side' of it by the tight security which dictates that we can only enter by one door). Food in the restaurants, if nothing to write home about, is at least perfectly adequate, and some of it—notably the caviar—so cheap in comparison with prices in the shops that it must be subsidized. Downstairs in the foyer each morning (for anyone who gets up early enough) it is possible to buy copies of the previous day's London newspapers. If we wish to telephone London, a specially recruited team of English-speaking operators on the specially built new international exchange will put us through, usually in only a couple of minutes (instead of the more normal two hours). Elsewhere in the foyer are endlessly helpful, friendly interpreters ready to assist with any enquiry. On a balcony overlooking the foyer, the Rossiya has its own 'mini-Press Centre', with a bar and another team of special interpreters (it is only after a day or two, when one has passed the same faces first thing in the morning and then sees them again eleven or twelve hours later, that one notices what extraordinarily long hours they seem to be working).

Only half a dozen steps outside the hotel there is the fleet of special press buses continually available to take us to every conceivable

The Looking-glass Olympics (*16 July–4 August 1980*)

'Olympic destination'. At the Main Press Centre, down on Sadovoye Koltso, the Caspian sturgeon, the Georgian champagne, the caviar ('by the cupful' as one of my colleagues put it) are even cheaper and more plentiful than in the Rossiya. Here too are as many telex machines, telephones and instant translation services as a journalist could want, not to mention more rows of helpful faces behind desks, working their twelve-hour shifts. While if one wants to buy a bottle of vodka or 200 English cigarettes (or a Russian doll souvenir or binoculars or a transistor radio or a colourful scarf or hand-painted wooden bowls or a hand-painted box showing Lenin standing in front of the Kremlin) one only has to pop a few yards down the side of the Rossiya to the huge 'Beriozka' supermarket to exchange a few pounds or dollars.

This is only one aspect of the 'bubble' we are living in—and it would be perfectly possible to stay inside it, performing one's task as a journalist efficiently and comfortably, all day and all night long. But perhaps one wishes to venture a little further, to see more of this fascinating country? Security is tight, of course, but then it has to be at a modern Olympic Games (you should hear some of the hair-raising stories my colleagues have to tell about Montreal, where the policemen were armed, and seemed to have no hesitation about pushing a loaded sub-machine gun into your chest). In fact there is nothing to stop any of us wandering at will all over this city, and of course, we are not just limited to the round-the-clock service of press buses. Our journalists' identity cards hanging round our necks entitle us to free travel on the metro or the city's own crowded buses wherever we wish to go (although in fact the flat-rate fare for Muscovites is only 5 kopeks, or about 3p, as it has been for years).

One way we can explore this country is vicariously, by means of the splendid array of programmes on Soviet television, which we can watch either on the huge telescreen in the foyer, or on the large colour set which most of us have in our rooms. There is a lot of Olympic coverage, of course, but there are also operas, ballets, concerts, folk-dancing, marvellous circus acts, films and documentaries of Soviet life with romantic shots of sunlit corn waving to the horizon down on the collective farm.

Or we can take advantage of the lavish programme of guided tours advertised in the Rossiya Press Centre: a visit, for instance, to the 'Bolshevik Collective Vegetable Farm', or on another day to the 'V. I. Lenin Collective Dairy Farm', on a third to the 'V. I. Lenin Automobile Factory'. Next week there is a day-trip to the famous religious centre of Zagorsk, sixty miles out of Moscow along a specially preserved tourist route lined with traditional carved and painted Russian villages, to see the ancient cathedrals and the young Orthodox priests training at the (state-supported) seminary, while on Tuesday, to mark 'Soviet Music Day', there is a visit to the 'House of Composers', to 'meet Soviet composers' and to talk with them about their work.

In fact there is one aspect of these Olympics which most people at home will probably not hear much about, but which is just as impressive in its own way as the sporting arrangements, and that is the quite astonishing 'Festival of Culture' which is being staged here (and throughout the other four 'Olympic cities'). It is customary for the host-nation of an Olympics to put on some sort of a 'cultural show'—indeed it is written into the Olympic rules (and up to the London Games in 1948 there were actually competitions and Gold Medals for poetry, music, sculpture and other artistic endeavours). But never has an Olympics seen anything resembling the culture *fest* which is taking place here: even the Soviet Union has known nothing quite like it, in all its sixty years. Every night there are plays, operas, ballets, poetry-readings, gypsy concerts and folk-dancing displays being staged all through the city, in every available auditorium, theatre, park (even, for the busy journalists, in the Main Press Centre itself, where one Georgian folk-ensemble is giving a programme entitled 'From The Suburbs of Tiflis'). According to our handouts, all this has already been going on for over a year, since 1 June 1979, and will not finish until October 1980, although these few weeks obviously mark the zenith of activity.

At the Bolshoi one can see *Boris Godunov* or *Romeo and Juliet* or *Ruslan and Ludmilla*, or a new ballet, *Chaika*, specially written for the festival by Rodion Schedrin, based on Chekhov's *The Seagull*. Almost every Russian work of note ever written is being presented somewhere, in some form—including Schedrin's ballet based on *Dead Souls* and a play (which must be rather long) based on *The Brothers Karamazov*. There are dance ensembles from the fifteen Republics; there are the Red Army Choir and the Leningrad Dixieland Band; there is a special programme at the Moscow State Circus called 'Laughter is the Best Medicine', starring 'People's Artist of the USSR O. Popov'. One can see Plisetskaya dance, hear Alla Pugacheva sing, Gilels play Beethoven or Yevtushenko read his poems. Among foreign works on show there is Shakespeare (*Hamlet, Richard III, Twelfth*

Night), Tennessee Williams (*Streetcar Named Desire*), Robert Bolt (*Vivat Regina!*). There are exhibitions of everything from 'Man and Space in Art' to 'Russian Samovars'. Films range from *The Battleship Potemkin* and *Diamonds for the Dictatorship of the Proletariat* to *The Misadventures of the New Satan*, though I may give a miss to the programme at the Pervomaisky Cinema:

> *A Mother's Heart*
> *October*
> *Lenin in October*
> *Lenin in 1918*
> *Stories About Lenin*
> *The Man With a Gun*

This somehow lacks the poetry of the fare at the famous Taganka Drama and Comedy Theatre, which runs:

> J. Reed, *Ten Days That Shook the World*
> W. Shakespeare, *Hamlet*
> M. Gorky, *Mother*
> V. Vasilyev, *The Dawns Are Quiet Here*
> V. Mayakovsky, *Listen!*
> F. Dostoievsky, *Crime and Punishment*
> K. Simonov, *The Fallen and the Living*
> Y. Lyubimov, L. Tselikovskaya, *My Friend, Have Faith!*

It should, in short, be a joyous and marvellous experience to be here, the holiday of a lifetime—yet somehow it is not. One clue as to why it is not may be gleaned from the armfuls of books, magazines and handouts we have been given, all written in that curiously naïve, stilted, self-congratulatory prose which soon becomes so familiar to the student of official Soviet publications. Everything has to point so relentlessly in the same direction, from the endless flow of statistics ('There are 660 gardens, parks and boulevards in Moscow. On average there are twenty-two square metres of green per Muscovite, compared with only seven square metres per person in New York, eight in London and four in Paris') to the equally remorseless quotation of compliments paid by foreign visitors to the beauties of Moscow, the achievements of the Soviet Union and the splendours of the Olympic arrangements. There is one glossy publication, *Olympic Panorama* (dressed up to look like a Western magazine, with advertisements for Chanel No. 5 and Mercedes Benz—much glossier than anything on sale on Moscow's news stands) which actually works through every single 'Olympic facility', appending such quotations as:

> Fencers have never in the history of the Olympic Games and world championships competed in a better gym. The conditions are superb here.
>
> > Carlo Montano, Italy, many times foil-medal winner at world championships

> I can only say that this facility is marvellous, a wonder!
>
> > Fred Oberlander, Canada, Vice-President, International Wrestling Federation

> I must praise the Games' organizers for doing their utmost to build the best shooting range in the world ...
>
> > George A. Vichos, Greece, President, International Shooting Union

Possibly 'Dr Alexander Brown, Great Britain, Chief Veterinary Officer' did not mean quite what he was quoted as saying about the 'Trade Union Equestrian Complex': 'I have seen everything here and found the equestrian complex grandiose.' But the thought strikes that all these people must have been specially flown to Moscow months, even years before the Games, precisely in the hope that they would provide such glowing references; otherwise the brochures could not have been put together in time to ensure that every piece in the dazzling mosaic of universal international acclaim was in place and complete.

In this context I cannot help recalling a comment made in *Through Bolshevik Russia* by Mrs Philip Snowden, as a member of one of the very earliest foreign delegations to make an official guided-tour of the Soviet Union in its infancy, exactly sixty years ago:

> The way in which our clever hosts contrived to place us under a very real and lasting obligation by their generous regard for our physical welfare ... and at the same time to extract from us for their own purposes the last ounce of propaganda usefulness excited my warmest admiration.

One of the troubles about this glowing picture of the Soviet Union we are being given is that it is *so* perfect, so utterly without flaw that it is completely dead. It is all so carefully composed, like a Victorian family photograph, that there is no longer anything remotely real or life-like about it. Indeed, another trouble is that, apart from the novelty of the Olympic ingredient, it is all so familiar, so stereotyped. The Bolshoi, the Lenin Motor Works, the caviar, the proclamations of 'Peace and Friendship', the visit to Zagorsk, the collective farms with their sunlit vistas of waving corn—we *know* that is what coming to the Soviet Union is all about. It has been like that for sixty years (almost literally—already in 1920, when the Revolution was scarcely two years old, Mrs Snowden could describe the 'vivid pictures portraying . . . Communist fields bursting with grain yield to the sickle of the happy, sunbrowned, well-fed harvester', in between her delegation's visits to the Bolshoi and consumption of caviar).

We know all this is intended to create the image of a perfect, prosperous, efficient society full of well-fed, happy workers and laughing, exuberant folk-dancers—yet one only has to keep one's eyes open and one's human sensibilities attuned, to see that it doesn't ring true for a minute. The gap between the image and the shabby, bleak reality is only too glaring: the queues, the shoddy goods and empty shelves in the stores (in such contrast to the brightly-lit abundance of the Beriozkas—which of course are only open to those able to pay with foreign currency),* the ubiquitous 'Repair' shops.

So *much* effort has been made to impress us. Even the announcements of 'mind the doors' in English on the metro, one senses, have been thought out not just to aid visitors, but also to create a certain effect. Indeed almost everything we are surrounded with is intended to create that effect, right down to the fact that, in our press buses, the driver (who speaks only Russian) so often just *happens* to have his transistor radio tuned to the English-speaking service of Radio Moscow, relaying eulogies of the Soviet Union by Olympic visitors, or interviews such as the one Ian Wooldridge and I heard yesterday, in which the manager of the Puerto Rican team was complaining at the

* These shops, originally known as *Torgsin*, have been a feature of cities open to Westerners since soon after the Revolution. Their intention is quite simply to insulate the foreign visitor against the rigours of Soviet life, by enabling him to buy a whole range of Western and Soviet-made goods not available in normal shops, and at the same time to provide the USSR with a useful source of foreign currency. The institution is found all over Eastern Europe and has frequently been the subject of protests by local populations (e.g. in Poland in August 1980) who see the bright lights and well-stocked shelves of these shops contrasting to the empty shelves of their own drab shops. *Beriozka* mean 'Little Birch Tree'.

'brutal pressure' which had been put on his athletes back home to persuade them from coming.

In fact it is all as obvious and as two-dimensional as one of old Grigory Potemkin's villages must have been to anyone who actually walked up to it and looked round the back of the cardboard. Untold millions of roubles must have been spent on regilding and repainting and restoring thousands of buildings all over the centre of Moscow, yet you have only to walk into GUM, right on Red Square, to see that cracked, leaking roof, closed-off galleries, and scaffolding that looks as if it has been there since the Revolution. However hard they try, the façade just keeps on slipping. To end with just one more tiny example: the other night one of the television channels was showing a Chopin concert from the Great Hall of the Tschaikowsky Conservatory. Occasionally the camera strayed across the well-dressed audience, pausing to pick out some suitably representative figure rapt in the music. Finally it fastened on a large lady who stood out from everyone else because she looked so obviously working class. The camera lingered on her, I had no doubt, because in someone's mind she provided such a perfect image of what the Soviet Union is meant to be all about—the rough-hewn proletarian who still has time to pursue a deep love of culture. The only trouble was that, at that very moment, the lady chose to give off a yawn of total boredom—and the camera hurriedly panned away.

If it looks like this from inside the bubble, how does life look outside it, in those serried ranks of jerry-built flats, where the ordinary people of Moscow live cheek by jowl, one, two or more to a room; in those drab shops where the arrival of a special 'Olympic consignment' of fruit or sausage is sufficient signal for a line of several dozen people to form instantly? Perhaps nothing more clearly indicates the 'closed-off' nature of what is going on in Moscow than the fact that none of the tickets for the Lenin Stadium have been on open sale to ordinary Muscovites at all—they have all been allocated to officials, sports organizations, the Red Army and special delegations.

I have already begun to feel a nagging sense of discomfort. Partly it is because, cocooned in our unreal little archipelago of hotels, restaurants and buses, scattered across the city, I feel so cut off, so privileged for all the wrong reasons—as when I can march into the Beriozka shop for a packet of cigarettes, knowing that none of the dozens of people passing the window can follow me. Partly, as Mrs Snowden put it, it is because of the sense of obligation one naturally feels towards such generous, thoughtful hosts—when I know that I am constantly trying to peer round the back of their generosity for all sorts of hidden motivations. Perhaps, above all, it is just a new awareness of how far and how deeply, beyond the brightly-lit bubble we are living in, the darkness actually extends.

As I put it in my article:

> It was predictable that the Soviet authorities would make fullest use [of the Olympics] to build the biggest and brightest Potemkin village of them all . . .
> What was not predictable until it began to emerge a few months ago was just how far, in order to maintain the artificial sunlight, the Soviet authorities would feel it necessary to increase the darkness over their own people, from the mass-rounding up of dissidents to the ransacking of the Soviet empire for meat to create an impression of abundance.
> The real underlying horror of these Games is just how dark is the pall which has fallen behind that bright façade. Not for nothing is the name Potemkin much the same as the Russian word *potemky*—which means 'obscurity, darkness'.

I wrapped up my piece, telephoned it over to London—to a cheerful copytaker, who said he 'wouldn't mind some of that caviar'—and wandered down to the bar.

Many people may wonder how it is that foreign correspondents manage to jet in to some trouble spot, where they have never been before, usually without speaking the language, and within twenty-four hours are filing out reams of authoritative copy telling the world just what is happening. Now I began to discover. It is remarkable how, surrounded by hundreds of journalists, in the bar, over dinner, or just through chance exchanges in the lift, one can pick up a general picture of what is going on without even trying.

Around the Rossiya that evening, for instance, I soon learned that Britain's swimmers had won two silver medals out at the Olimpisky Pool on Prospekt Mira ('Peace Avenue')—Philip Hubble in the 200 Metres Butterfly, and four of our girls in the 4×100 Relay. Our pentathlon team had come a bit of a cropper—partly because they had drawn some particularly unmanageable Russian-trained horses in the equestrian event. The first six gold medals of the Games had been distributed according to a pattern everyone expected most of the rest would follow—four to the Soviet Union, two to East Germany. As for that pistol shooting gold medal which the Soviet planners had known from 'studying the hourly timetable of Olympic events' two years before would be the first to fall of the XXII Olympiad—at precisely 11.30 am on 20 July 1980—the winner had been Red Army marksman Alexander Melentev, for the Soviet Union.

Inside the bubble, at least, everything was going according to plan.

8

Settling Down

The mounting influence of socialist sport on the world sports movement is one of the best and most comprehensible means of explaining to people throughout the world the advantages which the socialist system has over capitalism.

> *Teoriya i praktika fizicheskoi kul'tury* (Theory and Practice of Physical Culture)—the leading Soviet sports monthly—1973, No. 1

Thus Soviet authorities do not miss an opportunity to point out the success of athletes from socialist states in international competition and to draw conclusions which would lead one to believe in the superiority of the social system existing in most East European countries. An excellent opportunity of that kind presented itself after the XXth Olympic Games in 1972 in the city of Munich. The Soviet press emphasized that the Soviets won 50 gold, 27 silver and 22 bronze medals as opposed to only 33 gold, 30 silver and 30 bronze medals won by American athletes ... it was further stressed that while athletes from socialist states made up only 10 per cent of all participants, they won 47.5 per cent of all medals, and five socialist states were placed among the first ten in the unofficial team standing ... it was claimed that the successful appearance of Soviet athletes on the international scene was 'first of all the result of the great concern of the Communist Party and the Soviet government over the development of mass sport and the health of the working people'.

> N. Norman Shneidman, *The Soviet Road to Olympus: The Theory and Practice of Soviet Physical Culture and Sport* (1979)

Today there were still echoes of the nervy atmosphere of Saturday, although there were many more people on the streets, and there were few signs of the vast security operation which had closed off the centre of the city during the opening ceremony.

The big talking-point among the journalists was an incident that had occurred in Red Square at midday. A crowd of Western photographers had gathered in one corner of that great expanse in the expectation that they would be able to take pictures of the world-record-breaking British middle-distance runner Sebastian Coe, who had arrived in Moscow the previous day with his father and coach, Peter. In fact Coe was giving one of the biggest press conferences of the Games down at the Main Press Centre and never turned up in Red Square. But as the knot of photographers waited in hope they noticed that several dozen Russians were also standing around them, looking like ordinary bystanders—except for the curious detail that they were all holding identical little stubby, collapsible umbrellas.

Suddenly another man nearby unfurled a banner and began handcuffing himself to some railings. The photographers were just rushing over to take pictures when they were set upon from all sides by the umbrella-carriers. One photographer had his camera broken, another had his spectacles smashed, several more (including the *Daily Mail*'s Monty Fresco) had their films removed—and four journalists were arrested.

It turned out that the lone demonstrator was Vincenzo Franconi, a member of an Italian 'gay rights' group, campaigning for the release of two Russians who, it was claimed, had been put in prison for homosexuality. The journalists were released by the KGB after an hour, having been warned that in future they should 'concentrate on the Olympic sports rather than demonstrations'.

It was a silly little affair, although as Monty Fresco pointed out, if an Italian had chained himself to the railings of Buckingham Palace probably no one would have heard any more about it—whereas, thanks to the KGB's heavy-handed intervention, this incident was now destined for the front-pages of the world's press.

Away from such peripheral alarms and excursions, the second day of the Games proceeded as smoothly as ever. In the splendid new Sports Palace next to the Lenin Stadium at Luzhniki, Nataliya Shaposhnikova of the Soviet Union returned a perfect score of ten points in the vault (a triumph only slightly dimmed in Russian eyes by the fact that her great rival Nadia Comaneci, the Romanian ex-world champion, recovered from a long period out of form to take 'a full ten' in the beam exercises). In the Olimpiskiy swimming pool, Barbara Krause, a member of the East German security forces, broke her second world record in successive swims in the 100 Metres Freestyle. Other world records fell in various parts of the city, in sports ranging from pistol shooting to bantamweight weightlifting—and it is becoming clear that this is something of particular importance to the Soviet authorities. They are emphasizing it on every possible occasion; for the more records that are broken, the more clearly does it demonstrate that these Olympics are of truly world standard, and that therefore the absence of 'certain countries' through the boycott is irrelevant. The ladies of the USSR beat the ladies of the Congo by 30 points to 11 in handball. The Soviet Union beat Czechoslovakia 3 to 1 in volleyball. The Soviet Union beat India by 121 points to 65 in Men's Basketball. Everything is still going according to plan.

Tuesday 22 July

Today the atmosphere really has lightened. After last week's tension things are now getting easier, more relaxed. The security checks on the door of the Rossiya are getting noticeably more perfunctory. No longer do we get that initial exhaustive scrutiny, as the militia men look first at our identity card, then into our eyes. As one says '*pazhalsta*' (please) and '*spaseba*' (thank you), they are even beginning to smile.

This morning I took a stroll up to the Ploschad Nogina (named after the obscure 'Old Bolshevik' Nogin who was first Commissar for Industry after the Revolution). The sun was shining, the air pleasant and fresh. There were markedly more people about, even than yesterday. Young girls strolled hand in hand—as they often charmingly and quite innocently do in this country. Smiling officials from the grey, pre-Revolutionary building nearby, which houses the offices of the Central Committee of the Communist Party, paused to chat with each other, clutching briefcases.

I made a short tour of the Museum of the History and Reconstruction of Moscow, housed in a former church. Though it contains some archaeological and historical exhibits, as my guide book tactfully put it, 'Special attention is paid to the Revolution and later development of Moscow.' A small boy was having a bronze bust of Ivan the Terrible explained to him by his father (actually it portrayed the most notorious of all the tsars as quite a kindly old boy). There were busts of Lenin and Mr Brezhnev, and quotations from Lenin and Mr Brezhnev on the walls. A glass case contained editions of Mr Brezhnev's books, reverently laid out open as if they were some illuminated manuscripts or rare incunabula. But although there were plenty of exhibits from the dark days of the 'Great Patriotic War' (as they call World War Two)—drawings of Moscow in 1941 under barrage balloons, military parades in a sandbagged Red Square—there was nowhere, of course, a single sign or picture of the 'Great Leader' whose courage and military brilliance were once alone supposed to have saved Moscow and Russia in those times, Josef Stalin.

I walked on up to Dzherzhinsky Square where, right opposite the KGB headquarters in the Lubyanka, an almost equally large building houses Moscow's famous department store for children, Detskiy Mir ('Children's World'). If it was true that all the children had been moved out of Moscow for the Olympics—and certainly there seemed to be very few children and almost no teenagers in evidence on the streets—here would be as good a place to check as any.

In fact there were quite a few children with their parents in the store, though none more than about six or seven years old. The Moscow equivalent of Hamley's is a huge building inside, with three balconied floors running round a central hall. In the centre of this stood a large, rudimentary wooden model of an old pirate ship, about twenty feet long, with figures of sailors and pirates. There were several counters offering 'war toys'—tanks, guns, aircraft—but certainly no more and probably less than you would find in a Western toy store. In fact the main impression I formed, a sad one, was how crude and shoddy the toys were in comparison with their Western equivalents; they were almost all made of plastic (particularly sad because Russia was once so famous for its carved wooden toys—here there was no sign of craftsmanship whatever).

The truth about the 'mass exodus' of children, which aroused so much comment in the Western press, seems to be this. It is customary for children to go off each year to summer camps, organized by the Pioneer, Young October and Komsomol organizations to which every Soviet child and adolescent belongs. In 1980 the authorities have simply made sure that attendance is even more complete than usual. A great many other people have also chosen for one reason or another to be out of Moscow during the Games. Residents say they have never

97

seen the city so empty (evidently at least a third of the normal population is absent). And of course it is known that quite a number of people have been forcibly removed—e.g. the vast numbers of drunks who are normally such a depressing feature of Soviet cities; the unemployed who, theoretically under this system, do not exist. Like many of my colleagues, I have also noticed a complete absence of crippled or disabled people around the city.

I had lunch today in a shashlichnaya ('shashlik' or 'kebab' house) near the Bolshoi. It was fairly crowded. Very few of the dishes on the menu were available. I had a knuckle of some fairly indeterminate meat—there was very little on the bone, and the quality was noticeably poorer than anything we had seen in the press restaurants. One of the Russians sitting at my table, an unshaven man in his thirties, was wearing a large lapel button reading, in English, 'Vote for Miss Rhode Island'.

I can understand why Western journalists are struck by the Russians' fascination with things Western. So many reports from the Soviet Union centre on Russians coming up to tourists in the street offering anything up to 100 roubles (£70) for a pair of Levis, or on the popularity of Western rock music (a British colour supplement recently carried a picture of a sign in a remote town, out towards the Afghan border, carrying an advertisement for an evening of '*punk rok*', which does look very odd in Russian script). This morning, one of the ladies who clean my room in the Rossiya offered me two roubles (thirty shillings in real money) simply for a plastic carrier bag carrying the coveted legend 'Marks and Spencer, Oxford Street', which she wanted partly for the label, and partly because Russian shops, except those for tourists, do not provide such useful, wasteful items; if goods are wrapped at all, it is in very cheap 'utility' paper and string. Of course I gave her the bag—but it is perhaps worth bearing in mind David Satter's strictures against regarding the Russians as 'animals in a zoo', and pondering on some of the deeper reasons for this fascination with the more garish, meretricious aspects of our Western throwaway culture. It is a reflection on the extraordinary drabness and poverty of Soviet life, and a small outward sign of the tantalizing mystery in which the USSR shrouds the 'forbidden West', seemingly so strange and far away.

Despite the relaxation of tension, it would be a mistake to suppose that Moscow has suddenly taken on the jolly, festive air associated with previous Olympics, the streets full of dancing, laughing sports fans drunk on Olympic and holiday high spirits. Apart from the Olympic slogans and Misha Bears, there are few signs that the Games are on. One sees few foreigners, apart from the 'delegations' of Eastern Europeans. Another thing is that the foreign visitors really are isolated from each other, in their archipelago of hotels and Olympic venues. We journalists, for instance, never see the television and radio correspondents, except in the stadiums and arenas, because they are all quartered in the north of the city, in a huge, new hotel called the Kosmos, behind a security screen as tight as the one surrounding the Rossiya.

One of the few areas of common ground we may meet on is in the fifteen or so 'tourist restaurants', several of which specialize in the regional cuisine of the Soviet republics. I visited one of these with the *Sunday Times* team—the Uzbekistan, described in Mr Fodor's ineffable guide book as 'one of the better nationality restaurants ... colourful', and specializing in such appetizing Uzbek specialities as *pilaff*, *shashlik* and *tkhum-dulma* (Scotch eggs). As we entered through a dark passage, we heard distant sounds of singing, dancing and laughter. 'At last, the festive Olympic spirit!' we thought. Nameless Uzbek delights beckoned. Alas, *pace* Mr Fodor, we found nothing more ethnic and 'colourful' when we entered than two drunken groups of Colombians and Finns singing Colombian and Finnish pop songs, and regularly breaking off for toasts to 'Viva Finlandia' and 'Viva Colombia'. As we munched our way through a plate of fairly unappetizing cold meats (not a *tkhum-dulma* to be seen), I discovered to my delight that one of the *Sunday Times* journalists, Dudley Doust, a genial American, lived six miles from me in Somerset, and somewhat improbably was a keen follower of the Somerset county cricket team. Indeed he had just written a biography of one of its star players, the new England captain Ian Botham. My attempt to raise a toast by shouting 'Viva Somerset' met with little response from the Colombians and the Finns.

The big sporting excitement in the British camp tonight was the gold medal victory of Duncan Goodhew in the 100 Metres Breaststroke, beating a strongly favoured Russian into second place. It is hard not to react favourably to this idiosyncratic twenty-three-year-old, who stands out from the normal bland run of British Olympic competitors as no one has for years. He is completely bald (as a result of a childhood accident). After the death of his father, his mother married an Air Vice-Marshal called Crawford-Compton, who now lives in retirement in Sussex and has refused to accompany his wife and stepson to Moscow because he is a fervent supporter of Mrs Thatcher's boycott policy. Despite his decision to ignore the boycott, Goodhew, an articulate ex-public schoolboy educated at Millfield, is intensely patriotic, and made his own mute protest at the lack of a Union Jack at his medal-winning ceremony by wearing a red-white-and-blue bathrobe with the British flag prominently displayed on the breast pocket.

This was one of the first gold medals in these Games to be won by a competitor from one of the sixteen nations which have refused to allow any use of their national flags or anthems (in fact the very first, earlier today, was the medal for trap shooting won by an Italian). The form is that an Olympic flag goes up the flagpole instead, while the band plays that awful Olympic hymn. But as Goodhew stood on the top step with his medal hanging round his neck, the Russian televiewers were still treated to a close-up of the Union Jack. It just happened that one was being waved by a spectator in front of the grandstand—in convenient view of the Soviet television cameras.

Actually the Russians had even more to cheer about than the British at the Olimpiskiy Pool tonight. Until last Sunday they had never won a swimming gold medal, in a sport traditionally dominated by the United States. Now they have several—while today Vladimir Salnikov became the first man in history to break 'the magic fifteen-minute barrier' in the 1,500 Metres Freestyle, swimming's equivalent of the four-minute mile. This is a triumph not even the absence of the Americans can diminish.

Another tiny puzzle about this strange country. I mentioned the Kosmos, the huge new hotel specially built for the Olympics in the north of Moscow, where the television people are staying. The Kosmos was not only designed, but even constructed by Frenchmen, with materials (down to the last bath tap) supplied from France—just as the swish new Olympic air terminal out at Sheremetyevo was designed, built and supplied (down to the last baggage trolley) by the

West Germans. I remember first learning of this strange Russian habit of letting out building contracts to foreigners—materials, labour and all—back in 1976, when I called one day in London on the architect Richard Seifert. The British property business was in the middle of a major collapse at the time, and the only sign of a new project around in Seifert's office was the model of a large hotel which he told me he was hoping to get the contract to build in Moscow. It appears that in the end even the Soviet authorities balked at allowing Colonel Seifert to add his distinctive touch to the skyline of Moscow (or perhaps it was just the possible consequences of allowing several hundred British building workers into the Soviet Union which worried them). Anyway, it fell in the end to the French to build the Kosmos. But just as you might be thinking what an extraordinary comment on the inefficiencies of the Communist system, that they should have to get in foreigners to build their hotels and airports, you may recall that this aspect of Russian life is scarcely new. Peter the Great hired hordes of Italian architects and craftsmen to build his grandiose new capital, St Petersburg; while even the Kremlin—just about the most Russian thing in all Russia—was largely the work of an earlier team of Italian architects, back at the end of the fifteenth century.

Wednesday 23 July

The *Daily Mail* is in trouble with the Soviet authorities for the way we covered the opening ceremony on Saturday. At the daily press conference given down at the Main Press Centre by Vladimir Popov, a deputy-chairman of the Olympic Organizing Committee, he was asked by a representative of Novosti, the Soviet news agency, to comment on an article published by the London *Daily Mail* containing 'insulting attacks on the host country'.

Mr Popov replied that he had not yet seen the article but that it would be examined, and if necessary reported to the International Olympic Committee with a demand for 'strict measures with regard to the authors of the article'. There was quite a stir among the hundreds of newsmen present when he added the reminder that, in 1968, the Mexican Government had deported two journalists for 'insulting the national dignity of the host country'.

It turned out that it was not my article which had inspired the Novosti man's question, so much as one by Ian Wooldridge. On Monday, the *Mail* had printed my opening despatch on the left-hand side of a double-page spread, under the headline running across both pages: 'THE SHAM AND THE SHOWMANSHIP OF THE EERIE GAMES'. In the middle was a map of Moscow showing not only the Kremlin, GUM and the Bolshoi, but also the Lubyanka, Lefertovo, Butyrki, the Serbsky Institute of Psychiatry (where Bukovksky, General Grigorenko and many other dissidents had been certified as 'insane') and some twenty or so other Moscow prisons and psychiatric hospitals which had been used for political purposes. On the right was a piece by Ian Wooldridge, describing in his usual lively prose the joylessness of the opening ceremony. But what had really got under the Soviets' skin was a couple of paragraphs in which, almost in passing, Wooldridge had touched on Mr Brezhnev's vulnerability to a terrorist attack as he sat in the Lenin Stadium. The Soviet President had been sitting in such a way, Wooldridge observed, that any one of the hundreds of photographers who had managed to smuggle in a rifle disguised as a long-lens camera could have taken a shot at him.

Later, a friendly Western correspondent resident in Moscow passed on to us the private message that the Soviet authorities had taken a fairly dim view of the whole spread. No action would be taken, but from now on Wooldridge and I were advised: 'Take special care to keep your noses clean: no black market currency deals, no girls.'

In fact the Soviet authorities were not the only people to disapprove of the *Mail*'s apparent 'line' on the Games. At lunch today in the Press Centre, I kept an appointment to meet Ian Jack of the *Sunday Times* and Michael Binyon, the resident Moscow correspondent of *The Times*. When I arrived at the table another journalist who was sitting with them—a senior sports correspondent whom I had not met before—began spluttering with rage. He said that the article I had written on Monday had made him 'puke'. He also seemed to think that I had been responsible for the map of the Moscow prisons (which I still had not, in fact, seen), and that my presence in Moscow was all part of some devilish right-wing *Mail* plot. It was an unpleasant little incident, but it brought out into the open the resentment which I know a number of the sporting journalists felt, that I was in Moscow to comment on what they call the 'political' aspects of the Games, and that there was something rather wicked about this.

By way of complete contrast, I stepped this afternoon into a kind of time machine, by walking over to take tea at the British Embassy. It is hardly surprising that the Soviet Government has for some years been pressing the British to surrender this building, an imposing nineteenth-century mansion built by the sugar king Haritonenko, in exchange for a new embassy somewhere else in the city. Quite apart from the splendours of the building itself, the Embassy site, directly across the Moscow River from the Kremlin, is one of the most desirable in the city.

I walked in off the Quai Maurice Thorez, past Russian guards chatting outside their sentry box (the Union Jack no longer on the flagpole), and entered a splendid, dark-panelled reception hall. I was shown into the office of Andrew Wood, the Head of Chancery, to whom I had my introduction. While he went out to organize a cup of civil service tea (most welcome), I admired what I took to be his library—shelves full of scholarly tomes on Staffordshire pottery and the works of little-known nineteenth-century English painters. He quickly shattered my illusions; these were in fact 'Embassy presents' for official visits to Soviet provincial cities. The mayor of Omsk or Kishinov, if he is kind enough to receive the British Ambassador, is rewarded with *The Life and Works of John Martin* or a history of the Wedgwood family.

Our Ambassador, Sir Curtis Keeble, had, in fact, (like those of the United States, West Germany and several other countries) been withdrawn from Moscow for the duration of the Games, and the British Government's disapproval was being marked by a general 'low profile' all round. There were to be none of the usual Embassy parties for British medal-winners or officials. The Embassy staff had been discreetly given to understand that their presence at any Olympic event was not considered desirable. Worst of all, one of the most distinguished visitors to Moscow, had there been no boycott, would have been the Duke of Edinburgh in his capacity as President of the International Equestrian Federation—and undoubtedly at least one glittering reception would have been held at the Embassy in his honour. I caught just the faintest whiff of regret from the Embassy staff that they were being deprived of all this fun and games.

Indeed, at the best of times it must be a very strange, unreal sort of existence living in this splendid enclave in the middle of Moscow. As I was shown round, the sense of being out of time only deepened. Vast oil-paintings of Edward VII and Queen Alexandra, George V and Queen Mary looked down from the walls of splendid reception rooms. The Ambassador's drawing-room was closed for the duration, its floor and furniture covered with a forest of pot plants ('it makes them easier to water while he is away'). From a room in the front, large French windows above the portico open up to give an unparalleled view of the Kremlin across the river, its white and gold palaces and gilded cupolas shining in the golden late-afternoon sun.

As I walked round I recalled R. H. Bruce Lockhart's description in that remarkable book *The Memoirs of a British Agent* of how, shortly after his arrival in Moscow as a very young man in 1912, he had been invited to this mansion by the Haritonenkos, to a very grand reception attended 'by every millionaire in Moscow', when 'the whole house was a fairyland of flowers brought all the way from Nice' and 'orchestras seemed to be playing in every ante-chamber.' During dinner the Russian officer sitting next to him was called away to the telephone, and never returned. Later Bruce Lockhart learned that the call had been from the officer's mistress, the wife of a Governor in St Petersburg, to tell him that it was all over between them. Without letting go of the telephone, the officer had pulled out his revolver and shot himself through the head.

Even though the parties which might have been given here for the 1980 Olympics would scarcely have been so dramatic (or so splendid), the visit certainly reinforced my suspicion that the boycott had removed an important layer of the festivities which normally give colour and atmosphere to an Olympic Games. Throughout the Olympic period there would have been a round of diplomatic parties and receptions all over the city, attended no doubt not just by the international community but also by the Soviet leaders. Thanks to the boycott, this programme had been drastically curtailed, or cancelled altogether. Indeed, perhaps not the least measure of the hidden impact of the boycott on the Soviet authorities was that, immediately after the opening ceremony, President Brezhnev had retired back to his villa on the Black Sea, and was not planning to return to Moscow until the Games were over.

Another even more striking measure of the boycott's 'hidden' impact on the Soviet authorities can be seen from studying the coverage of the Games in *Pravda, Izvestia* and the rest of the Soviet press. Plenty of publicity is given to the amount of world records being broken (and there are a lot of them—world-record times were broken on thirteen occasions in just two events yesterday at the superb 'Velodrome' where the cycling events are held). But there is one feature of normal Soviet Olympic coverage which is conspicuously absent. For the first time since Helsinki in 1952, when the Soviet Union first competed, the papers are not publishing medals tables. A look at the position after four days may show why:

	Gold	*Silver*	*Bronze*
USSR	17	10	5
East Germany	6	13	7
Hungary	3	2	2
Bulgaria	2	1	4
Sweden	2	—	—
Great Britain	1	2	—

Even for the Soviet authorities this might be thought to be becoming just a little bit too much of a good thing.

9

In the Compression Chamber

What can I say by way of summary? Russia's political system is
more crude than people not living here imagine.
Westerners—particularly those who visit briefly—do not really
believe the power of the KGB over people's lives, and their
viciousness towards those they consider to have challenged that
mastery. Western tourists cling to a sanguine confidence that not
even the KGB could really be so unreasonable . . . nor can
Westerners appreciate the quantity and quasi-religious tone of
the political propaganda. The preaching, chanting and
twenty-four hour a day broadcasting of Marxist–Leninist slogans
and jargon is as frighteningly manipulatory as anyone can
imagine; it is the Party force-feeding newspeak and doublethink
to helpless masses, hypnotising them to love the Party. It is truly
Orwellian.

A Message from Moscow by 'An Observer' (1969)

I am sure that many Westerners reading these words may imagine that
they were written by some rabid anti-Communist, full of preconcep-
tions and determined to paint life in the Soviet Union in the blackest
possible light. In fact they come from one of the subtlest and most
sympathetic accounts of life in Russia ever written by a Westerner—George Feifer, who spent some time in the Soviet Union as a
student in the late sixties and published his book under a pseudonym
partly because he was still living there.

After a week here, I find a curious sense of timelessness is setting in
I am having to think hard in order to remember which day of the week
it is. Partly, of course, this is because we are cut off from any normal
routine or those little things, such as the morning newspaper, which,
at home, give a background framework to life.

But it is more because of the strange atmosphere of this city. I lie in
my room at night hearing the Kremlin chimes, or I wander out to see

convoys of military lorries rumbling down the deserted river embankment. I listen a lot to Radio Moscow, in an attempt to see the world through Soviet eyes. I have almost lost interest in what is happening back in Britain. It is as if we are completely cut off from the outside world here, wrapped in our series of cocoons. After the 'bubble' a new image has come into my mind: it is as if we are in a diving chamber, far below the surface of the sea. We are living in an artificial atmosphere, preoccupied with what is going on in the brightly lit foreground immediately around us: there is a sense of compression, while outside the shell of the diving bell stretches a vast dark submarine world, from which we occasionally hear muffled noises we do not understand.

It is hard to explain this as yet, because there is still so much I don't know, but like many Western visitors to Russia before me I am certainly beginning to feel very strongly how little we in the West understand this country, or can imagine what it is like to live here. As what was just a two-dimensional caricature develops into three dimensions it is beginning to look in some ways very different from my preconception. And so far I feel this in four main respects.

The first is how extremely attractive, warm and impressive many of the Russians are as people. One must dispel any lingering notion that the Soviet Union is made up of 265 million dehumanized, brain-washed zombies all marching happily to the same tune. From one point of view it may sound curious, from another patronizing—but one of the shocks about coming here is how strongly the Russians come across as individuals.

I say this partly because I have at last begun to have some long conversations with Russians—some of them no further away than here in the Rossiya itself. Thanks to the peculiar nature of the Olympic operation, there is a particular group of Russians working in this hotel of a type most Western visitors would not normally meet—some of the thousands of young foreign-language students and graduates who have been specially recruited to help with the Games. They have no doubt been carefully chosen for the job, and are no doubt under careful supervision from behind the scenes, but they are by no means regulation Intourist guides and indeed almost without exception are helpful, remarkably charming, intelligent and pleasant to talk to.*

There is, for instance, Valeriy, one of the interpreters and general helpers working in the Rossiya Press Centre, a chubby, bespectacled figure who usually wears a bright orange tee-shirt. He doesn't put a foot wrong as far as the Party line is concerned. He is a Komsomol (Young Communist League) group leader at the Maurice Thorez Foreign Language Institute, where he and some of his colleagues, for example two pretty girls, Lena and Yelena, have just graduated. When we first began chatting there was a tendency to tease him a little. We inevitably got on to the subject of Afghanistan, and he naturally argued the copybook Soviet case, that the Red Army had been 'invited in' by the Afghan Government, and that therefore it was all right. When it was put to him that the Americans had been 'invited in' to South Vietnam and that therefore the American presence there must have been equally justified, Valeriy looked awkward: 'I'm sorry, I do not understand.' We had reached the limits of what it was permissible for him to think about, at least in such a public place. Similarly, we asked him what he thought about Western newspapers, knowing that it was unlikely he would have seen many. He replied (not knowing which paper I worked for) that he had the other day seen the *Daily Mail*, and did not like it at all: 'Why is it so full of crimes and murders and poisonings?' We asked him which paper he did like. 'The *Morning*

---

* I say all this despite having come across (on my return to England) one of the more revealing 'behind the scenes' descriptions of how the cocooning of foreign visitors is organized in Communist countries, by a guide formerly assigned to such tasks in China: 'In Shanghai, as in other selected cities, the Communists organised a special Committee for the Reception of visitors . . . it employed a large number of graduates as interpreters and receptionists, whose qualifications were, in order of importance: (1) membership of the Communist Party or Young Communist League, wholehearted devotion to social-ism and political alertness; (2) good presence and manners; (3) knowledge of at least one foreign language. After they were engaged, they attended frequent political lessons . . . they had to go early in the morning to receive instructions from the reception committee; each night, after saying goodnight to the visitors . . . they had to submit a written and verbal report to the Committee and discuss any problems which might have arisen during the day, such as unsympathetic attitudes or questions by foreigners or clumsy behaviour by any Chinese.' Robert Loh, 'Setting The Stage for Foreigners', *Atlantic Monthly*, December 1959 and quoted by Paul Hollander in a fascinating article on the whole theme of Western visitors to the Communist world 'The Ideological Pilgrims' (*Encounter*, November 1973).

I have reason to suppose that our 'reception' in Moscow in 1980 was organized on similar lines—but I also have reason to suppose, without being more specific, that such exchanges do not always go strictly 'according to plan'.

Star, of course,' Valeriy replied. 'It has very good articles and reports fairly.'

Valeriy's use of the phrase 'of course' is one of his mannerisms which I have on occasion to tease him about, particularly when he uses it in completely inappropriate contexts. But since we have got over the initial fencing, and away from subjects which require strictly ideological treatment, he has turned out to be a most engaging companion—and in the broadest sense as good an advertisement as the Soviet system could wish for. It is extremely interesting to hear someone like him talk about the West (where he has never been, although he had been due to come to Oxford on a three-month cultural exchange course, until such contacts became a casualty of the post-Afghanistan 'freeze'). When he criticizes Western newspapers for their sensationalism, their obsession with crimes and scandals, for instance, I tease him by saying that these were exactly the charges made by Solzhenitsyn in his famous Harvard speech in 1978. But more seriously, it is not surprising that any Russian might feel these things on first exposure to the Western mass-media. Their own newspapers, in particular, are so stupefyingly boring, with nothing but propaganda and an almost eerie lack of hard news—yet ours too often fall into the opposite stereotype of such relentless and puerile superficiality that we no longer realize how odd to an outsider they must look.

It is 'of course' (as Valeriy would say) a commonplace that Western visitors to the Soviet Union over the past sixty years have been prone to accept a lot of truth in the criticisms they hear there of the 'decadent' West. After all, that is one reason why so many of them have gone there, or to other socialist countries, in the first place—because they are weary of the materialism and the vacuity which they see in life at home. But it cannot be denied that many of the criticisms which Valeriy and other Russians make of the West today—the weakness of its leaders, the obsession with money, the triviality and disorder of Western society—do ring uncomfortably true. Moscow Radio is making a good deal at the moment of the 'Billygate Affair'—President Carter's brother's squalid cash involvements with the Libyan Government. What could be more pitiful? Yet at the same time I have a strange feeling, when we talk about these things, that the Russians are curiously worried about what they hear of the West these days. It is almost as if, after sixty years of being told that the West was contemptibly 'decadent' they are actually beginning for the first time to believe it—that there really is some kind of a moral crisis going on in those mysterious, romantic 'affluent societies' they have been taught by rote to despise—and I have more than a suspicion that it rather alarms them.

In general, one of the most impressive things about almost all the Russians I have talked to here is that they have such an easy mixture of seriousness and humour. They can be serious about things where we in the West would only be earnest. They can laugh in a simple way about simple things, where we in the West are too often merely facetious, or just childish. I am beginning to like the Russians very much.

Another way I feel I am beginning to see Russia more three-dimensionally is hard to explain—but it is partly a matter of geography. From this country one really does begin to see the world in a quite different perspective. For a start, one feels right in the middle of a great land mass, stretching away for thousands of miles in every direction. Western Europe seems a long way away, and rather small. Looking out at the world, one feels that—however big the Soviet Union is—it is somehow surrounded by a vast ring: all the way round from Western Europe, via the Islamic world in a great crescent to the south—Turkey, Iran, Pakistan—to the vast, threatening hordes of China to the East. For the first time in my life I begin to understand emotionally something I have hitherto only grasped intellectually—the essentially defensive psychology of the Russian people. The outside world does seem like a threatening ring, for all sorts of reasons.

In the West we are accustomed to think of the Soviet Union as an aggressive power—and not without cause. In fact Russia has been almost continuously extending her boundaries outwards, not just in the past sixty years, but for centuries: the Ukraine, Siberia, the Crimea, the Caucasus, the Baltic lands—all these territories were taken over by the original little kingdom of Rus or Muscovy, long before the Communists arrived. It is true that since the Revolution that process of aggrandizement has gone further than ever before, as the Russians, under Soviet rule, have not only reconquered lost territories, such as White Russia, Moldavia, the Baltic states and Georgia, but have made further huge additions to the *cordon sanitaire* round their borders in the shape of the 'new Soviet empire' of Eastern Europe, not to mention the latest attempted addition of Afghanistan.

But, in a curious way, to see this as somehow comparable with the aggressive nationalism of, say, the Germans under Hitler is to get the whole thing psychologically upside-down. German expansionism under Hitler was a truly outward-looking type of aggression, fuelled by the urge to bust outwards from those claustrophobic rolling plains of central Germany and northern Bavaria. The Russians' reasons, on the other hand, for extending their frontiers and their zone of influence, have been defensive and protective: the results may, to the outside world and to the unfortunate victims, look remarkably similar—but the true underlying psychological motivation has been different, and this is extremely important.

The point is—as I have more than ever been aware since coming here—that the people of this country suffer from a colossal national inferiority complex. For centuries, as they have looked at the achievements of post-Renaissance Europe, they have felt inferior to the West, the pioneers of technical and cultural progress. In the past hundred years, and particularly the past sixty, the Russians have felt inferior in relation to America, as the world's number one 'super-power' in everything from nuclear weapons to consumer goods. 'We are number two, we try harder,' feel the Russians, and that is one of the reasons why they have concentrated so much of their effort on such dramatic, glamorous, obvious symbols of national virility as space rockets, hydro-electric schemes and military hardware. All this is not irrelevant to the Olympics, because it is one of the reasons why the Russians' successes in international sport are so desperately important to them—why it is so vital that these should be the biggest, best and most efficiently organized Olympic Games in history. *Nasha luchshe*, the Russians are fond of intoning, in almost any context: 'Ours is best.' But like all people with a massive inferiority complex, deep down they don't really believe it—even when it happens to be true.

All this doesn't make the Soviet Union any less dangerous: if anything, more so. But an awareness of these factors does make Russia seem somehow more vulnerable, more comprehensible in human terms—even, in a curious way, rather touching. I begin to understand more clearly just why the Soviet Union genuinely feels so constantly misunderstood by the outside world; why the average Russians I have talked to (in so far as they can be average) genuinely see the boycott of the Olympics as just another attempt by the superior outside world to spite and spoil a Russian achievement (a pathetic attempt to win votes for Carter by whipping up anti-Soviet hysteria); even why many Russians genuinely believe that the Soviet Union *had* to take its 'action' in Afghanistan to help a sympathetic government in a strategically sensitive country.

I discussed these points over lunch with a resident Moscow correspondent not unfriendly to the regime. He admitted that the Soviet Government is privately deeply embarrassed by its miscalculation over Afghanistan, not so much in terms of the reaction by the rest of the world, but simply because it had not realized how hostile and intractable to Soviet intervention the local population would be. 'They are bogged down, they don't know which way to turn—and what worries them not least is the sheer cost of the operation. The Soviet Union is not a rich country.'

I told him that I would like to have a talk with a really intelligent, sophisticated, persuasive spokesman for the Soviet point of view. Could he help? He said that he had someone in mind—Alexander Pozna, a senior commentator with Radio Moscow—and would do what he could to arrange a meeting.

A third thing I am feeling more and more strongly here is how desperately little we in the West can imagine, or even begin to imagine, what it is really like to live in a totalitarian country. I do not just mean an authoritarian country, like so many in the world, but a truly, 100 per cent totalitarian country, where literally everything is controlled by the State and the Party—every shop, every factory, every school, every newspaper, every film, every book; where not even something as trivial as a theatre programme or a cloakroom ticket can be printed without first being submitted to the censor; a society where the pressure to conform to the Party line is an ever-present reality of life twenty-four hours a day, from the cradle to the grave; where the State begins instructing you in what to think and what to feel about every subject under the sun from the moment you begin to speak; where there is an omnipresent army of informers (*stukachi*) to make sure that you keep in line, whether they be among your fellow-students or colleagues in your place of work, or the 'trusties' who are stationed in every apartment block to keep an eye on their neighbours, or the teachers at the local nursery school who keep a constant ear open for any hint of 'incorrect' thinking in what your child may unwittingly have picked up at home; a country where the State controls your job and where you live and can hand out or withdraw every privilege; where the two largest professions, employing tens of millions of people, are the armed forces and the police, a vast, privileged presence dedicated to making the power of the State an ever-present reality in everyone's life; a country so ruled by fear and intimidation that such things are part of the air you breathe; where every newspaper article, every television and radio programme, every work of art, every lesson in school is dedicated to the same end, of perpetuating just one 'correct' line of thought, one 'correct' mode of behaviour; while over it all broods the mysterious 'Party' itself, run by remote grey figures who are only seen on television, or at huge, carefully staged public occasions, and about whose private life the average Soviet citizen knows nothing at all.

Even living here as we journalists are, in conditions of isolation and privilege, one cannot but be at least a little aware of what it is like to live in such a world. For those with eyes to see, it is around us all the time, like the policemen patrolling night and day in the passage outside our doors. One gets used to the idea that every conversation in one's room is listened to; that there are certain names which it would be inadvisable to use on the telephone when talking to London; that there are certain remarks which it would be unsafe to repeat (unsafe, that is, not for us, but for those who made them in the first place).

Two other little things I have noticed in this country—policemen's eyes, and the way they make an arrest. As you walk around the streets, one way you can tell a policeman, whether a KGB man or an ordinary militia man, is that he always looks right into your eyes. I notice this particularly, because it has always been my habit to look at people's mouths—but here I find I am beginning to stare straight back. It is also noticeable how ordinary Russians tend to look everywhere except into the eyes, as if they have got used to avoiding these trained stares.

Another obvious sign of training is the way the police here carry out an arrest. I saw a girl being arrested outside the Rossiya the other night. Two men almost threw themselves on her with a great shout, and dragged her off to a van waiting in the bushes. It could not provide more of a contrast to the way English policemen are trained to make an arrest—the hand on the arm, the quiet voice, everything as relaxed as possible. Here it is only too obvious that the mode of arrest is part of the general policy to make the imposition of *poryadok* or 'order' (a much-used Russian word) as intimidatory as possible.

This is something of what I mean when I say that being here is like living underwater, in a compression chamber. And yet the Russians who have to live in this strange element all the time, like those species of deep-sea fish which have learned to live perpetually under the weight of thirty atmospheres, can still laugh and think and build their own little private worlds and remain individual human beings. It is another puzzle, perhaps one of the most important of all.

A fourth thing I am becoming vaguely but unmistakably aware of is just what an appalling economic mess the Soviet Union is getting into—again, far worse than most Westerners can begin to imagine. Every night, in those unreal, soothing tones of Radio Moscow, one can hear what a terrible state the West is in—how the recession is deepening, inflation and unemployment soaring—while 'in the socialist world, production has risen by a quarter in the past five years', or 'in the first six months of 1980, output in the Soviet Union rose by 4.7 per cent, and in East Germany by 5.9 per cent' (and of course there are no unemployment or inflation at all). For years, on the other hand, able Moscow correspondents like Hedrick Smith or more recently Michael Binyon of *The Times* have been trying to tell us of the horrifying inefficiency of the Soviet Union's economy; how it is riddled with corruption to an unimaginable degree; how the black market flourishes; how you can get nothing done except *na levo* (literally 'on the left', on the side, under the counter); how a large part of most people's lives is devoted to tracking down even the simplest household item, a saucepan which doesn't break, a pair of boots which don't fall to pieces; how the few necessary or desirable items which are produced are inevitably *defitsiny* ('in short supply'). Even Mr Brezhnev, in a remarkable speech last November, admitted something of how bad this situation had become, saying that if shortages of such essential goods as soap, nappies or needles and thread continued, 'it would be necessary to find particular people to blame for each scarcity, and punish them' (it is never, of course, the system itself which is to blame). Only a few days ago *Izvestia* announced that two senior officials had lost their jobs for personally causing the great shortage of light bulbs in the Soviet Union in recent months).*

---

* This was, in fact, a perfect example of how these things are explained to the Soviet people. The real reason why light bulbs had become almost unobtainable, according to the Communist Party Central Committee, was that, thanks to the efficiency of Soviet industry, there had in fact until recently been a surplus of light bulbs. This had lulled

In the Compression Chamber

And, of course, Western correspondents can only base their direct observations on what is happening in Moscow, Leningrad, Kiev, Minsk and a handful of other 'closed cities' (closed, that is, not to foreigners, but to other Soviet citizens who can only live in them with special permits); cities which are deliberately organized to enjoy a standard of living far above that of most provincial towns, or those vast areas of the USSR where foreigners are never permitted to penetrate at all. As Solzhenitsyn put it in a recent essay in *Foreign Affairs*, 'Moscow has come to be a special little world, poised somewhere between the USSR and the West; in terms of material comfort, it is almost as superior to the rest of the Soviet Union, as the West is superior to Moscow'—while as for the mass of provincial towns, strictly out-of-bounds to outsiders, there are many which 'have not seen meat, butter or eggs for decades, and which can only dream of even such simple fare as macaroni and margarine'.*

Despite the gigantic effort which has been made to put on a good show for the Olympics, all sorts of stray clues are beginning to accumulate to suggest that things are getting immeasurably worse, not just in the hidden parts of the Soviet Union, but throughout the Soviet empire.

There is, for instance, the continuing unrest in Poland we are hearing about on the BBC World Service. Despite the 'settlement' of last week's strikes in Lublin, trouble seems to have spread to several other parts of the country (on Monday a walkout by drivers even halted deliveries of the official Party newspaper *Trybuna Ludu*) and it is obvious that something fairly remarkable is going on there.

The other night I read a long transcript summarizing a description of two serious strikes which took place in May this year in the Soviet Union itself, in the great car plants at Gorki and Togliatti. For two days, the city of Togliatti, which is almost entirely dedicated to manufacturing the little Zhiguli Fiats, came to a virtual halt in protest against rising prices, meat shortages and a range of other problems. As had happened before when faced with such crises (though these seem

---

the two officials responsible—Mr Tezhnikov, head of the All-Union Electric Light Production Association, and Mr Umnov, of the State Planning Committee—into 'slackening their attention' to light-bulb production, with the result that a few months later scarcely a bulb was to be found.

* Solzhenitsyn's essay was later published in book form as *The Mortal Danger* (Bodley Head, September 1980).

to have been particularly serious examples), the Soviet authorities simply 'bought off' trouble by switching more supplies to the two cities to keep their workers quiet—but the reserves for such operations must be running fairly low.

Then there is what is likely to be the most remarkable piece of journalism to come out of these Olympics, a long article by George Feifer in this week's *Sunday Times* (20 July). Feifer, the author of the book from which I quoted at the head of this chapter, went back to the Soviet Union earlier this year for the first time since he had been expelled by the KGB in 1971. He was so pleased and surprised to get a visa that he determined to write nothing more than a harmless travel article about his return visit. But when he was reunited with all his old friends in Moscow—'painters, journalists, engineers, a lawyer'—he was so shocked to find how things had changed since he was last there that he knew he had to write about it.

'Watch ordinary people trudging to work in the mornings,' said one friend, 'see if you can discover what is making them gloomier day by day.' Feifer found the whole atmosphere of Moscow 'harder', more tense, more wracked with misery and frustration. The day-to-day problems of finding food were far worse than when he had last been there ('in 1971, even mediocre local shops stocked a range of items, from pepper to frozen cod, that are now as unavailable as caviar. The overriding impression of Moscow's shops is one of bareness'), and the quality of what remained had deteriorated sharply—*ersatz* sausage, milk ('chalky water, sour before you open it') reduced in butterfat content from 3.6 per cent to 2.2 per cent. Almost everyone was drinking in a way he had never known ('I had seen much drinking before, of course, but now it seemed to have developed into a devastating addiction'). Despite the recent claim of the Chairman of the State Committee of Prices that 'with the exception of the war years, there has never been any inflation in the Soviet Union', prices of everything from vodka to carpets, petrol to coffee had soared. 'Every Russian I talked to at any length was convinced that things were bad now and rapidly getting worse.' 'Everyone's weary to death, silently miserable,' said the director of a chain of hardware shops, 'I *know* we're headed for total breakdown.' As for conditions outside Moscow, 'massive evidence supported the dismay of Muscovites who returned from provincial cities' reporting that things out there were 'terrible', 'dreadful', 'appalling'. 'Sober travellers told me that Gorky is without butter, meat, fruit and flour ... talk focussed on the meat shortage, described as severe to almost total in huge areas of the country.' 'The Soviet economy is drifting into chaos . . . "breakdown" is the favourite new word' . . . 'to buy (*kupit*) is disappearing from the daily vocabulary; its replacement is *dostat*, "to obtain"'.

Amid this collapse and misery, such idealism about the 'Socialist path' as Feifer had known when he was in Russia ten years ago seemed to have completely evaporated.

'We can't turn on the television set because the propaganda is so awful,' said a former Young Communist organizer at the University, 'can't open a newspaper because they're worse. Can't get good books because they're even harder . . . to find than good food. So we drink. In recognition that this emptiness is our life.'

Hatred of the privileged class, the self-perpetuating group of officials and Party functionaries, with their special shops, special car lanes, special schools, seemed total.

'One day I had to visit the Tashkent Party headquarters,' one elderly lady told Feifer, 'and I saw their special food store. It made me blink, even though I knew about it. Amazing fresh produce, from eggs to meat to smoked fish, delivered every morning—while everyone else is frantic for usable potatoes. No waiting, no bother—the orders were neatly put together for the "Communists" to take home at the end of the day.'

Feifer concluded:

Bezizhkodnost, the word most people used to sum up their condition, means literally 'exitlessness'. They see no way out, as well as no way forward. Perhaps it is true that every people deserves the government they get, but this calamity for the Russian people seems, as so often, far worse than their 'crime'.

For the first time I begin to get the feeling that these Olympic Games, intended to be the ultimate showcase for the achievements of sixty years of Soviet socialism, may in fact be taking place at precisely the moment when the whole system is sliding towards some huge and unprecedented crisis. What *is* it that has happened to Russia in the past sixty years? What is this terrible shadow which has fallen over her people; this strange system which has the whole nation in its grip? In the hope of some illumination, I thought that it was time to go off to the central shrine of this whole strange system, the tomb of Lenin.

In fact, I had already tried to get into the Lenin Mausoleum a couple of times, and been told that it was only open to 'delegations'. I now went to Valeriy and asked him, 'How many people constitute a delegation—two, three? Can we form one of our own?' He agreed to make the necessary arrangements, while I rounded up Ian Jack and Peter Hildreth, a former Olympic hurdler who is here to cover the athletics for the *Sunday Telegraph*. The next day, at ten o'clock prompt, we set off from the Rossiya on the most important pilgrimage in the Communist world.

10

The Lie at the Heart of
the Soviet Union

How could you tell how much of it was lies? It *might* be true that
the average human being was better off now than he had been
before the Revolution. The only evidence to the contrary was the
mute protest in your bones, the instinctive feeling that the
conditions you lived in were intolerable and that at some other
time they must have been different. It struck him that the truly
characteristic thing about modern life was not its cruelty and
insecurity, but simply its bareness, its dinginess, its listlessness.
Life, if only you looked about you, bore no resemblance not
only to the lies which streamed out of the telescreens, but even
to the ideals which the Party was trying to achieve. Great areas
of it, even for a Party member, were neutral and non-political, a
matter of slogging through dreary jobs, fighting for a place on
the tube, darning a worn-out sock, cadging a saccharine tablet,
saving a cigarette end. The ideal set up by the Party was
something huge, terrible and glittering—a world of steel and
concrete, of monstrous machines and terrifying weapons—a
nation of warriors and fanatics, marching forward in perfect
unity, all thinking the same thoughts and shouting the same
slogans, perpetually working, fighting, triumphing,
persecuting—three hundred million people with the same face.
The reality was decaying, dingy cities, where underfed people
shuffled to and fro in leaky shoes . . .

George Orwell, *Nineteen Eighty-four*

I had always imagined that a visit to Lenin's tomb was, for the
Western visitor at least, just another tourist sight, a curiosity. You
joined that eternal queue ambling across Red Square. You would go in
off the Square, straight into a darkened room, and there would be the
old boy in his glass case. You'd stop for a quick peer, there'd be the
usual sort of conversation around you that you might hear in any

tourist spot: 'Haven't they done a neat job?' 'Doesn't he look well preserved?' Then you'd stroll out the other side of that funny, dumpy little building and go off for a coffee or a visit to the Kremlin.

It is not like that at all.

In the sixty years since the Russian Revolution, few things have struck outsiders more forcibly about Communism than its quasi-religious character—its processions, its rituals, its use of 'sacred texts', and above all its deification of its prophets and leaders. Supposed originally to be an attempt to capitalize, if that is not the wrong word, on Russia's great religious tradition, this 'religious' element in Communism first amazed foreign visitors in the very earliest days after 1917, when the chief object of the new Socialist hagiolatry was Karl Marx. In his fascinating account of his visit to the Soviet Union in 1920, *Russia in the Shadows*, H. G. Wells admitted that for all his sympathy for Lenin and Co. in the appalling difficulties they were facing, the one thing he could not stomach was the extent of the homage to the author of *The Communist Manifesto*. He had never been desperately keen on Marx in the first place, he confessed ('I have always regarded him as a Bore of the extremest sort. His vast unfinished work *Das Kapital*, a cadence of wearisome volumes about such phantom unrealities as the *bourgeoisie* and the *proletariat* ... impresses me as a monument of pretentious pedantry'). But after a few weeks wandering round the new Russia, he exploded; his 'passive objection' had turned to 'active hostility':

> Wherever we went we encountered busts, portraits and statues of Marx. About two thirds of the face of Marx is beard, a vast, solemn, woolly, uneventful sort of beard that must have made all normal exercise impossible. It is not the sort of beard that happens to a man, it is a beard cultivated, cherished and thrust patriarchally upon the world. It is exactly like *Das Kapital* in its inane abundance, and the human part of the face looks over it owlishly as if it looked to see how the growth impressed mankind. I found the omnipresent image of that beard more and more irritating. A gnawing desire grew upon me to see Karl Marx shaved ...

Over the sixty years since then the objects of devotion have varied. We have all become familiar with pictures of vast parades carrying huge icons of Marx, Engels, Lenin, and at different times Stalin, Khruschev, Brezhnev; while perhaps nothing has impressed upon us the lengths to which Communism can take this attribution of supernatural status to its leaders more than the cult of Chairman Mao which reached its apogee in China in the ten years before his death.

Even so, the average Westerner cannot conceive how intensely and ubiquitously these cults permeate Communist life. In the USSR today, Karl Marx has in a sense been 'kicked upstairs', still accorded supreme honour, but a much less prominent figure than he was. In the past few years, a massive formal homage has come to be paid to President Brezhnev as the present incumbent. But the real cult of the god-made-flesh today centres on the figure of Lenin.

I remember once in the Russian bookshop in Budapest coming across a cupboardful of packets of postcards of every city in the Soviet Union worthy of the name, hundreds of them. Each packet contained half a dozen cards showing the main features of the town in question—innumerable vistas of dingy tower blocks or Parks of Culture and Rest in Sverdlovsk, Kuubyshev, Ulyanovsk, Dneprodzerzhinski, Kabarovsk, Bratsk, heaven knows where. But the one thing they all had in common (apart from the tower blocks) was a statue of Lenin—which is hardly surprising because there is a statue of Lenin in every town in the Soviet Union. Every town also has its Lenin Museum or Library. There is at least one picture of Lenin in almost every room in every public building, and the grade of an official is marked by the size of the portrait of Lenin above his desk. Every wedding in the Soviet Union is solemnized under a picture of Lenin. In every school there is a shrine to Lenin, decorated with flowers on the anniversary days with which the Soviet calendar is full. Every art gallery has its idealized paintings and drawings of Lenin, not just as the heroic inspirer of the masses during the Revolution, but in more intimate, timeless guise: Lenin as friend, as teacher, as guide in every eventuality of life; Lenin with his hand on the shoulder of two workers, pointing the way forward to his vision of the future, inspiring them to ever greater output; Lenin standing with an artist in front of his easel, inspiring him to paint ever more glorious canvases furthering the ideals of the Revolution; a kindly Lenin surrounded by an adoring group of children. Lenin's picture appears in every newspaper, he is quoted every day in every newspaper, it is almost impossible to publish a book without quoting liberally from his writings. There is no subject, no theme, no problem—historical, moral, even technical—on which the words of Lenin cannot be quoted as ultimate authority, as revealed truth. He is the one towering, indisputably holy figure who not only created the Soviet Union, but continues to shape and to guide its destinies. As countless slogans proclaim, 'LENIN LIVES', he is still amongst us, and the proof of it lies there in that red granite mausoleum on Red Square.

The sun was shining as our little four-man 'delegation' walked across the cobbles of Red Square. Thanks to Valeriy we immediately got a place in the queue down at the far end, where the hill climbs up into the square from the Square of the Fiftieth Anniversary of October. We handed bags and books in to an office. There were a number of men in uniform about, and still puzzled by the distinction between KGB and militia men, I asked Valeriy who they were. 'They help to keep everything in order,' he replied. I did not pursue my line of enquiry.

The first surprise was to find just what keeping order meant in the context of a visit to Lenin's tomb. As we came to within two hundred yards or so of the squat tiered structure beneath the Kremlin walls, the uniformed men began to marshal us rigorously into pairs. Ahead of us a woman and a man were made to change sides, to match up with the man and woman in front of them. as we came nearer still, the guards began to straighten out people's clothing—I had part of my jacket caught up at the back, and this was pulled free.

As we approached the doorway, beneath the one word LENIN in large yellow letters, all conversation ceased. On each side of the door the immaculate KGB guards, their bayonets shining silver in the sun, stood stock still. We entered and instead of seeing Lenin straightaway found that we were turning left and going down, some thirty granite steps into the earth. The whole way down the staircase was lined with more silent, motionless guards. We turned right and right again, and finally, in the bowels of the earth, we entered the chamber. All around us were more guards—four standing permanently at each corner of the catafalque. It was dark except for one concealed light illuminating the features and top half of the corpse itself, just head and hands protruding from a black cloth, in its glass case.

The dapper little bearded figure, shining a dull yellow in that darkened room, looked so like a waxwork that it was hard not to cry out. My companion on my right, Peter Hildreth, had once written a brief popular biography of Lenin, in the course of researching which he had carefully studied as many surviving photographs of the founder of the Soviet Union as he could. He was familiar with the pictures of Lenin in his last years, when he was racked with pain and the arterio-sclerosis which eventually killed him in 1924. He had seen pictures of Lenin's mummified corpse taken in 1928, when the remains had been taken off for two years' work by experts in preservation while the original wooden mausoleum was replaced by the present solid granite structure. Hildreth was convinced that, however brilliant a job had been performed by the cosmeticians and taxidermists, this idealized, neat little waxy bourgeois effigy in front of us could not be the same as the shrunken corpse which was taken off in 1928, its face still showing signs of the terrible pain and illness which Lenin had suffered in the last years of his life.

We were not allowed to pause for a moment. The procession of pilgrims was kept moving, at a barely reverent pace. We climbed more steps at the far end of the burial chamber and emerged into the sunlight in a narrow garden running down the Kremlin wall, blocked off by another wall from Red Square, and lined with those silver-grey fir trees that always looked as if they had just had a dusting of snow.

Here, after that darkened chamber we had left, was the second most holy spot in the Communist world. In the wall and along the path are dozens of plaques, recording the ashes of the heroes and heroines, the saints and evangelists of the Revolution. To begin with are some of the foreign Communists who played their part in the years immediately after 1917, both in Russia and abroad: John Reed, the wide-eyed American journalist who wrote *Ten Days That Shook The World* and died in the 'flu epidemic in 1920; Inessa Armand, Lenin's special friend; a Scotsman, Arthur McManus, one of the founders of the British Communist Party, who died in 1927; 'Big Bill' Haywood, an American Communist, the other half of whose remains are buried in Chicago.

Then the row of plaques along the Kremlin wall commemorates the founders of the Revolution itself, the 'Old Bolsheviks', Lenin's trusted colleagues: Lunacharsky, the first Commissar for Education; Kirov, whose assassination by the NKVD in Leningrad in 1934 was used by Stalin as the excuse for launching the waves of purges which, over the next few years, were to sweep several million Communists to their deaths and millions more into labour camps; Ordzhonikidze, the Commissar for Heavy Industry, who unveiled the great Dnieper dam project in 1937, and died shortly afterwards—as many suspected, murdered for having protested to Stalin against the purges. One almost automatically checks off all those who played leading roles in the setting up of the Soviet state who are not here—Trotsky, Bukharin, Zinoviev, Kamenev, Radek, all eventually murdered by Stalin's NKVD, to become complete 'unpersons' never publicly named again.

Gradually the line of plaques works up to modern times: here are the ashes of the Soviet Union's great military leaders, Koniev, Zhukhov, Malinovsky; Gagarin, the world's first man in space is here; three cosmonauts who died during the re-entry of Soyuz-11 in 1971; Kurchatov, known as the 'father' of the Soviet atomic and hydrogen bombs; Korolyov, original organizer of the Soviet space programme.

But halfway along, immediately behind the Mausoleum itself, a special plot is reserved for eight heroes who each have a pillar topped by a crude granite bust, some seven or eight feet high: Sverdlov, the first head of state; Kalinin, his successor; Dzerzhinsky, founder of the secret police; Zhdanov, associated with the notorious post-war 'Zhdanov Decrees' and the complete stranglehold which the Soviet state eventually established over painting, music and literature; and finally, at the left-hand end, identical in size with the other seven, given no identification except his name and dates, J. V. Stalin (1879–1953).

It was hardly surprising that the two Russians in front of us excitedly whispered to each other, 'Stalin'. Once, for six years, he had lain alongside Lenin in the Mausoleum behind us. The great letters over the door had proclaimed 'LENIN–STALIN' in complete equality. For nearly thirty years he had ruled over this country, deified like no other living man before him. He had completed the transformation of the Soviet Union into one vast prison camp. Tens of millions of human beings had died as a result of his megalomaniac will, his insatiable paranoia. In 1941 he had nearly plunged his country into total disaster, and had then led it to the most glorious and complete military victory in its history. He had rebuilt Moscow. More than anyone else he had made the Soviet Union as we know it today. He had taken over his country when it was still almost broken by revolution and civil war and turned it into one of the two great 'superpowers' of the world. It was once estimated that there were more than a billion statues and pictures of this man—the 'Little Father', the 'Great Protector' of his people—on display in every corner of the country. Yet this was the first time since we came to the Soviet Union that we had seen even the slightest indication of his existence. Of the succession of figures who have presided over the Soviet Union's destinies in the pasty sixty years—Lenin, Stalin, Malenkov, Khruschev, Brezhnev—only two have not been totally written out of the script: Mr Brezhnev, because he is still there, and, of course, Lenin.

I was haunted by the experience of visiting that holy ground at the heart of the Soviet empire as by nothing else since I had come here. The quasi-religious symbolism of that shrine is something which cannot be conveyed to those who have not seen it. It brought home again the measure of what has happened to the largest country in the world since 1917. It also helped me to crystallize a view of just what it is that I believe may be wrong with this whole colossal, dark enterprise.

The deification of Lenin has gone so far in the sixty years since his death that it is almost impossible to see the man any more beneath the mountain of legend. Perhaps the nearest one can get to some kind of human picture of what this strange little bearded figure was like when he was alive is through the scattered descriptions by those who met or knew him—H. G. Wells, Valentinov, Bertrand Russell. Russell, after his meeting with Lenin in 1920, wrote in a description often quoted since 'I had much less impression of a great man than expected; my most vivid impressions were of bigotry and Mongolian cruelty . . .'. Another often-quoted story is Gorky's reminiscence of how Lenin expressed his profound impatience after hearing a performance of Beethoven's *Appassionata* Sonata:

> This is astonishing, superhuman music . . . but I can't listen
> often to music, it affects my nerves, makes me want to say kind
> stupidities and pat the heads of people who, living in this dirty
> hell, can create such beauty. But now one must not pat anyone's
> little head—they would bit off your hand, and one has to beat
> their little heads, beat mercilessly, although ideally we're against
> any sort of force against people. Hmmm—it's a devilishly
> difficult task.

The one thing which comes across from all the descriptions of Lenin is his astonishing single-mindedness. From the time he wrote his famous pamphlet *What Must Be Done?* in 1902, he realized that the only way the Revolution, the Dictatorship of the Proletariat could be established in the crumbling, decaying shambles of Imperial Russia was an absolute, superhuman concentration of effort. The Party must be small, totally disciplined, the embodiment of one undivided will—his will. Only if every ounce of effort, of thought, of imagination were channelled towards that one end could sufficient force be accumulated to bring about the distant, unthinkable miracle—the toppling of the Tsars.

Despite the help they gained from the chaos of World War One, the Communists are, of course, right to give supreme honour to Lenin, because it was entirely due to that superhuman concentration of will-power that, when the moment came, they were ready and able to seize power. In the years immediately after the Revolution, it was still Lenin's tireless single-mindedness which drove the whole thing on, for now a new task beckoned—the need to summon forth, from the sea of mud and dissolution to which Russia had been reduced, an entirely new kind of society, like nothing the world had ever seen before. Again it could only be done by a deliberate, superhuman act of will. The new world would not just evolve into existence, it could only come about by being planned down to the tiniest detail. Everything had to be harnessed to that one task, of reforging the people of Russia into one monolithic mass, marching forward in perfectly disciplined unity towards the sunlight of the perfect society. There was no time for disagreement; one of the greatest ironies of the country which still calls itself the 'Soviet' Union is that one of Lenin's earliest tasks, in 1918, was to begin the destruction of the 'Soviets' (the word just means 'Councils'), those ramshackle, anarchic talking-shops, full of all sorts of people who thought the Revolution meant discussion, the clash of ideas (and, as Lenin realized, getting nothing done). The whole nation now had to become an embodiment of the Party's—Lenin's—will. Even the gigantic educational effort to stamp out illiteracy was set in train, not so that the people of Russia could sit back and enjoy the riches of literature, but simply, in Lenin's eyes, so that they could more easily follow the Party's directives, and thus carry out the great universal task more efficiently.

The vision which Lenin conjured up of a wholly selfless society, millions of people totally abdicating their individuality to work together as One Man (or Machine), was stupendously powerful and appealing—the most persuasive psychological creation of the twentieth century. But the point about subordinating literally everything in human existence to one great abstract ideal—not just education, the arts, economics, but even the most basic issues of morality and human relationships—is that you really are putting all your eggs in one basket. You have got to have your central interpretation of human nature and human needs absolutely right. There is no room for even the tiniest misjudgment, or eventually the whole, unified structure goes wrong. And that is why, in terms of symbolism, nothing haunted me more as we walked round Lenin's tomb than the possibility that this little figure who lies there, still spiritually, mentally, doctrinally guiding this vast empire in everything it does, may be just a waxwork. A piece of Madame Tussaud's artistry, decked out with a few tricks of cosmetics. A fraud.

Would that not be a perfect and hideous symbol for what has happened to Russia in the past sixty years? Here was the Revolution, the greatest event in the history of mankind, that was going to tear down the old order, the old privilege, the old hierarchies, the old superstition, the old chaos, the old misery and suffering that had been the lot of Russia since time immemorial. And what has replaced them? A new order, a new hierarchical privileged society, new oppression, new superstition, new chaos, new misery and suffering far, far worse than anything that had gone before—weighing more heavily on men's souls than anything the world could have dreamed of sixty years ago. It is an act of deception, of self-deception, so terrible, so far-reaching, so hard to take that even now there are few people anywhere who really dare face up to what has happened to Russia in our time. They will make any kind of excuse: that the Soviet Union has at least got great achievements to its name; that it can't all have been a mistake; that the Russians are not like other people; that they take quite naturally to this kind of regimentation; that they are genuinely proud of their society.

Perhaps the most subtly demoralizing thing of all about life in the Soviet Union is the ceaseless, unwearying public insistence through newspapers, through television, through teaching in schools and every conceivable medium, that, thanks to the flawless planning of that embodiment of the general will, the Party, conditions of life are constantly getting better.

Even the Constitution states it unequivocally:

> In the USSR . . . the advantages of the Socialist way of life are becoming increasingly evident, and the working people are more and more widely enjoying the fruits of their great revolutionary gains . . . the well-being of the people is constantly rising.

Every graph, every statistic is constantly pointing in the same upward direction, towards that distant perfect society. We are used in the

West to living surrounded by millions of little untruths (there is scarcely a single advertisement or political speech, after all, which is not based on some attempt to distort or 'enhance' reality). But in the Soviet Union there is only one story being told all the time, only one tune being played, only one product on offer—the Party, and the wonderful, ever-improving society which its planning is bringing about. You may believe some of it, or none of it, but in the end the effect is the same. Everyone knows in his heart of hearts that things are by no means as perfect as they are being painted, and such is the nature of totalitarianism that it has to be all or nothing. You have to accept all of it, or none of it. Commumism, in short, becomes for almost everyone involved one enormous, all-pervading Lie—and it has to be like that because of the central view of human nature on which the whole theory of 'Scientific Socialism' is based.

Socialism sees the individual human personality, apart from the group, as something of no importance at all, an aberration, a 'bourgeois delusion'. Man is essentially a collective creature, who can only develop or have significance as part of a group, a class, a delegation, as an embodiment of 'social and historical forces'. Socialism sees truth and morality not as absolutes, but as nothing more than a function of group self-interest. It sees man as the highest thing in the universe, subject to no restraints other than his own ever-expanding physical and mental capacities. The perfect material society is within reach, and only requires organization, planning, discipline and perfect loyalty to the Socialist ideal for its realization.

This is such a hideous caricature of the fullness of human nature, such a gross misconception of the realities of the world both visible and invisible that a constant gigantic effort has to be made to preserve the fiction in being. In reality, it is quite impossible to squeeze human beings into such a mechanistic, artificial little mould, denying them so much of what it is that makes them feel human. That is why such a vast hidden apparatus of terror and conformity and pressure has had to be built up, to force people at least outwardly to accept the roles which the caricature is placing upon them. But it does not, and cannot work, because of the central lie on which the whole system rests.

There is one statistic which reveals more of the truth about what has happened to Russia since the Revolution than any other. Of all the different ways in which Russia has been forced into the inhuman framework of this stupendous mental abstraction, none was more cruel or caused more untold human suffering than the collectivization of Russian agriculture in the early thirties: the tearing apart of the old organic relationship with their animals and their land of tens of millions of peasants, to force them into the straitjacket of a fully 'planned', fully 'collectivized' agriculture. Anything up to 15 million people are estimated to have died as a consequence of this upheaval, but it was all justified because it was the only way Russian agriculture could be mechanized, brought up to date, harnessed to the great common cause of Socialism. A few years ago—fifty years after the collectivization programme was carried out—it was officially admitted (though not very widely publicized) that more than a third of all the food produced at that time in the Soviet Union was grown on just 1 per cent of the cultivated land—that 1 per cent which, in 20 million little plots of an acre or less, was still permitted to be worked privately by individual citizens. In other words, on official figures, productivity on those private plots was roughly fifty times what it was on land worked collectively. You can say that this is only a testimony to the surviving greed and selfishness of the Russian peasant (and anyone who does say that should immediately go off to live in the Soviet Union). But the fact remains that, without this last pitiful vestige of the old private, personal, individual relationship of the Russian peasant with his soil and with the opportunities of the marketplace, denying every principle the Revolution stood for, the whole Soviet experiment would long since have come crashing down in ruins because the Russian people would have starved to death.*

I am feeling my way to the realization that something of enormous importance has begun happening to Russia in the past few years. I can understand how for twenty, thirty, fifty years after 1917 it was possible to preserve idealism about the Revolution, to suppose that one day it might work. In the twenties, the great experiment was still new. Thanks to the limited private enterprise allowed under the New Economic Policy, people were no longer starving as they had been during the Revolution and the Civil War. In the thirties, as the vision of a classless society remained, as Stalin's vast heavy industrial projects rolled forward, the dams, the huge tractor factories, the

* Figures taken from *The Russians* by Hedrick Smith, who derived them from an article by A. Yemelyanov published in the Soviet journal *Problems of Economics*, March 1975. Smith also quoted, from *The Economy of the USSR in 1973*, figures for individual crops: private enterprise produced 62 per cent of the country's potatoes, 32 per cent of fruit and vegetables, 34 per cent of meat and milk and more than 47 per cent of eggs.

rebuilding of Moscow, there was still for many a genuine sense that Russia was being carried by this new religion towards some better world (see, for instance, that remarkable book *Into The Whirlwind* by Evgenia Ginsburg; although as the wife of a prominent local official she was thrown into a succession of horrifying prisons and camps, during Stalin's purges, she still retained her ultimate faith in Communism). In the forties there was the huge new emotional impetus generated by the 'Great Patriotic War', welding Russia together against the common enemy. After Stalin's death there was the sense of relaxation which followed the release of millions from the prison camps, the 'Khruschev Thaw', the dream that Communism might be 'liberalizing', the pride that came from the first great achievements in space. In the sixties and early seventies, under Brezhnev and Kosygin, there was a marked general increase in the standard of living, the availability of consumer goods. But the importance of the past few years is that the one thing on which the whole of the Communist system rests—the belief that somewhere, somehow things are going to get better—has crumbled away more seriously than ever before. No longer is there any excuse such as the war, or post-revolutionary 'teething troubles' for the fact that things are not only not improving, but getting worse. After sixty years, Communist 'planning' simply has not worked, and everyone, even up to Mr Brezhnev himself, knows it. This is a society which has suddenly, more completely than ever, lost the most important props to its faith, sinking down into a sea of corruption, inefficiency and hopelessness.

All that is left is to 'keep order' and, without conviction, to go on proclaiming the Lie.

II

Comrade Popov's Thinking 'In the Correct Direction'

Since Soviet ethics does not recognize morality in general but rather class and communist morality, which differs considerably from the ethics and norms accepted in the West, the behaviour and actions of representatives of the Soviet state are often misunderstood by Western athletes, officials and spectators.

N. Norman Shneidman, *The Soviet Road to Olympus*

Thursday 25 July

Today, after a week of uncertain weather and sudden downpours, we went to the other extreme. The temperature rose into the 90s, Moscow lay under a heavy heat haze and we stewed in stifling humidity—much to the trepidation of the thousands of athletes who today began what many still regard as the central event of the Olympic Games, the intensive eight-day programme of track and field events in the Lenin Stadium.

What is rapidly becoming one of the star attractions of these Games, however, is not the Olympic competition as such but the regular press conference held each day at 1 pm down at the Main Press Centre by Vladimir Popov, a former Deputy Minister of Culture, now a vice-President of the Soviet Olympic Organizing Committee. Although press conferences are hardly a regular feature of Soviet life, Mr Popov has already vastly impressed Western journalists with his deft, often amused fielding of questions. Nevertheless what cannot help coming through on these occasions is the seemingly unbridgeable gulf between Soviet and Western ways of thinking, and today provided some particularly striking examples.

By one o'clock the hall was packed to the doors with several hundred journalists, radio commentators, television teams. Mr Popov, a well-built, greying man of fifty-five, with a humorous, intelligent face, took his seat in front of the arc lights, on a raised platform, flanked by two bulky, rubber-faced *apparatchiks* who seemed to be there only for decoration.

Mr Popov began the proceedings by expressing the hope that, after all the alarms and diversions of the first few days, 'the sports content' of the Games was now 'coming into the forefront', and that 'attempts to hush it up have not been successful'. As usual, he emphasized the world standard of these Olympics by underlining how many world and Olympic records were being broken: already existing world records had been broken thirty-seven times in Moscow, whereas 'in the same few days' at Montreal the figure had only been sixteen.

Mr Popov almost immediately went on to say: 'I would like to turn to other matters connected with sport and which touch the nature of the human being,' and proceeded to announce that the previous day a new Soyuz spacecraft had been sent into orbit from the Baikonur space centre, manned not only by a Soviet cosmonaut, Colonel Viktor Gorbatko, but also, for the first time, by a cosmonaut from an Asian country, Lieutenant Colonel Pham Tuan of the Socialist Republic of Vietnam. In the light of this 'most outstanding event' in the history of 'international co-operation', Mr Popov took the opportunity to send his best wishes to competitors from the Socialist Republic of Vietnam in their first Olympics.

There was a warm round of applause for this announcement from the large number of Communist journalists present, but Western journalists were stunned. Hardly surprisingly it was not long before a Dutchman was on his feet, to voice the immediate response of most of them, by asking 'what on earth has this Sputnik or Soyuz or whatever you call it got to do with the Olympic Games?'

Mr Popov's bland reply, scarcely calculated to dispel Western confusion, was that 'to get into the cosmos you have to be well-trained, a good sportsman. We give all our cosmonauts the title of Sportsman of the Soviet Union. I think this is something of a sports event, I am certain of it.' He pointed out that, after all, Soviet cosmonauts had a sports federation of their own. When Western journalists asked whether they had heard him correctly, he confirmed that there was an All-Union Federation of Aviation Sport and Astronauts, and also a Russian Federation.

This equation of launching huge rockets into space with conventional notions of what constitutes 'sport' came so oddly to most of the Westerners present (particularly since Mr Popov had been so keen

since the Olympics began to pour scorn on those who persisted in trying to confuse sport with politics) that for the rest of the Conference
they sat with expressions of bemused wonderment, as a dozen lesser
revelations followed of just how differently the world is seen through
Soviet eyes.

Mr Popov reeled off an impressive list of figures about the numbers
of people attending all the different Olympic events. For all any of us
knew, these may have been spotlessly accurate, but when he was
asked in a fairly routine manner how the figures were arrived at, he
replied—in a way which would have scarcely been enough to instil
total confidence at a Western press conference—'Those involved
know how it is done—so you can believe my figures.'

Addressing himself to Western visitors' surprise that so few children seemed to be in evidence in Moscow, Mr Popov patiently
explained that it was 'a local peculiarity' that all children should be
moved out at this time of year to summer camps, and that 'it was laid
down in the constitution and legislation' that this should be done for
their 'health'. He announced that he wished to correct a report by
Reuters' that 'sixty to eighty' members of the Irish team down at the
Olympic Village were suffering from food poisoning. A doctor had
inspected them at 11.20 this morning, and a smaller number of
competitors than stated were suffering from a mild form of stomach
complaint.

'Of course I understand freedom of expression,' said Mr Popov,
smiling, 'we are all there to tell the truth as we see it.' But the type of
reporting exemplified by Reuters' on this occasion had not been quite
'in the correct direction'.

Mr Popov was certainly handling with aplomb the kind of interrog-
ation Soviet officials do not normally receive. An example of the type
of questioning he would have been more familiar with came when a
reporter from *Volgograd Pravda* got up to ask whether he could give us
exact figures for the numbers of special buses, other types of vehicle
and drivers being employed as part of the Olympic transportation
service. Without batting an eye, Mr Popov promised that he would
contact the appropriate authorities and provide a full answer
tomorrow.

Then, just as we thought the conference was about to come to an
end, Mr Popov announced with a smile that he had a little surprise for
us. He looked towards the back of the hall, everyone craned round,
and there coming down towards the platform was a tiny old man.

The wizened, bespectacled figure climbed up next to Mr Popov, leaned into the microphone and told us in croaking English, with an American accent, that he had attended every Olympic Games in the modern era including the first in Athens in 1896. He could remember being taken by his father to see the winner of the very first modern Marathon—Spiridon Louis—running into the stadium.

We were all staggered. For a moment we were all so transfixed by this amazing historical phenomenon who stood before us that we almost forgot where we were. Could there be anyone else in the world who could claim to have attended every single Olympics between Athens in 1896 and Moscow 1980?

It turned out that he was a Greek–American called Mr Nick Paul, and then, as he went on speaking, we all gradually came back to earth. He wished us to know how impressed he was by the way these Moscow Games had been organized: 'the opening . . . you cannot describe it. It was something I have never seen before, and you will never see again.' He was greatly impressed by the way he was being looked after in Moscow ('the people here receive us like royalty'). 'Sport is my religion,' he said, 'and politics shouldn't enter into sport.' Sport was an instrument for peace, which could 'finally erase war itself'.

We were back to earth with a bump. How had the Russians found this strange old man? How had they checked him out to make sure that he would only croak out precisely the right sentiments about 'peace' and the beauties of Moscow? Particularly since he was an American, it was inconceivable that he could have been wheeled on for our benefit unless the Soviet authorities could guarantee that his remarks would be 100 per cent 'in the correct direction'.

Gradually the performance began to disintegrate into farce. An Australian journalist called out, 'How old are you?' and another journalist yelled, 'A hundred and sixty-three.' In fact, Mr Paul replied, he was eighty-eight. On further questioning, it turned out not to be strictly true that he had attended *every* modern Olympics; no, he had not actually been at Berlin in 1936, nor in Melbourne in 1956, nor in Tokyo in 1964 . . . Mr Popov, with a huge smile, hastily brought the proceedings to an end.

The curious production of this bizarre figure like a rabbit from a hat, was another eerie little reminder of what a vast painted cardboard structure surrounds us in Moscow, in which nothing is ever quite so straightforward or natural as it seems. For some reason my thoughts went back forty-two years to a tiny incident during the great show trial of Bukharin, Yagoda and Co., as described by Fitzroy Maclean. Perhaps the most brilliant *coup de théatre* of the whole trial had come when Vyshinsky, the immensely smooth State Prosecutor, had accused one of the defendants, a veteran Bolshevik named Zubarev, of receiving bribes many years before from a local chief of the Okhrana, the Tsarist secret police. It seemed a startling, completely unprovable allegation—but then with a little smile, Vyshinsky had announced to the packed courtroom that he would like to call a surprise witness. Everyone had craned round—and there coming towards the witness stand was a tiny, wizened old man. Somehow, somewhere in the Soviet Union, years after everyone present assumed that every member of the Tsarist secret police must long since have been exterminated, the NKVD had been able to put their finger on the very man who was able to say precisely what was wanted—how, he was the police chief who, all those decades before, had twice paid Zubarev thirty silver roubles for informing on his comrades. One thing for which you have to take your hat off to the authorities of this country is their stage-management.

After spending the afternoon writing another article for the *Daily Mail*, I went off in the evening to the Kremlin to see *Aida*. I had decided to do this, partly because I had never seen *Aida* before, and partly because it was being staged in the vast glass-and-concrete Palace of Congresses, built in 1961 as a setting for the famous XXII Communist Party Congress at which Khruschev had shocked the entire Soviet Union by his denunciation of the 'Stalin cult', and his revelations of some of the horrors of Stalin's slave-camp system. A shameful little pun about 'coming to the *Aida* the Party' died on my lips, as I sat in that huge, bare concrete hall through one of the worst and tiredest performances Verdi's most spectacular opera can ever have been given. The famous scene in Act Two when, at Verona, the arena fills with live elephants was so obviously staged on the cheap that the victorious Egyptian army consisted of little more than the same half dozen members of the chorus marching round and round, off stage and back again, changing their weapons each time to make it look as if there were at least a few dozen of them. To be fair the audience, apparently consisting of bored delegations of Bulgarians and East Germans, was so dead that it can hardly have inspired the 'Bolshoi Company' (presumably a third string) to give of its best. Even my hopes of exploring a little more of the Kremlin in the interval were dashed, as a line of militia men prevented us from walking out any further than the stretch of concrete immediately in front of this austere and not inelegant piece of modern architecture.

I returned to the Rossiya to the usual buzz of gossip and stray snatches of information among the hundreds of pressmen in the restaurants and bars. The Soviet Union has now won so many gold medals—considerably more than all the rest of the competing countries combined—that these Olympics are in danger of becoming ridiculous. The Romanians are still apparently furious with the Russians over the handling of the Women's Team Gymnastics final yesterday (Wednesday), when the Soviet Union beat the Romanian ladies, including Nadia Comaneci, into second place—but only, according to the Romanian officials, because Romanian competitors had been subjected to all sorts of unexplained delays in starting their performances, and because the Soviet judges had shown 'gross partiality' towards their own team (such incidents between the two countries are not new—three years ago the Romanians pulled out of the European Championships in Prague because of their complaints about Soviet judges). For the first time today in any event in these Olympics all three medals in the 4,000 metres team pursuit cycling went to countries who insisted on having the Olympic flag run up instead of their own—the Russian audience apparently responded with a storm of boos and catcalls.

But the big news of the day for most of the British journalists is that at last they have been able to spend the day at the Lenin Stadium watching athletics. Britain's Allan Wells has got into the semi-final of the 100 Metres with the fastest time of the day. Sebastian Coe and Steve Ovett both cruised into the semi-finals of the 800 Metres. My colleagues have finally been able to get down to what most of them came to Moscow for. And it is time I said a little more about this group of people with whom, during these few strange weeks, I am so closely sharing my life.

12

Blunts and Smudges

British Journalist (over breakfast at Rossiya, to German
colleague): 'What did you do last night?'
German Journalist: 'I vent to ze Bolshoi to see Ivan ze Horrible.'
British Journalist: 'Terrible.'
German Journalist: 'No, it vos excellent.'

Popular story among British journalists
at the Rossiya

One of the little things I was apprehensive about in coming to my first
Olympic Games was how I would get on with one of the largest but
most isolated groups of people in my profession—the sporting
journalists. Fleet Street is made up of a series of little self-contained
worlds—the political journalists, the crime reporters, the book critics
and so forth—which rarely, if ever, come into contact with each other;
and the 'circus' of sporting journalists is one of the most specialized
and self-contained of all. In purely statistical terms, their words are
probably read more avidly than those of anyone else in our trade. They
include some of the best-known 'names' in journalism. But as they
travel round together, from Wembley to Wimbledon to Las Vegas,
through the sequence of great popular rituals which make up the
sporting calendar, they inevitably get to know each other a good deal
better than they do the other specialists on whatever paper they work
for. And of course there is no more important date in their calendar,
when more of them are gathered together, simultaneously, than that
which comes round every four years as the supreme sporting event of
the modern world, the Olympic Games.

As for my own reception by this tightly-knit group, despite the
reservations many of them have about what I am doing here, I need
not have worried. With only one or two exceptions, they could not
have been more friendly and helpful, and one of the things which has

helped to make these last few days enjoyable has been seeing an increasing number of familiar faces wandering down the interminable corridors of the Rossiya, chatting late at night in the bars, and wrestling alongside them with some of the mysteries we are all faced with in this luxurious prison, such as how to get our washing back from the Rossiya's laundry department.

Inevitably I have had most contact with my own immediate colleagues on the *Daily Mail*: the irrepressible Ian Wooldridge, who shares the room opposite mine with the *Mail*'s athletics correspondent Neil Wilson, a pleasant, dark-haired man in his mid-thirties, married to an ex-ballet dancer, who lives in Surrey. Perhaps the most 'colourful' of all the *Mail* team is our photographer Monty Fresco, a little ex-East Ender in his sixties, who shares a room down the corridor with his nephew Monte (with an 'e') Fresco, also a photographer, with the *Mirror*. 'Old' Monty has accumulated round him a host of semi-apocryphal stories, many relating to his legendary capacity for turning an Olympic Games, with its usual plethora of handouts from camera firms and other commercial sponsors, into a going concern; although one of the first stories I heard was about Monty's visit last year to Poland with a *Mail* reporter, to cover the Papal visit. The Pope was due to visit Auschwitz, and with enormous difficulty Monty's colleague managed to wangle that they should be allowed into the camp, which was under very tight security, before the crowds arrived. Monty turned up for the assignment half an hour late, and the police strictly forbade him to enter, leaving Monty shouting at the gate, 'It would happen to me—the only Jew in history they wouldn't let into Auschwitz.'

It was in fact Monty who is supposed to have coined the nickname 'Blunts and Smudges' for the circus of sporting journalists— 'smudges' being an affectionately dismissive old Fleet Street term for photographers, while the 'blunts' was added by Monty, presumably in reference to the blunted pencils which we hacks are constantly sucking as we take down our shorthand.

Someone else I have seen a lot of is Frank Keating of the *Guardian*—a sensitive soul of great charm, just three days older than me (which makes him forty-two), brought up as a 'Catholic Socialist' in Gloucestershire, given to bestowing 'love' and 'bless you' in all directions (much to the puzzlement of the Rossiya waitresses) with an air of slightly harassed eccentricity. Frank forms a kind of double act with his *Guardian* colleague John Rodda, a mine of statistical and other Olympic information who wrote a history of the Olympics with Lord Killanin (particularly when I saw them in action later at the Lenin Stadium—Keating all wild 'artist's impressions', which he jotted down in a surprisingly tiny pencil handwriting, Rodda all stop-watches, charts and cool efficiency—I came to think of them as a kind of latter-day Quixote and Sancho Panza).

Then there is the *Sunday Times* team, including Dudley Doust, my cricket-loving American neighbour in Somerset, who seems to have been covering everything this week from riding, rowing and swimming to boxing and gymnastics; Norman Harris, a gangling, purposeful-looking Australian; Ian Jack, a bearded, mildly left-wing Scotsman in his early thirties who, again, I see a lot of, because he and I are the only special correspondents here to write about everything except the sport.

Another thoughtful, intelligent man who I can never quite associate with the paper he works for is David Miller of the *Daily Express*. His veteran colleague Sidney Hulls is the only journalist whose preparation for these Olympics has been so thorough that it included a two-year course in learning to speak Russian. Of the 'popular' journalists, the doyen is Frank Taylor of the *Daily Mirror*, an amiable roly-poly figure who only just survived the Manchester United–Munich air crash of 1958. There is Peter Hildreth, my companion on the Lenin Mausoleum pilgrimage, a tall, thin introspective estate agent, who only covers athletics for the *Sunday Telegraph* on the side. There is Pat Besford, the tireless, grey-haired lady who organized all our travel arrangements, and is still to be seen each night at a desk in the Rossiya Press Centre poring over administrative details, in addition to filing her daily copy from the Olimpiskiy swimming pool for the *Daily Telegraph*. There is the legendary Hugh MacIllvanney, the *Observer*'s belligerent Glaswegian 'colour writer', who can churn out in half an hour 2,000 vivid words on any sporting event in the world (though preferably a heavyweight boxing contest), and is to be seen here every night propping up the Rossiya Press Centre bar. And last but not least, as another kind of doyen amongst us, there is his bespectacled *Observer* colleague Chris Brasher, who won a gold medal in the 3,000 Metres Steeplechase at Melbourne in 1956, and will reminisce at the drop of a hat about the great days when he first visited the Soviet Union in 1955 to run against his old friend Vladimir Kucs, or was agonizing with Chris Chataway in their hut in the Melbourne Olympic village at the news from across the world of the simultaneous invasions of Egypt and Hungary. Despite smoking almost as many of my cigarettes as I do when we are together, Brasher makes a valiant attempt to go out jogging each day through this unwelcoming city, where 'lone joggers' are unheard of (his consequent experiences with the Soviet police, faithfully reported to the *Observer*, were, I gathered later a major 'Olympic talking-point' back in Britain).

Such then are some of the eighty or so British journalists with whom I have been sharing my life out here. I have not mentioned the handful of resident Moscow correspondents whom we also come across, such as Nigel Wade, a burly Australian here for the *Daily Telegraph*, who is always a combative presence at Mr Popov's press conferences, or Michael Binyon, the tall, thin, thoughtful *Times* correspondent, who lived here as a student some years ago and speaks good Russian—because one of the more fascinating things for me over the past week has been to observe the effect which being in this strange city has had on the 'Blunts and Smudges'.

The past six months leading up to these Olympics have not been easy for Britain's sporting journalists. For many of them sport is not just their professional preoccupation, something which they spend their whole lives following and writing about. Particularly for the more idealistic among them, such as Chris Brasher, sport is one of the few human activities left which pits the human being against himself, which is concerned with a lonely search for excellence and perfection, involving enormous sacrifice and dedication for its practitioners and bringing people from all over the world together regardless of their politics or nationality. Despite all the rows over drugs and 'shamateurism' and other corrupting influences which have been brought to bear to undermine the almost sacred purity of sport in recent years, the shining ideal remains—and there is nothing on earth which embodies that ideal more clearly than the Olympic Games.

So, as the Moscow Olympics, since the invasion of Afghanistan, has fallen further under the shadow of 'politics' than any other in history, there is almost no one among the journalists here who has not been passionately hostile to the boycott (often in newspaper offices, like the *Daily Mail*'s, where the editor and his political staff were equally passionately in favour). These journalists have more than anyone championed the line that sport should be kept as clear as possible from political interference. They have supported the claims of British athletes to go to Moscow against all comers. They have not seen why Britain's sportsmen and women should bear the brunt of a boycott campaign which the politicians have often seemed reluctant to support in more practical and meaningful ways themselves, such as by cutting some of the lucrative trade links with the Soviet *bloc*, which have only too obviously remained open.

In addition, it must be said, there has been a particular reason why Fleet Street's sporting journalists have been so keen that Britain should not withdraw from these Olympics; and that is that it has for some time been clear that Britain's athletes were poised to make their strongest challenge for years against world-class competition: notably Daley Thompson, the half-Nigerian, half-Scot who, until a few weeks ago, held the world Decathlon record; Allan Wells, the Scottish sprinter, who has a strong medal chance in both the 100 and 200 Metres; and above all, the two middle-distance 'supermen', Sebastian Coe and Steve Ovett who, over the past twelve months, have been vying so strongly with each other to pull down world-record times in the 800 and 1,500 Metres that they have left the rest of the world out of sight.

When we arrived here, in short, most of my colleagues were simply grateful that finally the months of bickering were over and that sport could at last proceed without the politics. In particular they looked forward to what has been widely billed as 'the athletics duel of the century' between Coe and Ovett who, although they are such deadly personal rivals, have only once before met face to face on a track—and that two years ago, before either had reached his present peak of performance (and on that occasion the winner was in fact an East German).

Of course the journalists knew that an Olympic Games in the Soviet Union would not be quite like any other. There was a lot of excited speculation in the first few days about where the KGB might have hidden the bugs in our rooms—rumour had it that an ITV technician over at the Kosmos had discovered his hidden in the colour television set. Monty Fresco, having been to Russia before, came out prepared for the worst in terms of food, and has been sitting in his room munching his way through innumerable tins of sardines, washed down with British tea, bemoaning the lack of opportunities for a little harmless private enterprise at an Olympics where generous commercial sponsors are so conspicuously absent (something of an irony, since the economy of this country, as much as any in the world, runs on the principle of *na levo*).

As they settled down to their work, the first few days' despatches were plentifully scattered with grouses about the 'security overkill'. Wooldridge, in particular, after months of attacking the boycott back home, was keen to show that he was nobody's man. His first article began, after security men had moved in to stop Monty Fresco photographing a queue in GUM on their first morning, 'First round score: *Daily Mail* 0; Soviet Union 1', and he has since weighed in with a series of robust pieces sending up everything from the joylessness of the opening ceremony to the ludicrous wheeling-on of that little joke 'Soviet–American' at yesterday's press conference.

One potential source of strain seems to have been miraculously taken care of. A number of journalists soon found that if they made a reservation for a table in one of the tourist restaurants, when they arrived an appropriate number of pretty, English-speaking Russian girls would almost invariably be sitting at the next table, eager to strike up an acquaintance. After the girls' dinner had been paid for, they would suggest going home to their flats where, for either a small currency deal or just the pleasure of English conversation ... Wooldridge (although, like many others, he did not take advantage of this unforeseen aspect of the Soviet Union's Olympic arrangements) was nevertheless filled with admiration. 'You've got to hand it to the KGB or the Olympic Organizing Committee or whoever thought this one up—they know they've got 3,000 randy journalists on their hands, in a town where nobody speaks the language, so what do they do? They think the problem through, realize it is a potential source of trouble, and make sure that anyone who wants a girl can find one. Stupendous!'

But gradually the experience of living inside our 'compression chamber' has begun to have its effect on even the most ebullient of my colleagues. Despite all the trouble which has been taken to ease our path, there is the sudden difficulty of getting some very simple thing done. Two journalists came home very late one night, and were presented by the 'floor lady' with a bill for their laundry. They did not have the necessary handful of roubles on them. They were told, with the usual policeman standing menacingly by, that they could not enter their rooms until they had paid. Complete impasse, which took half an hour to sort out.

There is the eerie sense of being so cut off from the outside world. Stray scraps of news percolate through—the deaths of Peter Sellers, of Kenneth Tynan, of the Shah—seemingly from another universe. One journalist's response to the news of the Shah's death is supposed to have been 'Oh good, perhaps that means that the Rossiya will now release my laundry.'

Curious little incidents constantly remind us of how the apparently normal, brightly-lit foreground of these Olympics are surrounded with a world of shadows. David Miller told me that Sebastian Coe's father was a regular reader of my articles in the *Spectator* and would like it if the three of us could have dinner together at the Rossiya. At the last minute, a mysterious message came to say that he couldn't make it. I later heard that Mr Coe had been 'advised' by someone on the British Olympic Committee that, in view of the general line of my articles in the *Daily Mail*, it was not thought appropriate that he should be seen dining with me.

After turning a ghastly shade of yellow, poor Peter Hildreth has vanished into the obscure depths of some Soviet hospital, where they won't tell him what's wrong with him. It looks like a severe attack of food poisoning, but apparently the authorities are reluctant to admit that Soviet food could cause such problems.

One person who seems particularly hit by the experience of being in this country is Frank Keating. He has spent a certain amount of time with Russians. Every time I see him he is more depressed, and wanting to know about Solzhenitsyn.

There is no doubt that in the past day or two a strange heaviness of soul has been settling over the British journalists here. It is well known that journalists drink, but one or two people have told me they have never known such hitting of the bottle as has been going on here (I myself found that, after finishing the best part of a bottle of Stolichnaya the other night I lost half of the next day). In the last twenty-four hours more than half a dozen people have told me how they wish they could go home. I doubt whether, five days after the opening, you would ever have heard that at an Olympic Games before.

But at least over the next few days there is the sport. Tomorrow, Friday, sees the final of the 100 Metres and the first day of the Decathlon, while on Saturday we are due for round one of the 'Duel of the Century', the 800 Metres final in which the two 'giants' meet at last. The contest could not have been more beautifully set up. To a man, the press here loves 'Seb' Coe, the charming, boyish extrovert from Sheffield University, 'the gentleman of the track' who is never too busy to answer their questions—and hates the aloof, sulky Ovett, the 'solitary' from Brighton, who is full of himself and won't so much as pass the time of day with a pressman. The journalists ruefully concede that Ovett may just have a chance in next week's 1,500 Metres, the event in which he recently took the world record off Coe. But as for Saturday's 800, there is not a journalist in this hotel who does not expect 'Seb', the world-record holder, to win.

13

British Weekend at the Lenin Stadium

Physical education and sport and high athletic results are in the
Soviet Union not an end in themselves; they are rather a means
through which the Communist Party and the Soviet government
intend to further certain ideological and political objectives.

N. Norman Shneidman, *The Soviet Road to Olympus*

Friday 25 July
The atmosphere of the Lenin Stadium with the sporting programme
in full swing is about as different from that of the heavy, regimented
spectacle of last Saturday as could be imagined. To come out high
above that vast bowl, to look down on runners, jumpers, discus
throwers, different sections of the crowd following and cheering
different events in various parts of the arena, with occasional bursts of
stirring or solemn music, is intoxicating.

I arrived just before six o'clock, for the semi-finals of the Men's 100
Metres. I took a seat on a bench right up behind the banks of press
desks, with a militia man sitting next to me in his shirt sleeves, and the
finishing line exactly below us.

In the first heat, a burly black Cuban, Silvio Leonard, won by a
couple of feet in 10.45 seconds from a Russian, with Don Quarrie of
Jamaica, the silver medallist in Montreal, and Mennea of Italy both so
far behind that they failed to make the final. The Montreal gold
medallist Hasely Crawford of Trinidad was also knocked out, in
yesterday's first round, so that placed the Cuban as the main chal-
lenger. A few minutes later Allan Wells from Edinburgh, in the
second semi-final, beat another Cuban, coming home in 10.27. For
the first time this evening the letters 'GBR' went up at the top of the
giant electronic screens at each end of the stadium, and Wells's hopes
for the final were obviously high.

Then came the 800 Metres semi-finals—three heats. After the first. 'GBR' was up at the top again, as Steve Ovett won in 1 minute 46.6 seconds. In the second, Nikolai Kirov of the USSR won in the same time, to the nearest split second. After the third, 'GBR' was up again as Sebastian Coe had won in 1.46·7. I smiled at the militia man next to me. He smiled back.

A few minutes later the tens of thousands of Soviet spectators throughout the stadium were on the edge of their seats to see how one of their greatest heroes, Victor Saneyev, would perform in the Triple Jump (or 'the Hop, Step and Jump' as we called it thirty years ago when I came second in the school sports to the first 'Russian' I ever met in my life, a boy called Michael Pasternak-Slater who was Boris Pasternak's nephew). Saneyev, a Georgian from Tbilisi (where according to my handout, he 'graduated in agronomy, specializing in citrus-fruit and tea-growing') had won the gold medal at Mexico, Munich and Montreal, and was in line to become only the second man in history to win an athletics event at four consecutive Olympics (the other being the American discus thrower Al Oerter). In fact he was just beaten into second place by a Russian. Saneyev, with his dark, almost Mediterranean face, understandably looked a little sad as for the first time in the evening we stood for the Soviet anthem.

At about seven o'clock 'GBR' was again at the top of the board when Joslyn Hoyte-Smith (a name which gave peculiar trouble to the Cyrillic spellers on the scoreboard, since the Russian alphabet lacks 'j', 'y', 'h', or 'th') won her heat of the Women's 400 Metres. As the moment of the 100 Metres final approached, the stadium looked quite beautiful—the arena bathed in golden, late afternoon sunlight, with a dark slate-grey sky behind, and against it, burning high above the whole scene, the bright orange of the Olympic flame.

The 100 Metres is over so quickly that you scarcely have time to focus. Leonard of Cuba seemed to be leading throughout the second half of the race—but just as he reached the finishing line, exactly below me, I could see Allan Wells in the near lane duck his head sharply forward to the right in a final desperate plunge. Was it enough? Wells obviously thought so, setting off on a lap of honour, although he had run only a few yards before a covey of Soviet officials closed in to usher him off the track.

Again and again the giant screens played recordings of those closing seconds, in slow motion, and the race had obviously been so close that it was a full ten minutes before it was finally, officially confirmed that Wells had beaten Leonard by so tiny a margin that they were both credited with the same time, 10.25 seconds. He was the first British gold-medal winner in the 100 Metres for fifty-six years, since Harold Abrahams won in Paris in 1924. Again 'GBR' went to the top of the board, as Wells received his medal to the bathos of the Olympic flag and Olympic anthem.

The last event of the evening was the 400 Metres of the Decathlon, the fifth ordeal out of the total ten. Daley Thompson had already led the field in two. Now he again registered the best time, which put him at the end of the first day so far ahead of the nearest challengers, a group of three Soviet competitors, that he seemed almost certain of the gold the next day.

Returning home with the memory of those scenes, and the succession of 'GBRs' at the top of the board, dancing in my mind, I could understand why the sportswriters find their trade so hypnotic. As Ian Jack put it to me: 'You feel almost ashamed that it is so easy to get swept up in the excitement of it all—as soon as you walk into that stadium.' My thoughts went back to one of my few memories of the Montreal Olympics. I was staying in a camp site in the pouring rain by the banks of the Danube in Hungary. The only other people on the site were Hungarians and East Germans. As night fell, I heard cheering coming from the other end of the camp. I squelched my way through the mud to find several hundred Hungarians and East Germans shouting themselves hoarse in front of a large, open-air television screen, completely transfixed as they followed the fortunes of their countries' competitors on the far side of the world. I looked on pityingly to think that their lives were so drab that they had to invest so much emotional energy in sport. Just four years later in Moscow, I understood something of what they must have felt.

Saturday 26 July
Back to the Lenin Stadium.

7.25. At last, the great event—the 800 Metres final. 'The clash of the decade', 'the race of the century', 'the moment of truth awaited by the whole world' are only some of the more modest claims which have been put forward by my colleagues for what we are about to witness. Even the Soviet citizens among the 103,000 people present have been made aware that this is something special, partly because there is just an outside chance that their own man Kirov could win, but mostly because whatever may be said about other events on this track, such as the 100 Metres, there is no question that the absence of the Americans, the West Germans and fifty-nine other nations makes no difference at all to this one. It is a world-class event.

The first lap is slow. At the bell, Coe is in the middle of the pack, badly boxed in. As the group of runners moves round to the far side, Warren, the third British finalist, is still leading—but then, with 250 yards to go, Nikolai Kirov breaks clear. Ovett is following him, but the Soviet crowd is going mad—can their man perform the miracle? Where is Coe? Why is he still hanging behind, when is he going to unleash his famous punishing final spurt? The faces of the British journalists around me are filled with anxiety. Now the runners are in the final straight, and Ovett is surging ahead of the Russian. Coe is obviously making a titanic effort to catch up, but—it can't be, he's not going to do it! The world-record holder, the darling of the British press, is not going to win the 800 Metres!

Ovett won the gold, Coe just managed to throw himself forward on the line for the silver, Kirov took the bronze, and never can a British first-and-second in an Olympic event have been received with such long faces and looks of shock among the British pressmen. It was almost as much as they could bring themselves to do to watch the medal ceremony itself, with Ovett as usual making his silent signal of 'I Love You' through the television cameras to his girlfriend back in Britain, and giving a perfunctory handshake to Coe on the step below him. Afterwards Ovett declined to take part in the usual post-race press conference, leaving a stunned Coe to confess that he was 'choked', that he had run a disastrous race, and that all that was left was to start preparing to climb the second half of 'the mountain', the 1,500 Metres next week.

There was at least some consolation a few minutes later when, to the amazement of the British journalists, Gary Oakes, a twenty-one-year-old Londoner, took a quite unexpected third place and the bronze medal in the final of the 400 Metres Hurdles. And then all that was left was the tenth and final event of the Decathlon, the 1,500 Metres.

As the scoreboards indicated, after nine events Daley Thompson was now so far ahead of the rest of the field that he would only have to finish to take the gold medal, although there was still a chance that a really exceptional performance could give him back the world record that he had lost a few weeks before to a West German. As soon as the starting gun cracked, it was obvious which option Thompson had taken. In the Montreal Olympics, at the age of seventeen, he had come eighteenth. For four years he had never had any doubt that this would be his day. Earlier this afternoon he had seen his nearest rival, Valeriy Kachanov of the USSR, taken off in tears after ricking his ankle in the pole vault. Now Thompson ambled round that 1,500 Metres track as if his only concern was to conserve his energies for the lap of honour. Sure enough, when the moment of victory came, he accelerated away so fast, with the usual crowd of Soviet officials in hot pursuit, that he had already covered the best part of a fifth lap before he could be rounded up and sent back to his dressing-room.

A final 'GBR' went to the top of the giant screens.

Sunday 27 July

As I chatted over the telephone with John Bryant in London about a suitable theme for my *Mail* article, it seemed to both of us that something rather interesting has been happening during the past two days in the Lenin Stadium. As a marathon runner, whose greatest passion in life is athletics, John had been following the events of these last two evenings (or as much of them as British television showed) with almost as much fervour as I had. And it was he who first pointed out the curious way in which the string of British successes had all been, to a quite unusual degree, family affairs.

Apparently the image which most British viewers are likely to retain of Allan Wells's victory in the 100 Metres on Friday is not so much the headlong duck for the tape which gave him victory, but the alternating expressions of delight, despondency and finally exultation which crossed the face of his wife Margo, as she went through the uncertainty after the race as to whether he had really won. Mrs Wells is a sprinter herself, but in recent years she has sacrificed her own career to throw everything into supporting her husband—so much so that his first comment after Friday night's victory ceremony was that, if he had a sword, he would cut his gold medal in two and give half to his wife.

Steve Ovett, who runs a solitary 150 miles or more each week in training, has had no more vital protective and emotional support in the past few years than from his mother. Sebastian Coe owes so much to his father, who has coached him every inch of the way, that they are almost inseparable. Daley Thompson is proud to admit that no one has played a more crucial part in his climb to become the Olympic Decathlon champion than his 'Auntie Doreen', who adopted him when he was a child and has been his most fervent fan here in Moscow, dressed in a 'Daley Thompson' tee-shirt. Gary Oakes, the surprise bronze-medal hurdler, owes almost everything to the efforts of his father, a Camden Town coalman who works tirelessly for Harringay Athletics club. Even Duncan Goodhew, the swimming gold medal-list, has no trade mark, apart from his bald head, more familiar than the flat cap belonging to his dead father which he always makes a point of wearing at the poolside; while Sharron Davies, who won a swim-ming silver medal, is coached as assiduously by her father down in the West Country as Coe is by his up in Sheffield.

Now, to British ears, it may sound sentimental to go on about the family story behind all these sporting successes. But here in the Soviet Union it stands out as something quite extraordinary. Most people in Britain have a vague idea that Soviet sport is organized rather differently from the way it is back home, and that most of the Soviet sportsmen and sportswomen whose triumphs have so astonished the world in the past thirty years are the products of an incredibly well-organized and disciplined state system, specifically geared to turning out world-beating sporting performers. Certainly in the handouts which have been lavished on us in Moscow we have been treated to a mass of publicity and statistics about the wonderful sporting facilities in the Soviet Union, how all Soviet citizens are encouraged to take part in sports because it is so good for their health, how there are x number of stadiums and y number of gymnasiums per head of the population, and how this is all part of the wonderful, ever-improving society which the Soviet state provides. But I suspect that not even my colleagues here, who are understandably devoted to the notion that sport and politics should not mix, have really the slightest idea of just how differently sport and its organization are viewed in this country.

The story of the 'miracle' of Soviet sporting achievement goes back to the days shortly after the Revolution of 1917, when all sporting clubs in the new Soviet Union, and their equipment, were commandeered and handed over to the Red Army's new training organization *Vsevobuch*, whose 'main aim was to supply the Red Army with contingents of trained conscripts as soon as possible'.* Right from the start, a primary aim of sport in the new society was to bring its citizens up to a high standard of fitness for military purposes. A second aim was to improve the health of the citizens. A third, given in the twenties the title of *Proletkult*, was to involve as many citizens as possible in collective activities, 'labour exercises and mass-displays, pageants and folk-games', to encourage a collective feeling, and to make them feel part of the single, perfectly disciplined unit that was the ideal of Soviet society.

During the 1920s sport or 'physical culture' in the Soviet Union was placed entirely under Party control, and in 1925 an official decree confirmed that

> physical culture must be considered not simply from the standpoint of public health and physical education; not only as an aspect of the cultural, economic and military training of young people; it should also be seen as a means to educate the masses . . . it must be regarded, moreover, as a means of rallying the bulk of the workers and peasants to the various Party, government and trade union organizations, through which they can be drawn into social and political activity . . . physical culture must be an inseparable part of overall political . . . education.

What has all this to do with the Olympic Games in 1980? Simply that it was on these ideological foundations that the whole structure of sporting activity and organization in the Soviet Union, involving today between 26 million and 60 million people on a regular, organized (and to a degree compulsory) basis, was erected—with its aims to give all young people a basic military training, to promote health, and to draw all citizens into mass-activity which will give them the sense of being part of a disciplined whole. Eventually to these aims a fourth was added, which was to use success in international sport quite explicitly as an advertisement for the Socialist way of life, and it was only when they were confident that this could be done effectively that the Soviet authorities in 1951 finally joined the International Olympic Committee, as a preliminary to their sensational debut at Helsinki in the following year.

* From *Sport in the USSR* (Collet's, 1979) by James Riordan. Almost all the description of sport in the Soviet Union which follows is based either on this booklet, produced for the Olympic Games, or on the much longer study, *The Soviet Road to Olympus: Theory and Practice of Soviet Physical Culture and Sport*, op. cit.

The Looking-glass Olympics (16 July–4 August 1980)

Every Soviet citizen between the ages of sixteen and eighteen not only belongs to a sports club, but has to pass certain basic tests of skill and fitness, as part of the so-called GTO National Fitness Programme, instituted in 1931 to serve the twin aims of *masterstvo* (proficiency) and *massovost* (mass-participation). GTO stands for *Gotov k trudu i oborone*, 'Ready for labour and defence'. The first test is 'to have a knowledge of Physical Culture and Sport in the USSR'. The second is 'to know and carry out rules for personal and public hygiene'. The third is 'to be able to carry out the initial military training programme, to wear a gas mask for one hour, and to know the basic rules of civil defence'.*

But it is when you come to the organization of Soviet sport that the Western mind really begins to boggle, and it is here that the real contrast with the homespun nature of the British successes in the Lenin Stadium this weekend opens up. Soviet sport is run by thirty-seven different clubs or societies, under the USSR Committee of Physical Culture and Sport. Thirty-four of these are trade union clubs: each of the fifteen Republics has two, one rural, one urban, and four are 'All-Union', including those representing railwaymen (*Lokomotiv*) and office workers (*Spartak*). But to outsiders the two most interesting sports organizations, by far the largest and most powerful, are those run by the Red Army and the KGB. The KGB club in particular is well known to Westerners, because its footballers and athletes are the most successful in the Soviet Union, but very few Westerners recognize the presence of the Soviet secret police behind the innocuous-sounding name of its sports club, which is *Dinamo*:

> Dinamo . . . is the oldest sports society, having been established in 1923, several weeks before the Central Army Sports Club. Dinamo is in fact a para-military society, representing the Ministry of the Interior. Attached to it are the Soviet border defence forces and the state security forces. It was organised on the initiative of F. E. Dzerzhinsky, who was at the time the leader of the Cheka . . . presently the duties of the Cheka are carried out by the Soviet secret police or so-called KGB. Despite the fact that the human base of this society is rather small, it has held for many years a leading place in Soviet competitive athletics . . . in the XXth. Olympic Games (Munich) members of the Dinamo won 28 gold, 10 silver and 16 bronze medals.

* Among the specific skills required under a further heading are ability 'to hurl the hand grenade', and proficiency in firing 'a small-bore rifle or heavy weapon'.

Similarly in the 1976 Olympics, members of Dinamo topped the list of Soviet medal winners. Dinamo is successful not only because it is the oldest Soviet sports society but also because it is the richest, and it has the best sports facilities in the USSR.*

Mr Shneidman does not add the possibility that members of other 'societies' might be afraid of winning (and I particularly like the phrase 'Despite the fact that the human base of this society is rather small . . .'); but I rather suspect that anyone who announced in the West the near-certainty that the largest number of medals in these Olympics will be won by members of the KGB would be accused on all sides of wild anti-Soviet paranoia.

It is really on straightforward facts like these that the whole case for 'keeping sport clear of politics' in these Olympics ultimately falls down. It is indeed something of an ironic comment on just how far the modern Olympic movement has travelled from its founder Baron Coubertin's ideals that the most successful group of sportsmen in the world today should belong to the same organization which created the Gulag Archipelago, responsible for the deaths of anything up to five or six times as many people as were killed in Hitler's concentration camps. It also helps to explain why there is such an apparent confusion in the Soviet Union between 'peace-loving sportsmen' or 'gymnasts' on the one hand (like the ring of track-suited gymnasts who sit round the perimeter of the Lenin Stadium, or those men who goose-stepped in clutching doves at the opening ceremony), and on the other, soldiers and secret policemen. The answer is that they may well be—often are—the same: every member of the Red Army, every KGB man, is also, in another guise, a 'gymnast' or a 'sportsman', and a great many of them are winning medals in these Games.

There is one other aspect of the state organization of sport in this country which must be touched on, and that is the huge amount of money and effort which goes into nurturing any sportsman who is potentially a world-beater, and may thus further the prestige of the Soviet Union abroad. Westerners are vaguely aware of the mass of special schools and colleges where promising young gymnasts, swimmers or athletes can be taken off for concentrated training as early as eight or nine years of age. What is less well known is the complex hierarchy of distinctions which are available to Soviet sportsmen and sportswomen as they climb the ladder of success, each with its own

* Shneidman, op. cit.

privileges attached. According to a precisely defined 'points table' (e.g. so many placings in the first six in international competitions), you may rise through a succession of grades, up to 'Master of Sport of the USSR' and, at the very top, 'Merited Master of Sport of the USSR'. To be a member of one of these tiny elite groups ranks you alongside Party officials, Red Army officers, KGB officers, members of the Bolshoi, cosmonauts, leading scientists and writers, composers as one of the most privileged people in a society where privilege means such an extraordinary amount, with access to special shops and apartments, the right to jump queues for train or theatre tickets and, of course, not least, the chance to be able to travel abroad (which means not just being able to *see* other parts of the world, but, even more important being able to bring back foreign goods, such as perfumes, jeans or radio sets, for sale on the black market).*

But before getting too carried away by the dizzy idea of such privilege, it is worth recalling just what it may amount to in fact. Probably the most famous sports personality the USSR has ever produced is Olga Korbut, the elfin gymnast who entranced the world at Munich in 1972. In the West she would probably now be a multi-millionairess. As a holder of the most coveted title of all, Merited Master of Sport of the USSR, she has been brought to Moscow for the 1980 Olympics, to meet and be seen by foreign visitors. But her husband has had to stay at home in the provincial city of Minsk, where they live in a small three-room flat. Their sole 'asset' is a three-year-old car. And now that she is retired, she is no longer permitted to travel abroad.

In the shadow of such a vast state-organized machine specifically geared to mass-producing Olympic successes, the background of the little handful of British winners in Moscow this week seems almost painfully amateurish—Daley Thompson's Auntie Doreen, Allan Wells's solitary training runs at Meadowbank. As I summed it up in my despatch:

> The idea that an athlete's preparation for such a gruelling and prestigious event might be primarily a family affair flies right in

* The first ever Soviet Olympic gold medallist was Nina Romashkova-Ponomaryova, who won the Women's Discus at Helsinki on 20 July 1952. She became better known to British newspaper readers four years later when she was arrested for stealing a hat from the C. and A. store in Oxford Street.

the face of the whole ideology of Communism—which dictates that the first definition of any citizen is that he is a cog in the State machine, compared with which family ties are of virtually no importance. It would be absurd to say that family life does not exist in the Soviet Union—despite all sorts of pressures, it has survived here at least no worse than in Western nations. But from their earliest years children are drilled by schools, Pioneer and Komsomol organizations into believing that the collective and the State must always come before the family. One of the Pioneer heroes all good little Soviet citizens are taught to admire is Pavel Morizov, who was killed by peasants in 1932 for reporting on his own father for hoarding grain which should have gone to the State.

In his book *The Russians*, Hedrick Smith tells the chilling story of a Swedish diplomat who asked his young son, temporarily attending a Moscow school, which grown-ups did he respect? 'Instead of naming father or mother,' as Smith puts it, 'the little six-year-old replied "Lenin". "Well, after that who?"' was the next question. 'The boy went right down the line through the Soviet hierarchy, from Brezhnev to the District Communist Party Secretary, without naming his parents.'

It would be hard to imagine a more complete contrast to the ethos represented here in Moscow by such as Coe, Ovett and Thompson, who have not only been able to give thanks to the support of their families before anything else, but have performed here under the shadow of their government's active disapproval. Indeed . . . what has happened here provides a contrast not just to the Communist approach to sport, but also to the American system—in its own way equally collectivistic—which seeks to mass-produce athletics successes through the country-wide chain of colleges and special scholarships. The British athletes here, supported by their 'mums', 'dads' and 'aunties', have represented a third approach—as private, human and individualistic as the others are not.

When I had telephoned over my piece, I went off to the little seventeenth-century Church of the Resurrection in Nezhdanovoye. There were about three hundred people present, of all ages, though the largest groups were old ladies and young people in their twenties and thirties. Everyone was wrapt in his own devotions. The singing was beautiful and timeless. As incense rose before the icons, shining in the light of hundreds of candles, it was an hour of perfect inner peace—as far removed from the clamour and instant mass-enthusiasm of the Lenin Stadium as could be imagined. I was reminded of Maurice Baring's story in *What I Saw in Russia*:

> You live here, walk about, talk, and forget you are in a place which is quite unique, until some small sight or episode brings home the fact to you and you say, 'This is Russia' ... such a moment has just occurred to me tonight. When driving home through the empty streets at 11 p.m. I passed a church as the clock struck and I heard a voice speaking loud quite close to me. I turned round and saw a policeman standing on the pavement, having faced about towards the church. He was saying his prayers in a loud sing-song. His whole body was swaying as he crossed himself ... when I saw this policeman saying his prayers I experienced that peculiar twinge of recognition which made me say, 'This is Russia.'

Strange to think that Baring recorded that experience within the lifetime of one or two of the older people who were with me in that church tonight.

As the evening service came to an end, I went back across the city to the Stadium for the last race of the day, the 10,000 Metres. When I arrived, the race was already under way—it is very long, twenty laps of the track. By the halfway mark, the field was already divided into two quite distinct groups. So far out in front that the rest were of no importance were five runners, two blond Finns, including the great Lasse Viren, who won this event in 1972, and three black Ethiopians, including the ageless Miruts Yifter. Lap after lap they ran, the same five men doggedly pounding away, not more than a few yards between them, although occasionally one of the Ethiopians would surge forward, and they would all change places. It was hypnotic. Only as they came round the far side for the last time, did Yifter in an amazing final explosion of energy, considering they had been at it for nearly half an hour, surge away, to take the gold medal with apparently complete ease. It was a breathtaking spectacle. Not only was there not a Soviet athlete in sight, there was not even an Englishman. It was just the beauty of sport for its own sake, a truly Olympian struggle between the athletes of two tiny nations, and a perfect end to the weekend.

14
Visit to an Occupied Country

If any nation is retained by force within the limits of another
State, if, in spite of the desire expressed by it (it matters little if
that desire is expressed by the press, by popular meetings,
decisions of political parties, or by disorders or riots against
national oppression) that nation is not given the right of deciding
by free vote—without the slightest constraint, after the complete
departure of the armed forces of the nation which has annexed
it, or wishes to annex it, or is stronger in general—the form of
its national and political organization, such a union constitutes
an annexation—that is to say, conquest and an act of violence.

> From the first Revolutionary Proclamation, the
> so-called 'Peace Decree', drafted by V. I. Lenin,
> 8 November 1917

Monday 28 July
Back in London we had been told that there would probably be great
difficulty in getting to Tallinn, where the Olympic yachting events
were being held. It seemed that only accredited yachting correspondents were being allowed there. In the event, it turned out that
nothing was easier. Valeriy had arranged tickets and hotel bookings
for Ian Jack and myself. In fact the only minor obstacle came when,
after a long night talking to the interpreters, I awoke at eight-thirty
and realized that our scheduled flight had left half an hour before.

We jumped into a taxi and sped off to Vnukovo Airport, some
twenty-five miles to the south-west of central Moscow. This is one of
the main provincial airports of the capital, and the somewhat tatty
main terminal building was packed with Soviet citizens and their
families, many looking as if they had slept there. At the departure
desk we were told that, as foreigners, we should use the special
'Intourist' reception area in another building. This was new, clean and
empty. A smiling girl said that there would be no problem—we would

be booked on the next flight. We had an hour to wait and thought of finding something to eat. We tried the main airport restaurant, where a lengthy queue snaked down the stairs. Again we were told that, as foreigners, we could eat in a special cafeteria behind the Intourist reception area, where there were only two or three people eating, and we were served immediately.

As departure time approached, we were taken to a special departure lounge for foreigners, brand new for the Olympics, whence shortly afterwards we were led across the tarmac to a waiting Tupolev. As we took our seats we realized why we had got a new flight so easily. There were only half a dozen or so other passengers. At that moment, the 'ordinary' passengers streamed in, filling every seat in the aircraft. It looked suspiciously as if, in order for us to be given our seats, two other people must have been turned away at the last minute.

There were various reasons why I was particularly keen to visit Tallinn, capital of the Soviet Republic of Estonia.

Firstly, as the setting of the yachting events, it was the place where the effects of the Olympic boycott were likely to be most dramatically in evidence, since nearly half the original forty-odd competing teams had stayed away, including those of almost all the main yachting nations, such as West Germany, Canada and Britain.

Secondly, I had heard that Tallinn, set on a bay in the Gulf of Finland, is very beautiful—one of the best-preserved old towns in Europe, with its churches, medieval and baroque buildings and narrow cobbled streets.

Thirdly, Estonia—smallest in population and almost smallest in area of all the Soviet Republics—was reputed to be the most prosperous, 'free', Westernized corner of the Soviet Union. Its *per capita* income, based on the manufacture of precision instruments, chemicals, textiles and dairy products, is the highest in the country. The inhabitants of Tallinn are the only people in the USSR who can watch Western television, from Finland just fifty miles across the Baltic to the north (and which they can understand because Estonian, as one of Europe's handful of 'Finno-Ugrian' languages, is very similar to Finnish—the Estonians are really Scandinavian).

Not the least reason why Estonia is more 'Westernized' than any other part of the USSR, of course, is that it became part of the Soviet Union only forty years ago. In the twenties and thirties, like its Baltic

neighbours to the south, Latvia and Lithuania, Estonia was an independent country, run by its own parliament—or, as a booklet *Tallinn:
Olympic Regatta City* which we had been given back in Moscow put it,
a 'bourgeois dictatorship'. Eventually, according to the booklet, the
'bourgeois government' went over to 'frankly Fascist methods'. In
June 1940, 'the working people' of Estonia staged 'a general strike and
mass-demonstrations' which 'succeeded in bringing to power the
progressive People's Front, which held elections to Parliament—the
State Duma'. On 21 July 1940, the new Duma 'unanimously proclaimed Estonia a Soviet Socialist Republic' and a month later the
country was admitted at its own request into the Soviet Union.

Before leaving Britain I had in fact spent a certain amount of time
looking into the history of Estonia, and the version I had become
familiar with was somewhat different.

Although Estonia is so small, and has been occupied during most of
the past eight hundred years by Germans, Swedes and Russians, its
people have a very strong sense of their own national identity. They
have their own language, a rich folk-culture and their own national
myth, centred on the great hero Kalev. In the late nineteenth century,
when Estonia was under Tsarist rule, a great nationalist awakening
took place (as elsewhere in Europe), centred not least on the famous
university of Tartu. Around 1900 a number of nationalist leaders
emerged, including a radical newspaper editor Konstantin Päts. In
the general Russian collapse of 1917, the Estonians declared their
independence. In 1918 they were occupied and then abandoned by the
Germans, upon which a civil war broke out between the local nationalists and Soviet-backed Communists. The turning-point came in
December 1918, when a British cruiser squadron under Rear-Admiral
Sinclair anchored in Tallinn Bay, and supplied 1,000 machine guns to
the nationalists, under a Colonel Laidoner. The Communists and Red
Army units were routed, and in 1920, in the Treaty of Tartu, the
Soviet Union 'voluntarily and forever' renounced any further claims
over Estonia.

Estonia settled down to independent, democratic rule, under a
succession of prime ministers from various parties, including Päts. By
all accounts, it was a very pleasant little country to visit between the
wars. Apart from the beauties of Tallinn, the people were friendly,
hardworking, with a lively culture; a much larger proportion of the
population went to university than in Western Europe; they published the highest number of books per head of population of any

country in the world and had the highest rate of theatre-going. In 1934, faced with an economic crisis and violent political divisions, Päts assumed the Presidency, suspending all political parties for three years, and running the country as a 'benevolent dictator', with Laidoner as his minister in charge of public order. It was this which the Soviets describe today as 'fascist rule', although they omit to add that in 1937 constitutional rule, with Päts as elected President, was restored. In 1939, a secret protocol to the Nazi–Soviet Pact assigned Estonia, along with Latvia and eastern Poland, to the 'Soviet sphere of influence'. In March 1940, the Soviet Union unilaterally imposed on Estonia a 'Mutual Assistance Treaty' not dissimilar to the one signed with Afghanistan in 1978. In June 1940, while the eyes of the world were on the fall of Paris to Hitler, Stalin unilaterally invoked the treaty, sending the Red Army into Estonia, Latvia and Lithuania (presumably the 'mass-demonstrations' referred to in my pamphlet). By 17 June Soviet forces occupied the whole of Estonia. A month later, 'elections' were held, with only one list of Soviet-sponsored candidates—and from then on the Soviet version of events is reasonably accurate, except that it fails to mention the mass-arrests of President Päts, Laidoner, many other political leaders, writers and academics and some 60,000 other Estonian citizens who, over the next twelve months, were either killed or taken off in cattle trucks to prison camps in Siberia.

Between 1941 and 1944, the Estonians endured the rigours of Nazi rule. As the Soviet army returned, some 33,000 Estonians fled to Sweden, another 30,000 to Germany. In 1945 and 1946 another 20,000 were deported to Stalin's camps. In two days in March 1949, during the 'collectivization' of Estonian agriculture, some 40,000 more were deported. In other words, if you add up all those who were either killed, deported or fled between 1940 and 1949, it amounts to a total of some 180,000 people. The entire population of Estonia in 1940 had numbered not much more than a million—so nearly one in five had vanished in less than ten years, all but a handful never to return.

This was the country we were about to visit for the yachting events of the 1980 Olympic Games.

The sun was shining and a fresh breeze was blowing in from the sea as we disembarked at Tallinn's little airport. We were met on the tarmac by a smiling Estonian girl, who knew all about our arrival. We passed through the handsome new dark-brick-and-glass airport terminal, specially built for the Games by the Finns, where two or three more charming, English-speaking Estonians were waiting to accompany us in a mini-bus to our hotel, the Viru, in the centre of the city (population 500,000).

I could form little impression of Tallinn as we sped through, apart from a pretty lake, trees, trams, 'Western' spelling on the signs, a few modern buildings, including our hotel, an ultra-modern tower block, also built in dark brick and glass by the Finns. The view from my bedroom window on the twelfth floor was a great panorama of Tallinn Bay, under a dazzling blue sky. Over to the left I could see the Old Town rising on its hill, with battlements, towers, gabled houses and spires, including the famous Oleviste, St Olaf's, the tallest spire on the Baltic, used for centuries as a lighthouse. I had not realized what a relief it would be to get out of Moscow. The whole feel of this place, with its charming Estonians, Roman spelling and sea breezes seemed different. I felt quite in holiday mood.

When we came downstairs, an intense-looking, bespectacled young man materialized from the shadows (the hotel with its black brick and low lighting was very dark) and offered to 'show us around'. This was Martt, an English-speaking Estonian, who had trained in social psychology at Tartu. We gratefully accepted his offer, and began walking towards the Old Town, chatting amiably. We passed the Estonian State Theatre, a picture or two of Lenin, the sort of drab shop fronts typical of a Communist country, but after Moscow the whole scale of the place seemed smaller, more intimate. And as we climbed a steep little street up the hill to the Toompea, or citadel, it became clear just what an exceptional town this was, with its medieval walls and towers (each with a name—Fat Margaret, Long Hermann, Kiek-in-de-Kok, or 'peep in the kitchen', as in the fifteenth century a watchman could look down from its battlements into the kitchens of Tallinn below). Within the citadel itself, at the top of the hill, a group of handsome, beautifully restored baroque buildings, including the old Estonian parliament building, clustered round a tiny square. Further on, from a little belvedere on the edge of the Toompea we could look down on winding medieval streets and gatehouses, jumbled roofs with here and there a painted baroque façade. Beyond, in the late afternoon sun, lay Tallinn Bay, its beauty marred only by a great plume of yellow smoke stretching right across to the horizon from a chemical works further up the coast.

The Looking-glass Olympics (16 July–4 August 1980)

The Old Town of Tallinn is the largest 'conservation area' in the Soviet Union, and everywhere we looked we could see signs of the huge effort of restoration and repainting which had been under way for several years to show the city at its best to Olympic visitors (much of it under the direction of a team of Polish restorers, the best in the Communist world). We walked round the Town Square, with its fourteenth-century town hall, and street after street of magnificently restored high-gabled houses, looking very Hanseatic. Yet although it was beautiful, the whole town seemed curiously empty, like a great, dead stage-set.

I was keen to eat out in the Old Town, but although it was not all that late, the few restaurants seemed either closed or just closing. So, making our guide promise that we could return to explore the bars of the Old Town the following evening, with the hope that we might also hear some traditional Estonian singing, we went off for dinner to the Olympia Hotel, another gaunt new tower block, apparently constructed inside almost entirely of white lavatory-tiling, and virtually deserted. It was a relief to get back to the Viru, although, despite the posters everywhere proclaiming 'Tallinn Welcomes The Visiting Olympians', here too there seemed a distinct shortage of guests. We at last found the semblance of scenes of animation in a downstairs bar, where a small group of journalists were drinking with their Estonian guides. The most conspicuous figure present was an old Irish journalist, Mr Walsh, editor of the *Munster Express*, accompanied by his daughter Priscilla. They were here, we learned, because the following day—the last of the yacht racing—it seemed almost certain that an Irish pair would win a silver medal in the Flying Dutchman class, Ireland's first-ever yachting medal. Mr Walsh had been at every Olympic Games since Berlin in 1936, and was busy informing the Estonians present, 'You should take a leaf out of Ireland's book. Look what we did in 1916 and 1920. This lot are no better than the Black and Tans—you should put them all up against a wall and shoot them.'

As I went to bed in my little room on the twelfth floor of that empty hotel, with a uniformed policeman walking up and down the empty corridor, and a pretty young girl at the desk reading a novel by Heinrich Mann for hour after hour through the night, I thought of all the little clues during the day to what a strange country this was. And not the least strange thing was how few of the highly-educated Estonians we met seemed to speak more than a smattering of Russian.

Visit to an Occupied Country

Q. 'What is the largest country in the world?'
A. 'Estonia, because its coastline is on the Baltic, its capital is
Moscow and its population is in Siberia.'

Estonian joke

An Estonian was once sitting on the Toompea when a Red Army
soldier sat down on the bench next to him. They looked out at
Tallinn Bay, and the Estonian said, 'When I see such beauty, I
thank God.' The Red Army man muttered, 'I thank Mr
Brezhnev.' As they chatted on, whatever wonder of Soviet life
was mentioned, the soldier said, 'For that I thank Mr Brezhnev.'
Eventually the Estonian said, 'You thank Mr Brezhnev for
everything. But who will you thank when Mr Brezhnev dies?'
'Ah,' replied the Red Army man, 'when Mr Brezhnev dies, then
I will thank God.'

Another Estonian joke.*

I have often felt in, say, Czechoslovakia, that I was in an occupied
country—but I have never experienced that feeling so strongly as I
was beginning to in Soviet Estonia. It had even been glibly reported in
certain sections of the British press that Estonia was somehow more
'free' than other parts of the Soviet Union. It is true, as we learned
from the Estonians we had been talking to, that most weekends a boat
arrives from Helsinki full of what Estonians call 'the vodka tourists'—Finns who have been banned from buying alcohol under their
country's strict anti-drunkenness laws, and who come to Tallinn to
get drunk (a unique instance of Westerners being able to come into the
Soviet Union to enjoy a specific freedom which is denied to them at
home).

But the beautiful, deserted, frozen stage-set with which we were
being presented—with little more than its appointed cast of Olympic
officials in sight—was something much more eerie than Moscow, not
least because of the almost complete absence of Russians.

In the past thirty years, Moscow made extraordinary efforts to
'Russify' Estonia, by moving in tens of thousands of Russians,
not only to occupy many of the top jobs, but quite deliberately

* Since all our movements in Estonia were tracked, I hasten to add that these jokes,
like much of the information on following pages, came from sources other than people
with whom we were in contact in Tallinn—notably Andres Küng's excellent book *A
Dream of Freedom*, Boreas Press (1980).

to shift the whole balance of the population, so that today nearly half the inhabitants of Tallinn are Russian. The Russian 'occupation', as it is still seen by almost every Estonian, has never ceased to inspire seething resentment. The Estonians resent the exploitation of their economy, so that only a small proportion of what this tiny corner of the Soviet Union produces actually remains in Estonia. When outsiders point to the higher productivity and living standards of Estonia, compared with the rest of the Soviet Union, Estonians point back in turn at Finland, which, before 1940, was much on a par with Estonia in both respects, but which has since improved its position compared with Estonia by a factor of three. Estonians resent the way the Moscow 'planners' have exploited their natural resources: in particular how a vast tract of the north-east of their country has been reduced to a poisoned moonscape by the wholesale mining of oil shales (which are then wastefully fed into two huge thermal power stations to supply Leningrad with cheap electricity), in what is probably the worst single example of 'industrial pollution' in Europe.

In fact the outside world has remained almost totally unaware of the incredible courage which has been shown in the past thirty-five years by the peoples of these three little Baltic nations (including Estonia's two neighbours, Latvia and Lithuania, to the south) in their resistance to Soviet rule. For at least fifteen years after the occupation, in all three states, organized guerrilla groups continued to operate clandestinely in remote areas and forests (known as 'the Forest Brethren'), scarcely believing that somehow help would not one day come from the West. That hope was finally abandoned about the time when the fate of the Hungarian uprising in 1956 demonstrated how little the West was prepared to 'interfere' in East European politics.

In the late sixties, a new wave of protests, more open than hitherto, spread through all three countries: in Estonia it centred on the students of Tartu and Tallinn, who were too young to remember the days of independence. In the years since, despite constant pressure from the KGB, the spirit of rebellion has rarely been far below the surface. In 1972, two groups calling themselves 'the Estonian Democratic Movement' and 'the Estonian National Front' sent a long memorandum to the Secretary-General of the United Nations, pointing out among many other things that the three Baltic countries

were the only states—former members of the League of Nations—who after World War Two have experienced no implementation of the 3rd article of the Atlantic Charter, relating to the restoration of sovereign rights and self-government to those nations who have been forcibly deprived of them.

In 1975, at the very moment when Mr Brezhnev was in Helsinki putting his signature to the agreement on human rights, the KGB fifty miles to the south was engaged in a particularly ruthless wave of repression, in which several leading figures in Estonian life were dismissed from their jobs, including the director of the Sociology Department at Tartu University, the administrator of the Estonian Radio Symphony Orchestra and the country's best-known musicologist, while a number of others were sent off to labour camps.

In 1977 a letter was smuggled to the West signed by eighteen Estonian natural scientists, from Tartu University, Tallinn Polytechnic, the Academy of Sciences and the Nature Conservation Society of the Estonian SSR, protesting against the dangerous 'environmental situation' rapidly developing in northern Estonia, as a result of the devastating exhaustion of natural resources and the general pollution of water, air and soil—the 'direct result of a bureaucratic, short-sighted, extensive colonial administration'.

In the same year an even more remarkable collection of three documents was smuggled to the outside world. They were in the handwriting of Konstantin Päts, the last President of free Estonia. In one, dating from 1954 (when he had been just coming up to eighty), he had written:

> Since the year 1940 I am being held without a court order, without any charges, as a prisoner in Russia in a hospital for the Jewish poor, where I, as President of the Republic of Estonia, am being subjected to degradation in every way … my health here has deteriorated very much … I have even been refused to use my own name. Here I am only 'Number 12' …

The Soviet Government eventually admitted to the International Red Cross that Päts had died on 16 January 1956, but they would not say where.

Tuesday 29 July
The following morning the sun was again shining, as we drove a few miles out along the edge of the sea, on a specially built highway, to the

Olympic yachting marina, set among the pinewoods of Pirita.* Before
the war this had been a popular resort, but in recent years industrial
pollution has made bathing in Tallinn Bay rather less pleasant. The
lavishly-equipped Olympic yachting complex, a series of spacious
concrete structures looking out over the Baltic, seemed almost as
empty as the Old Town the previous night.† There was a muted air
about the place, as if everyone was carefully acting out a part. A
smiling press official came up and introduced himself to us. I said that
his name did not sound Estonian, and he said, 'No, I am afraid it is
Russian.' We wandered down to the marina, where the boats were
being prepared for the final day of racing. Within a few minutes we
had located the two pleasant young Irishmen who, after six races, were
standing second to Spain in the Flying Dutchman class. It turned out
that although they were born and brought up in Ireland, one of them,
David Wilkins, worked for Pedigree petfoods and lived near Melton
Mowbray; the other, James Wilkinson, was an IBM computer
development specialist and lived near Southampton. They trained on
the Solent and had often sailed with Rodney Pattison, who twice won
gold medals in this event for Britain at previous Olympics. One of
them was even wearing a British Olympic Association tracksuit. 'If
this isn't the nearest thing to a British yachting medal hope in these
Games,' I thought, 'then I'm a Flying Dutchman,' and we resolved
that we would spend the day out in the bay supporting 'our lads'.

Half an hour later we were chugging out to sea in a motorboat,
accompanied by an Estonian, a Ukrainian and a Byelorussian. Tallinn
Bay, where Rear-Admiral Sinclair's cruisers had anchored in 1918,
looked glorious in the blazing sun. Always in the background was the
skyline of the Old Town on its hill, the slender spire of Oleviste. Along
the flat, typically Baltic shoreline stretched pinewoods, broken by a
new Olympic television tower and a large shell-like structure which,
every five years, is the setting for an enormous Estonian folk-song and
dance festival (the last, earlier this summer, was attended by more
than a quarter of the country's population).

* Shortly before the opening of the Olympics there had been a mysterious car
accident on this stretch of highway, involving the death of Irina Kaplun, thirty, the
editor of a clandestine Leningrad magazine and wife of Vladimir Borisov, the 'free trade
union' dissident who had been deported by the KGB a few days previously. Borisov
later claimed that his wife had been murdered by the KGB.

† I later learned from an Estonian source (but not from anyone we met in Tallinn)
that this elaborate complex and other Olympic installations had only just been completed in time for the Olympics, by 'volunteer work brigades' of Tallinn citizens, forced
to work round the clock.

Visit to an Occupied Country

I had often wondered what Olympic yachting races were like, and I was surprised how closely, thanks to the skill of our Estonian captain, we could follow what was happening. There were six 'classes' operating on the Bay that day, each a gaggle of yachts, followed by a flotilla of launches carrying umpires, officials, commentators and spectators—all weaving in and out of each other, like a slow-motion marine ballet. On the horizon, further out, several larger ships were anchored, including what looked like a guided missile cruiser and an ocean liner, the *Baltika*—'Khruschev went on that to New York in 1960,' said one of our companions. A smart-looking scarlet cabin cruiser sped past, carrying a large sign reading 'VIP'. In the back lounged a fat man in dark glasses, reminding me of the late King Farouk. 'Who is he?' I asked. 'The Estonian Deputy Minister of Foreign Affairs,' replied one of our companions, with an apparently straight face. 'Foreign Affairs?' I asked, somewhat startled, 'with which countries does he have his foreign affairs?' The man smiled.

The Irish pair did everything that could be expected of them. The Spaniards, already assured of the gold medal, had decided not to race that day. Two Hungarians came first, with the Irishmen not far behind, and we were able to shout congratulations on their silver medal to them as they floated past us a minute or two later. Back at the marina a band was playing Sousa marches as the boats sailed back up the main channel, while pretty Estonian girls handed out bunches of red roses to the competitors as they came ashore. When we arrived in the press centre, we were surprised to find Martt waiting for us, looking rather anxious. 'We weren't expecting to see you here,' I said, 'I thought we were meeting at the hotel later, for our evening in the Old Town?' He looked troubled. 'I think we should go to the official party for the end of the Olympiad.' 'What about the Old Town, and the folk music?' I said, 'surely we can go out to dinner, and then come back to the party afterwards.'

Martt, who was joined by another Estonian, seemed curiously insistent that we should go to the party first, on the dot of eight o'clock, to 'reserve our tables—then we can go and come back later—and anyway, you will hear Estonian music at the party'.* It all seemed very odd, but the long and the short of it was that two hours

---

* An experience not unfamiliar to guests of the Soviet Union: as Bertrand Russell put it, 'While they assured us how splendid the banquet or parade was going to be, we tried to explain how we should prefer a quiet walk in the streets' (*Practice and Theory of Bolshevism*).

later Ian Jack and I were sitting having dinner in a large, darkened basement of the Viru Hotel, with a definite uncomfortable feeling that someone, somewhere, did not want us to be anywhere but where we were. The evening was indescribably awful. The nearest thing to 'Estonian music' was a rock group playing, under flashing strobe lights, absolutely deafening versions of such traditional local melodies as 'Blue Suede Shoes' and 'Rock Around the Clock'. As far as I was concerned, the only light relief came when, in a short period of respite from the band, I registered that the table just below our balcony was occupied by the team from Zimbabwe (all white). I shouted over to them, 'In honour of the glorious Zimbabwean revolution, a toast to Comrade Mugabe.' Their team leader, looking a trifle taken aback, raised his glass saying, 'Oh well, I suppose it makes a change.' Later he came over and we had a good chat. He turned out to be a policeman from Salisbury, and among other things told me the strange story of how the Zimbabwe Olympic team had got to the Soviet Union—which I only repeat because it was to have a rather curious dénouement after we returned to Moscow.

Apparently, in the months before the Games, when it looked as though the boycott was going to have a disastrous effect on the turnout, the Soviet authorities had made a tremendous pitch to the African countries, trying to persuade them to send as many competitors as possible. The Soviet Union would do everything—pay their bills, subsidize their expenses, even fly them to Moscow. Like other African nations, Zimbabwe rummaged around and dug up as many extra competitors as it could, including a ladies' hockey team, who had scarcely ever played together before. On the appointed day, they had all been flown up to Lusaka in three ancient Rhodesian air force Dakotas—and there waiting for them was a Soviet Ilyushin . . .

The din began again from the band, drowning all further conversation, and finally, when it was too late to visit any of the bars of the Old Town, we were at last able to go for a walk. It was almost full moon. We strolled through those deserted stage-set medieval and sixteenth-century streets, across the Town Square, and up on to the Toompea. We looked out once more over the city, to the Baltic beyond. Conversation with our hosts seemed stilted.

First thing the next morning we flew back to Moscow.

Visit to an Occupied Country

In November 1917, one of the first acts of the Bolsheviks after they had seized power was to issue the grandiloquent 'Proclamation to the Peoples of All the Belligerent Nations', read out by Lenin to a packed meeting in the Smolny Institute in Petrograd, with 'a thousand simple faces looking up in intent adoration'.* It included the paragraph quoted at the head of this chapter, unequivocally condemning the suppression of any small nation by one more powerful; another paragraph included the lines:

> By annexation or conquest of foreign territory, the Government means ... all union to a great and strong State of a small or weak nationality, without the voluntary, clear and precise expression of its consent and desire.

One of the most consistent boasts of Soviet propaganda is that the fifteen Republics making up the USSR have all been happily welded together into one great glorious whole, which yet allows each nationality to express and develop its own identity (as reflected in the folk-costumes and national dances of the Olympic opening ceremony). We worry today about Afghanistan, but it is worth recalling that fourteen of those nations actually making up the Soviet Union itself were conquered by force. All except two had been originally annexed by the Tsarist Empire. In 1917, their peoples took Lenin's stirring words in Petrograd literally, and over the next few weeks and months nine proclaimed their independence, setting up more or less free, democratic states. All but three were invaded and re-conquered by the Red Army over the next few years—and those three, the Baltic states, remained independent for just another twenty.†

---

* Eyewitness account by John Reed, *Ten Days That Shook The World*.

† The fourteen subject Republics round the borders of Russia fall into four groups.

To the north-west are the three Baltic states, all annexed by Russia in the late eighteenth century, independent from 1919 and reconquered by the Soviet Union in 1940.

To the west of Russia are:

Byelorussia—historically divided between Russia and Poland, and seized by the Soviet Union in 1939, under the Nazi–Soviet Pact. Ironically, although it is the only Soviet republic never to have been an independent state, it today has a separate seat in the United Nations.

Moldavia—once part of Austria–Hungary, then the Romanian province of Bessarabia 1919–40. Ceded to Soviet Union in 1940 under threat of force, and retained after 1944.

Ukraine—conquered by Russia in the seventeenth century, proclaimed independence 1917, reconquered by Red Army 1919–20.

To the south:

The Looking-glass Olympics (16 July–4 August 1980)

Not long before the opening of the Olympic Games, a document was smuggled to the West from Professor Yuri Orlov, serving a term in a labour camp in the Perm region for his part in monitoring the Soviet Government's observation of the Helsinki human rights provisions. During his first two years of imprisonment, he had sought to establish what proportion of Soviet political prisoners came from each of the fifteen Republics. Although in the West we hear almost exclusively about Russian dissidents, Professor Orlov found that the political prisoners from Russia were in fact the smallest group of all (despite the fact that Russians comprise 52 per cent of the USSR's population). A staggering 40 per cent of political prisoners came from the Ukraine, with only 16 per cent of the total population. Even more striking, however, was the fact that 30 per cent came from the three Baltic states with, between them, barely 2 per cent of the population.*

Georgia, annexed by Russia 1800–78, proclaimed independence 1918 under Social-Democratic government. Independence recognized by Western allies January 1920, and by Soviet Union May 1920. Invaded by Soviet Union February 1921.
Armenia—ruled for centuries by Turks, set up independent free republic 1918, recognized by West 1920, invaded by Soviet Union same year.
Azerbjjan—independent state from May 1918, invaded by Soviet Union April 1920.

To the south-east, the five Asiatic Moslem republics annexed by the Tsars between 1731 and the 1870s include Kazakhstan, Kirghizstan, Tadjikistan, Turkmenistan, Uzbekistan. The Kazakhs proclaimed independence under a nationalist government in 1917, reconquered by Soviet Union 1919–20. The Kirghiz rose against Tsarist imperial rule in 1916 (150,000 died), and were reconquered by the Soviet Union 1920–4, although armed opposition from local tribesmen continued for some years.

* cf. article by Bohdan Nahaylo, 'The Non-Russians: Alive If Not Well', *Index on Censorship*, August 1980.

Two months after the end of the Olympic Games, in early October 1980, reports reached the West that there had been two big 'anti-Soviet' demonstrations in Tallinn by schoolchildren, waving the forbidden blue, black and white colours of 'free Estonia', and protesting against 'Russian settlers'. Figures for the numbers involved ranged between 1,000 and 2,000. A few days later there were reports of further demonstrations, in Tallinn, Tartu and elsewhere, and of a number of arrests. The seriousness of what had happened was emphasized by the fact that, most unusually, the Soviet authorities admitted that disturbances had taken place, involving 'violations of public order' (*Daily Telegraph*, 18 October 1980), and on television the Soviet Estonian Home Minister Marko Tibar warned that 'hooliganism' would not be tolerated. Estonian exile sources reported intense interest in what was happening in Poland.

15

A Little Mild Hysteria

The situation for Soviet officials in international competitions is
indeed difficult: on the one hand, they must satisfy the Soviet
authorities in their selection of a winner, while on the other hand
they must maintain an appearance of objectivity in order not to
discredit themselves and their country in the eyes of a foreign
public.

N. Norman Shneidman, *The Soviet Road to Olympus*

Wednesday 30 July
We have returned to Moscow to find mild hysteria in the air. After two
weeks of life in the 'compression chamber', things seem to have been
getting ever so slightly out of hand.

Apparently trouble began in the Olympic Village on Sunday night.
A crowd of competitors who had already completed their events were
gathered in the 'Village disco' making merry when, at eleven o'clock,
the nightclub closed down. After months of hard training and absten-
tion some fifty competitors, including a contingent of Britons,
thought that this was too much, so they adjourned to the twenty-
four-hour restaurant where, to the astonishment of the phlegmatic
Russian waitresses, they began throwing buns and yoghurt at each
other, with cries of 'Free Afghanistan' and 'Russians out of Afghanistan'. Fifteen Soviet militia men burst in to restore order, and were
received with unflattering comments on the tight security arrangements. Enquiries had at once been set in train by tight-lipped officials
of the teams concerned, and on Monday a number of competitors had
been quietly flown home, including two Britons, one of whom, as luck
would have it, was a swimmer named Jimmy Carter.

Then today the big talking-points have been an incident at the end
of the pole vault, in the Lenin Stadium, and, more generally, 'Soviet
cheating'.

The pole vault was a particularly gripping affair, as everyone expected. It was the event which, in terms of suspense and record-breaking, promised a battle royal, between the Poles and the French. The Polish trio included the defending Olympic champion, Tadeusz Slusarski, and a cheerful, curly-headed giant named Wladyslaw Kozakiewicz. The French trio included the present holder of the (unconfirmed) world record Philippe Houvion, who recently vaulted 5.77 metres; the previous world-record holder, at 5.75, Philippe Vigneron; and a third man Jean-Michel Bellot, who had cleared 5.70.

At 5.65 the previous Olympic record of 5.60 had already gone, but there were only four men left—Slusarski, Kozakiewicz, Houvion and a Russian, Volkov. The man in supreme form seemed to be Kozakiewicz, who had cleared the bar at his first attempt all the way up. The Polish and French contingents in the crowd were going mad with excitement, but it was becoming noticeable that the Soviet spectators seemed to be trying to break the Poles' concentration by shouting, even booing, each time they ran up. At 5.70 Slusarski and the Frenchman went out. The Russian, having missed twice, chose to skip his third try, gambling on a do-or-die effort at 5.75. He failed, but took the silver, while Kozakiewicz, looking as if he was enjoying himself, as one of my colleagues put it, 'like a kid let loose in a sandpit', ordered the bar up to 5.78 to take the world record. He did it on the second attempt, and although he failed to become the first man in the world to top 19 feet, the French and the Poles in the crowd, after such a feast of enjoyment, surged towards each other to fraternize in an explosion of Olympic high spirits—only for a grim-faced mass of Soviet militia men to intervene, to restrain anything so unseemly.

This horror of anything spontaneous had been getting more and more on everyone's nerves here. Asked at his press conference yesterday why Soviet officials will not allow winning competitors to perform their traditional laps of honour, Mr Popov apparently replied with a straight face that these were 'not in the Olympic Charter' (they are very keen to be seen carrying out the Charter to the letter) and went on to say that such behaviour could 'excite the public unnecessarily'.

But what has irritated many competitors much more—the pro-Volkov attempts to put off the Polish pole vaulters were in a way a version of the same thing—is the widespread belief that Soviet judges and officials have been cheating in an effort to help Soviet competitors. Some of the allegations sound far-fetched, such as the opening of huge doors at the end of the Stadium to give wind assistance to Soviet javelin throwers, but others are rather more specific—for example, the claim that officials marked the Soviet javelin gold medallist Kula's winning throw a metre further than the javelin had fallen, and that the throw also landed 'flat'. Swedish pole vaulters complained that officials were helping Soviet competitors by holding out flags to indicate wind direction. The Australians were furious that a potential gold medal winning leap by their triple jumper Ian Campbell was ruled invalid for 'dragging'. The marking of the Soviet gymnasts' chief rival Nadia Comaneci from Romania last week sparked off a full-scale enquiry by the International Gymnastic Federation. Three nations protested when a Soviet diver was allowed a second chance and won the gold in the springboard diving.

Whatever the truth of all these charges, they appear to be remarkably widespread, which it is perhaps not altogether surprising, since the Soviet Union has a long record of this sort of controversy in international competition. As Mr Shneidman judiciously puts it in his invaluable treatise on Soviet sport:

> While judges representing any country . . . tend to support athletes from their own countries, representatives of the Soviet Union have much less freedom in exercising their duties than their Western *confrères*.

Commenting on the fact that the partisanship of Soviet judges 'has recently become the concern of a number of international sport bodies,' he adduces, among other examples, the decision of the International Skating Union actually to ban Soviet judges altogether for a year, because of 'repeated international partiality'.

A rather different example of the almost desperate importance the Soviet authorities attach to winning came yesterday evening, while we were out of Moscow. One of the events the Soviet Union was most confident of winning was the football competition, which has been building up to its final stages over the past ten days in Moscow, Minsk, Leningrad and Kiev. The grand climax, the final, at which the Soviet authorities expected their team to take the gold medal, was scheduled as the last major sporting event of the Games, in the Lenin Stadium on Saturday afternoon. Last night, however, something untoward happened. In the fifteenth minute of a semi-final, a bad mistake by a Soviet footballer allowed the East Germans to score, and it turned out to be the winning goal. As Ian Wooldridge, who was watching the game on Soviet television, put it 'it was quite extraordinary—the Soviet commentator appeared to see neither error nor goal. At least if he did, his voice registered no reaction. He just talked on in a flat, even tone, as if nothing had happened—it was like listening to Jim Laker studiously describing a Turner sunset over the pavilion while the West Indies captured a vital England Test wicket.' Later in the evening, as the Radio Moscow commentator on television summed up another day of keen competition, there was somehow no mention of the fact that East Germany had knocked out the Soviet Union. The entire football competition has become the sporting equivalent of an 'un-person'.

There have been other, less public signs of strain in the 'compression chamber'. One of our colleagues formed a liaison with an attractive member of the Rossiya staff, and several times spent the night at the flat she shares with another girl working here. Suddenly he was shocked when he passed her in the hotel to find that she would not speak to him or even register his existence. Later her friend managed to explain, with a very worried expression, that the KGB had visited their flat and warned the girl in no uncertain terms to have nothing more to do with foreign journalists.

Andrei Sakharov's wife has brought to Moscow an 'open letter' to Mr Brezhnev and Kurt Waldheim, proposing a seven-stage plan for a Soviet withdrawal from Afghanistan. The Soviet authorities will not be pleased; the letter accuses the Soviet Union of expansionism and of 'destroying Afghan sovereignty', and warns that unless the Soviet Union withdraws its invasion could have 'catastrophic consequences'. According to the BBC World Service, the situation in Afghanistan itself is scarcely improving from the Soviet point of view. There are reports that an entire Afghan division has gone over to the rebels, and that Soviet aircraft are mounting one of their biggest operations of the war so far in an attempt to wipe it out. The situation in Poland also seems serious—the Polish Government has admitted that the country's foreign debts are now so heavy that they may not be able to keep up repayments.

Thursday 31 July
A slightly bizarre day. A certain lightheadedness seems to be creeping into the proceedings, certainly here in the Rossiya. Everyone is all too

aware that there are only two or three days to go (the athletics programme comes to its climax tomorrow), and hysteria seems to be dissolving into a blur of surreal images.

Realizing how little time there is left, I decided to set off for the famous Pushkin Art Gallery. By mistake I found myself in the nearby 'Muzei Pushkin', on Khruschev Street; devoted to memorabilia of the poet Pushkin. An earnest lady curator began to show me round. I told her how pleased I was to discover a street named after Mr Khruschev—'We have a great respect for Nikita Sergeivich in the West.' She explained, in great confusion, that the street was not called after 'this man you refer to', but a quite different Khruschev, who had been a friend of Pushkin. As we continued on our tour, my inclination to tease got less and less. It really was a very sad museum, with almost nothing original on show at all; the manuscripts were all photostats, the few tatty bits of furniture were 'of the type which Pushkin might have used'. I felt a melancholy creeping over me, and when, at the end, I was offered the usual 'visitors' book' for comments, I wrote as kindly as I could. I was interested to see a few pages back some rather more effusive comments signed by 'Lord Ritchie Calder'. When I expressed interest in the presence of the former Chairman of Britain's Metrication Board, my guide said, 'He often comes to see us when he is in Moscow.'

There are a good many people in this town who are not quite what they seem. Ian Jack paid a visit today to a painter called Glazunov, who is at pains to point out that he has had terrible trouble with the authorities, who have banned many of his paintings. But he seems to live in unusual style, with a spacious studio and a handsome collection of icons. He even hands out expensive colour reproductions of one of his 'banned' paintings, an awful montage of famous figures of the twentieth century, which includes Khruschev, Chairman Mao and Solzhenitsyn. He seems to be what you might call an 'Intourist dissident'.

I fell into conversation with a Ukrainian journalist from Canada, who had just come back from Kiev. I was rather surprised when he told me how happy everyone in the Ukraine was, and how well they lived. It turned out that he and his wife were Marxists who had been students at Kiev University, paid a special 'foreign students' allowance' by the Soviet Government which, with odd translation fees, worked out at more than 500 roubles a month, far in excess of the average industrial wage (even the elite car workers of Togliatti get only 250 to 350 roubles); in addition to which he was, of course, as a foreigner, able to take advantage of the local Beriozka shops (or, as they are called in the Ukraine, *kashtans*, 'little chestnuts').

Then there was the rather creepy Labour MP hanging round the Rossiya Press Centre bar. It seems he is in Moscow because of his interest in sport—he was a boxing blue at Oxford. But how on earth did he get through the normally impenetrable security screen? I am sure there is an innocent explanation, but I wish I had asked him.

Walking back along the river embankment early this evening, I was surprised to see the bridge above me jammed with people. The explanation, half an hour later, was a spectacular show of fireworks along the river—even though it was still daylight. The last echoing series of explosions, sending a huge cloud of smoke drifting across the front of the 'Stalinist–Gothic' skyscraper just downstream from the Rossiya, was as memorable an end to a fireworks display as I have ever seen. A few minutes later I went up to find that Wooldridge had been enjoying a grandstand view from his window. 'Sensational! Fantastic! Have a vodka.'

Wooldridge is getting more lightheaded than anyone. The other night he danced till dawn with Olga Korbut. For days he has been accusing everyone in sight of being a *krot* (Russian for 'mole'). He has never quite recovered from his delight at Mr Popov's strictures after his article on the opening ceremony, and has been going round warning in a heavy Russian accent that the slightest complaint against the perfection of our arrangements was 'affronting dignity of host nation'. Now he is trying to work out, for one of his last articles, the Russian for 'sick as a parrot' and 'over the moon'.

Whether it has made the Soviet authorities 'sick as a parrot' or 'over the moon', I don't know, but today there was proof positive that the Russians have been cheating, even on the evidence of their own television cameras. All three medals in the hammer-throw went to a trio of hefty Soviet musclemen, Yuri Sedykh taking the gold with a world-record breaking heave of 81.80 metres, more than 250 feet. But the cameras clearly showed his front foot on the winning throw edging over the rim of the throwing circle, and he was not disqualified.

You might well ask, 'Why do they bother?' when, with two days to go, the top of the medals table reads:

	Gold	Silver	Bronze
Soviet Union	69	56	39
E. Germany	37	31	37
Italy	7	3	2
Bulgaria	6	12	14
Hungary	6	9	12
Romania	5	4	10

In addition the Soviet Union can lay claim to one very special record in these Games. No less than eight of their gold medals have been won by one man, the twenty-two-year-old gymnast Alexander Dityatin, who has thus become the winner of more individual gold medals at a single Olympics than anyone in history, breaking the record of seven medals set by the American swimmer Mark Spitz at Munich in 1972.

In one event, however—apart from the unmentionable football—'Soviet planning' has come unstuck in a delightfully bizarre manner. After all the effort and expense involved in flying the scratch team of lady hockey players from Zimbabwe to Moscow, the Salisbury housewives rewarded their hosts last Monday by knocking out the Soviet Union, in yet another event the Soviets had hopes of winning. Today the story had an even more bizarre ending, when the Zimbabwe ladies beat Austria 4–1 to take the gold medal.

For the British journalists, the only serious question left to be decided is: will their supreme hero and favourite Sebastian Coe manage to get his revenge on Steve Ovett in tomorrow night's final of the 1,500 Metres? Ovett is the world-record holder, but in today's heats it was Coe who put up the fastest time of the day.

Friday 1 August
At his press conference today, Mr Popov said that he would like to congratulate the sportsmen of Zimbabwe—the newly independent state—on the 'wonderful occasion' of their country's first Olympic gold medal. 'This is the first time a representative of the African continent has become a champion of the Olympic Games' (a rather unfortunate oversight of the 10,000 Metres triumph by Yifter). He

did not of course spoil the general impression these remarks might have been intended to convey by adding that all the 'Zimbabwe sportsmen' in question were white.

Another deeply wonderful and carefully organized press occasion took place this afternoon, when an official visit was paid to the Olympic Village by Patriarch Pimen, head of the 'official' branch of the Russian Orthodox Church. According to the handout released later by the Press Centre:

> Patriarch Pimen examined the discotheque of the Olympic Village, the halls for collective recreation and those for individual listening to music.
>
> 'Here everything has been thoroughly thought over, so that athletes could have a rest after tiresome trainings and very tense competitions. It is a fine Village . . .' Patriarch Pimen said.

Asked by a journalist, 'Have you been to a previous Olympics, or is this your first one?' the Patriarch must have amazed everyone present by admitting that this was his first. As if to show that Soviet priests are not behind their Western counterparts in certain respects, he added that he was a keen follower of 'Olympic contests on television'.

All is set for tonight's closing athletics events—the 5,000 Metres, the Marathon—and Coe v. Ovett, round two.

16

Pilgrimage to Peredelkino

Something in the world has been changed. Rome was at an end.
The reign of numbers was at an end. The duty, imposed by
force, to live unanimously as a people, as a whole nation, was
abolished. Leaders and nations belonged to the past. They were
replaced by the doctrine of personality and freedom. The story
of a human life became the life story of God and filled the
universe.

Boris Pasternak, *Dr Zhivago*

Nothing could demonstrate the isolation of the 'Olympic bubble'
which has been built in this city in the past few weeks more vividly
than the death of Vladimir Vysotsky.

Vysotsky was an actor and singer, perhaps best loved in Russia. He
was famous for his performance as Hamlet at the Taganka Theatre.
He was married to the French film actress Marina Vlady. But he was
also loved for his extremely daring 'underground' songs, dating back
to the years of his youth when he served in a labour camp. Publicly he
recorded 'acceptable' songs about cosmonauts and 'friendship'. But
before private audiences he mocked Party bosses and their life of
privilege cut off from the people, and sang bitter ballads about the
miseries of prison life. He was a symbol, protected from trouble only
by his enormous popularity, 'the unofficial voice of the people'.

Last week Vysotsky died, at the age of forty-eight, on the eve of a
performance of *Hamlet*. On Monday when he was buried at Vagonk-
ovskoye cemetery, in his Hamlet costume, tens of thousands of Muscovites turned out to follow him to his grave. Moscow had scarcely
ever witnessed such scenes. Thousands remained milling about for
hours outside the Taganka Theatre, discussing everything which
Vysotsky had stood for in their lives, until midnight, when they were
roughly dispersed by mounted police.

Nothing of this extraordinary event has penetrated the 'Olympic bubble'. Our contact with the regular life of the great city around us has been almost non-existent. Nevertheless, even from within our layer upon layer of cocooning, there *has* been contact with the Russian people, and the impact of this on many of the journalists here has been fascinating to observe.

In the past few days, behind the hysteria and lightheadedness, and despite all the obstacles erected by the regime—not just those which are visible, but even more those which are invisible—Russians and Western visitors have come together in a great wave of warmth. Even here in the hotel it has been plainly evident, in the conversation and presents and laughter exchanged with interpreters and waitresses and 'floor ladies', many of whom, far from being old dragons, are charming girls in their twenties and thirties, who have been unfailingly smiling and helpful, despite the appalling hours they work (one outside my room was on duty for nearly twenty-four hours the other day). Journalists have been meeting Russians in the street, almost desperate for a little contact with the 'forbidden West', and have been invited back to their flats. Some of the terrible drabness and inconvenience of the Russians' lives has come across—the queuing, the shortages, the terribly cramped housing conditions, the constant fear they live under. But above all what has come across is the kindliness, the good humour and patience of the Russians, and the fact, as I mentioned last week, that they are such unmistakable individuals. The contrast with the stereotype of 'Soviet man' and the 'Soviet system' could not be more striking. For years most of us have used the terms 'Russian' and 'Soviet' almost interchangeably—'the Russians invading Afghanistan', 'the Russians locking up dissidents', 'the Russians threatening world peace'. Here, where both 'system' and 'Russians' are in such evidence, it has come as a revelation to see what a profound distinction one is automatically beginning to make between the two, and furthermore how impressive the Russians are to talk to, even to look at—more impressive in a strange way than a great many people in the West are these days.

At the beginning of our last three days in Moscow, there were still several things I was hoping to do. On Sunday afternoon there would be the closing ceremony, and then I had tickets for *Boris Godunov* at the Bolshoi in the evening. On Saturday, I was planning to go out to the 'writers' village' of Peredelkino, just outside Moscow, where Boris Pasternak had lived and was buried. And on Friday evening I had been hoping to go to a rather special concert at the Tchaikowsky Conservatory.

A few days after my arrival in Moscow I had visited the flat of a Western correspondent who has lived here for some years, loves Russia and is very keen on music and the ballet. When I came in, his record player was playing Beethoven's *Archduke* Trio, with Rostropovich on the 'cello. When I was last in the Soviet Union, every record shop had on prominent display a whole range of Rostropovich recordings—the Beethoven 'cello sonatas with Richter, the Triple Concerto with Oistrakh, the Britten concerto specially written for him. Rostropovich was the most honoured musician in the USSR. Now, since his enforced exile in the West, all those records have vanished from Soviet shops as though they had never been. He is another 'un-person'.

My friend and I discussed the feast of cultural treats on offer during the Olympics. He recommended some, dissuaded me from others, but he said, 'There is one concert you absolutely must go to, if you can. On 1 August, there is a man called Vladimir Spivakov playing with his little string orchestra, the Virtuosi of Moscow. They're not allowed to play very often, because he and most of his players are Jews, and there will be huge demand—but if you can possibly lay your hands on a ticket, go.'

On the earliest day tickets were on sale, I had asked at eight in the morning and was told that not a ticket was to be had. This Friday morning, the day of the concert, I thought I would have just one more go. I was so pressing that a kindly Intourist lady got on the telephone, and after three tries she said, 'I've found you one.' So, armed with my ticket, shortly after five in the afternoon, I set off from the Rossiya to the Lenin Stadium, for the second half of the 'duel of the century', the 1,500 Metres final.

The once hyper-efficient press bus service is not what it was. Perhaps the organizers have realized that running buses every two minutes, round the clock, regardless of what is happening, means that all too often the drivers are driving empty, unwanted buses through the empty streets. Anyway, after waiting quarter of an hour, I can only get one to the Main Press Centre, to find a crush of increasingly impatient journalists waiting for anything that will get us to the Lenin Stadium for the big event. Time is running short.

I fall into conversation with a Russian girl called Lara, attached to Reuters'. She says that she is married to an Englishman and returning to London with him in September, and she is rather worried as to how she will make out, living in England. Unthinkingly I say to reassure her that I know one or two Russians in England who seem to be making out reasonably well, thinking of certain exiles and former dissidents. At last a bus comes, we arrive at the stadium, and hare off with a good deal of laughter to the press entrance, emerging out of the tunnel at the top of the steps to find that the big race has just begun.

After 200 metres, as the runners come round for the first time into the straight below us, the East German Jurgen Straub, in a dark vest, is just in front, with Coe at his shoulder, running easily; a third British finalist, the tall, curly-headed Steve Cram, is just behind, with the muscular Ovett outside him. As they come round to the same point a lap later, the order remains unchanged. After 1,000 metres, Cram is dropping back, Straub is still just in front, the boyish Coe still running well within himself at his shoulder; the noise from the crowd is mounting all the time—but there is not a British journalist around me who is not aware that, over the past three years, the world-record holder Ovett has won every one of forty-five consecutive races at this distance and the mile. For the last time they approach the final bend. Straub is lengthening his stride, but cannot shake off the two Britons. Now Ovett is creeping up slightly on Coe—but then, as they turn into the final straight, Coe accelerates away. The stadium seems like a mass of sound as Coe streaks across the line, with Straub a few yards behind, and a flagging Ovett left with only the bronze medal in third place.

Delirium from my colleagues. 'He's done it!' 'He's climbed his "mountain"' (as Coe's father was later to say, 'You've seen an athlete come back from the grave'). As we wait for the medal ceremony, Lara reveals that the Englishman she is married to works for the *Morning Star*, and I realize why she had been so worried about coming to London. When I introduce myself as 'Christopher Booker of the *Daily Mail*' she is horrified. 'How could you write those horrible, insulting things about my country?' End of a beautiful friendship.

As Coe climbs up on to the gold-medal winners' pedestal, I notice that the digital clock on the giant scoreboards is showing '18.12'. The band strikes up the Olympic anthem, almost drowned by the singing of 'God Save the Queen' from a section of the crowd. As always before when an Englishman has won a gold medal, a large Union Jack is being waved by spectators away to our left, picked up instantly by the Soviet television cameras in preference to the five-ringed Olympic flag rising to the top of the pole.

Every journalist in sight now descends to a crowded room in the Stadium press centre for the hero's conference. The hush is reverential as Chris Brasher asks the first question: 'Seb, you climbed the mountain. How did you do it?' The twenty-three-year-old Coe answers this and succeeding questions with pleasantly banal replies. What else can be expected of a young student, who has just stepped off a running track after winning the race of his life? The sportswriters don't just want him to do his own job properly. They now want him to play the artist, the psychologist, the philosopher as well. More than ever I find myself wondering about the way the journalists build up these young sportsmen as demigods: it is as if, unconsciously, they want to blow sport up into providing all the drama, the heights and depths that human life has to offer. For some of them sport really is a substitute for all that religion and art has given the human race—beauty, tragedy, death and resurrection, a vision of perfection—and it is too much to squeeze down into just one corner of the fullness of human experience. They are asking of sport that it should express not just the highest achievements of one part of the human personality, the body, but that it should carry all the rest, mind, heart and soul as well—and it is not surprising that such lack of a sense of overall proportion should all too often end up producing mere banality and sentimentality.

I wonder whether I should stay for the traditional climax to the sporting programme, thinking that I am unlikely ever again to be in an Olympic stadium for the end of a Marathon—but something persuades me to go to the concert.

Back in my room briefly, in the almost deserted Rossiya, I catch the end of the Marathon on television—won by the same East German who won in Montreal, very boring, I missed nothing. I set out across the centre of the city to the Tchaikowsky Conservatory, an imposing nineteenth-century classical building on Herzen Street. I run up seemingly endless flights of broad, imposing stairs, under chandeliers and oil paintings and busts of Glinka, Mussorgsky, Rimsky-Korsakov and the giants of Russian music. I just squeeze into my seat in time, in

183

the second row of the Great Hall—and there then follows one of the most remarkable concerts I have ever heard in my life.

For a start there is the look of the little orchestra, sitting on the platform just above me, all in impeccable white tie-and-tails—such good, strong, sensitive faces. The most imposing figure of all is Spivakov himself, in his late thirties, tall, thin and grave.

Then they begin to play. Apart from the opening work, the Bach double violin concerto, the pieces are comparatively slight—an early Mozart divertimento, K.136, two of Rossini's set of student string sonatas, and as a joke-piece, a heavily gypsified viola concerto of Paganini. But, although I have listened to most of the best string orchestras in the world, I have never heard playing like this—such delicacy and precision, such subtlety and colour of string tone. Each of these slight works is made to sound like a major masterpiece—one of the Rossini's almost like Haydn's *Seven Last Words*—with the exception of the Paganini, which is played with huge high spirits, Spivakov beaming all over his face. I am almost relieved that they are not playing anything more profound, because it would be unbearable.

The audience is in raptures. As is the Russian custom, people come up from all over the hall with bouquets, some looking like 'official' bunches of roses and carnations, others just a handful of four or five michaelmas daisies. By and large the audience here is the 'Moscow intelligentsia', people who look as though they think and feel, deeply and privately. In a precise, grave voice Spivakov announces an encore—'Praeludium, Dmitri Shostakovich'. When it is finished, more rapturous applause, a second encore—'Sergei Prokofiev'—a third, 'Mozart'. We are at it for a full twenty minutes, before finally we are streaming down the stairs.

What intense feeling seems to be aroused in this country by its leading artists and performers, something much deeper than we are normally familiar with in the West. How even more strange it must be therefore when so many of these leading musicians, artists, ballet dancers, writers simply, unaccountably, disappear from view overnight, to become 'unpersons'—no longer usually because, like so many of their predecessors, they have been shot or carried off to camps (Stalin was supposed to have disposed of 600 writers in this way), but nowadays because, for one reason or another, they have vanished to the 'forbidden West'. Rostropovich, Ashkenazy, the sculptor Neizvestny, ballet dancers like Nureyev, Mikhail Baryshnikov, the Panovs, the poet and ballad singer Alexander Galich, writers such as Solzhenitsyn, Joseph Brodsky, André Sinyavsky, Yuli Daniel, Vladimir Maxmiov, Andrei Amalrik, the list goes on and on. In the past year alone, three of the leading dancers with the Bolshoi have defected—Alexander Godunov, Leonid and Valentina Kozlov. One can only begin to imagine what an appalling extra shock must be the loss of someone like Vysotsky, at the age of only forty-eight.

In Herzen Street on the way home, a solitary man asks me for a cigarette. He turns out to be a Moldavian from Kishinov, down on the Romanian border. He wants to know why the British Olympic Committee is not in Moscow. We stop in the vast open space of the Square of the Fiftieth Anniversary of October as I try to explain to him that the British Olympic Committee *is* in Moscow. 'No,' he says, 'Mrs Thatcher and British Olympic Committee are against being in Moscow.' I try to explain that Mrs Thatcher and the British Government were against the British Olympic Committee being here, because of the Soviet invasion of Afghanistan, but that they came all the same. He simply cannot comprehend that the British Olympic Committee and the British Government are not the same thing. Understandable.

Saturday 2 August
Still half-asleep, I reach out to switch on the BBC World Service, only to hear a familiar voice proclaiming 'Sensational! Fantastic!' It is a recording of Wooldridge being interviewed about Coe's victory the previous evening.

My friend Valeriy has said that he would like to accompany me to Perekelkino (pronounced Pyreredelkina). We take the metro to the Kiev Station, to catch a suburban line train out to the west of the city. Peredelkino is the fifth stop. After four stops we are still very much in the city, grey apartment blocks looming over the willowherb by the railway track—but then, quite suddenly, we are out in the countryside, with fields and birch trees. Arriving at the little station of Peredelkino is like being transported back a hundred years. All is peaceful. Birds sing. The level-crossing keeper's cottage is surrounded by what looks just like an English village garden, pink hollyhocks and brimstone butterflies above a riot of colour. We see the onion domes of the little village church gleaming not very far away through the trees. We walk up a road, past a crumbling old wooden house. There are few signs of the luxurious *dachas* (pronounced dachya) where leading Soviet writers are supposed to live in these parts.

We walk right round the church, trying to find a way in. The scene on the far side reminds me of so many villages in Eastern European countries. A weed-filled pond amid trees, with a rotting bridge over it. A few scrawny hens clucking about through the undergrowth. Piles of building materials looking as if they have been there for years. Everything pleasantly untidy, lazy and decayed. Eventually we come back to the main door of the church, which is now open, because half a dozen *babushkas* with shawls round their heads are cleaning it. They are fairly unwelcoming, but Valeriy does his stuff with the lady in charge, and reluctantly they let us in. The church is being restored, very dark and full of scaffolding, not much to see.

I have not told Valeriy that I wanted to see Pasternak's grave, but as I look in vain for it among the tombstones of former priests around the church itself, I think it is time for me to come clean. A black-bearded man with an extremely fine face, who seems to be connected with the church, directs us a few hundred yards away, to the main cemetery, set in a wood. It is a typical Eastern European graveyard, with iron railings round each grave, and usually a photograph of the deceased on the stone or wrought-iron Orthodox cross. We amble round for about twenty minutes, often losing our way in the maze of railings and trees, occasionally asking groups of old ladies or gravediggers whether they know the whereabouts of 'the grave of Pasternak'. Eventually a woman insists on taking us there, saying that we would get lost otherwise—and there finally it is. Quite unlike any of the others: a simple rough block of stone about five feet high, carved with an impression of Pasternak's head and his signature, on a little patch of lawn, surrounded by a hedge, under the trees. Next to it is a field, the simple, wooden *dacha* where he lived for many years amidst the trees on the other side.

There are two other Russians in the little enclosure, photographing the grave. Pasternak is 'half allowed' in Russia, for his poetry rather than *Dr Zhivago*, which is still of course banned. Every 30 May, the anniversary of his death, large crowds of people come out from Moscow to put flowers on his grave and to recite his poems. But above all, as I stand there, I think back to the day more than twenty years ago when that haunting novel mysteriously emerged from Russia, and of the message it brought to us all in the West.

Pilgrimage to Peredelkino

No country in history has ever unveiled itself more dramatically to the world than Russia did through its writers in the nineteenth century—Pushkin, Lermontov, Turgenev, Tolstoy, Dostoievsky. And what was it that marked them out above all? Nothing more than the endless pageant of instantly recognizable individual human beings who walked through their pages, projected larger than life against a universal backdrop—making, say, the characters of Dickens look like nothing more than cosy, parochial cardboard cut-outs. All human life was there, on the grandest scale—war, peace, tears, joy, children's games, grand parties, gambling, weddings, remorse, Natasha singing in the moonlight, Prince Andrei looking at the oak tree in the forest, Pierre gazing up at the comet trying to fathom the mysteries of existence, Levin making hay with his peasants, old Platon Karataev with his ancient folk-wisdom, Bazarov the nihilist, Prince Myshkin, Pechorin, Onegin. To our great-grandfathers this mysterious land of Russia was a fairy-tale world—the country of snow and *troikas* and wooden dolls and bearded *muzhiks* and Fabergé eggs and beautiful princesses skating in furs. But above all, through its literature, it seemed a land of magnificent individuals where everyone, regardless of class, seemed somehow able to express the glory and the suffering of human existence, in both the outer and the inner worlds, more fully and intensely than any other people on earth.

Then, amid the confusion of World War One, came news of a great upheaval—chaos, blood, unimaginable disorder, huge crowds running willy-nilly through the streets—followed by a blanket of silence. 'The Bolsheviks have taken over.' Slowly a new image emerged of a whole country welded together under the hammer and sickle, under new leaders, new icons, marching purposefully into the twentieth century—tractors, dams, electrification schemes, Five Year Plans, soaring pig-iron production, the familiar corn waving to the horizon on collective farms, Young Communists in red kerchiefs, the 'Dictatorship of the Proletariat' on the march—all very impressive and powerful, but strangely impersonal. Where were all those individual human beings? Out of all that old, rich, fairy-tale mess came nothing but these endless parades, Parks of Culture and Rest and neat welfare clinics, under the benign gaze of 'Uncle Joe' Stalin. Admittedly there were stray hints that all was not totally well behind the bright, hygienic façade—rumours of millions starving, labour camps, the 'Show Trials'. But then came World War Two, and here at least for many seemed proof that the new 'Soviet man' and 'Soviet woman' were a reality: despite initial defeats, the eventual contrast to Russia's performance in the previous war could not have been more marked, as they struggled heroically through unimaginable sufferings, those terrible winters, those battles on a cosmic scale—Stalingrad, Kursk, Kharkhov, Leningrad—to their final stupendous victories on the eastern front and the taking of Berlin. In the post-war years came a new, grimmer image of Russia—the 'Russians' as a major threat to world peace, replacing the 'Germans' as our main imaginary enemy, the 'Russians' as a Superpower, under their succession of enigmatic, post-war leaders, Stalin, Malenkov, B. and K. The fairy-tale land of larger-than-life characters, each living life with an almost child-like intensity and directness, seemed to have vanished altogether beneath the new, grim image of the regimented masses behind their unsmiling leaders, always saying 'Nyet'.

And then suddenly, in 1958, came *Dr Zhivago*. The clouds of ice-crystals parted, and here at last, in all their warm, chaotic humanity were real Russians again, real individuals, with an inner life, with hearts and souls, still capable of speculating about the meaning of existence, God and the universe. So this was what had happened to the line of Turgenev and Tolstoy and Dostoievsky! It had simply flowed underground, like a river still running warm beneath the ice when the world is covered in snow! We followed the story of the doctor-poet Zhivago from his childhood, through the parties and loves of his youth, with off-stage rumbles of the approaching cataclysm, through the mighty whirlwind of the Revolution and the Civil War, sweeping him and Tonya and Lara like autumn leaves from one end of Russia to the other and back again, up to his unhappy death in a Moscow Street in the thirties, and to two friends reminiscing about him in the years after World War Two. We read of a Russia that we thought we would never see again—and yet here it still was, in our own time! We read such lines (unbelievable to us that they could have come out of Russia in the 1950s) as:

> 'Of course one does meet brilliant men,' said Nikolay Nikolayevich, 'but they are isolated. The fashion nowadays is all for groups and societies of every sort. It is always a sign of mediocrity in people when they herd together, whether their group loyalty is to Solovyev, or Kant or Marx. The truth is only sought by individuals, and they break with those who do not love it enough. How many things in the world deserve our loyalty? Very few indeed. I think one should be loyal to

immortality, which is another word for life, a stronger word . . .'

Everything established, settled, everything to do with home and order and the common round, has crumbled into dust and been swept away in the general upheaval and reorganization of the whole of society. The whole human way of life has been destroyed and ruined. All that is left is the bare, shivering human soul, stripped to the last shred, the naked force of the human psyche for which nothing has changed, because it was always cold and shivering and reaching out to its nearest neighbour, as cold and lonely as itself. . .

All the movements in the world, taken separately, were sober and deliberate but, taken together, they were all happily drunk with the general flow of life which united and carried them. People worked and struggled, they were driven on by their individual cares and anxieties, but these springs of action would have run down and jammed the mechanism if they had not been kept in check by an overall feeling of profound unconcern. This feeling came from the comforting awareness of the interwovenness of all human lives, the sense of their flowing into one another, the happy assurance that all that happened in the world took place not only on the earth which buried the dead but also on some other level known to some as the Kingdom of God . . .

It was also in that book that most of us read for the first time a word which was later to become a great deal more familiar; when one of the characters, after World War Two, recalls:

'We are told, "Here you are. This is your camp." An open snow field with a post in the middle and a notice on it saying "GULAG 92 Y.N.90"—that's all there was . . . we broke saplings with our bare hands in the frost, to get wood to build our huts with. And in the end, believe it or not, we built our own camp . . . our prison and our stockade and our punishment cells and our watch towers, all with our own hands.'

But the most important thing about that novel was the profound optimism which ran through it, the constant symbolic emphasis on the fact that wherever there is untold suffering and death there is also resurrection. It was no accident that Boris Pasternak chose for his hero the name Zhivago—for in Russian that can only suggest one thing, the mass of words which derive from *zhivot*—'life'.

Part of the optimism which marked the closing pages of *Dr Zhivago* derived from Pasternak's own belief when he wrote it in the fifties that, at long last, after forty years of darkness and imprisonment, the atmosphere in Russia was lightening, that what his fellow-writer Ehrenburg called the 'Thaw' was under way, that better times were coming, in which, for instance, books like *Dr Zhivago* itself could be openly read. When the novel was published in the West, however (even more when it won for its author the Nobel Prize for Literature), Pasternak was stripped of all his honours, expelled from the Writers' Union, and two years later, in 1960, died in disgrace. Word of his funeral somehow got out, through Western news broadcasts beamed back to Russia. Tens of thousands of people came out from Moscow to this little graveyard to see him buried. Among those carrying his coffin were two young writers, André Sinyavsky and Yuli Daniel, whose imprisonment five years later was a sign that the 'Thaw' was finally at an end. Both, of course, are now in the West.

As Valeriy and I walked back down the road to Peredelkino Station, the sun still shone bright and warm, but the sky over Moscow was almost black. We just reached the little shelter next to the platform in time, as the heavens opened in a tremendous cloudburst. I noticed that no less than three of the older men in the shelter with us had lost a limb or were walking on crutches—the first I had seen since I arrived in Moscow two-and-a-half weeks before.

In the rackety train as we travelled homewards, standing in the corridor, Valeriy told me a little of the funeral of Vysotsky the previous Monday. He had been in those vast crowds, paying tribute to one of the few larger-than-life artistic heroes left in Russia.

Back at the Rossiya there was a good deal of talk of a mysterious incident in Red Square that morning. The Irish athletics coach and one or two passing journalists had seen flames and smoke: it seemed that a man in a straw hat had been trying to burn himself to death. But instantly the KGB had moved in, swept the man away and removed all trace of the incident except a small dark patch on the cobbles. What was he protesting about? We shall never know.

For days there had been rumours that French athletes were planning to make some kind of a protest about Afghanistan. This afternoon four of them, with their team manager, had a brief 'interview' with Soviet officials, led by Mr Popov. They also handed over a written statement, which included an appeal to the Soviet Government to free people held in prison for their political beliefs. Afterwards, a smiling Mr Popov said the discussion had only been in general terms, that the word 'Afghanistan' had never been mentioned, and that the only point on which he could disagree with the Frenchmen was that concerning political prisoners. There were no political prisoners in the Soviet Union: 'If there are prisoners, as in any other civilized state, they are in prison for violations of the penal code.'

Much later that night, somewhere in the Rossiya, I ran into a very drunk Swedish journalist. He was more full of voluble, outspoken contempt for the Soviet regime than anyone I had met in Russia. He had married a Russian girl the previous May, and was hoping, when he travelled back through Leningrad, to be able to take her home with him. Up to now she had not been given a visa.

He said that, when he was in Leningrad last year, he had got drunk with a KGB man who was working on arrangements for the Olympics. 'He told me, because he knew I would never use it, that they were planning to recruit 24,000 foreign-language speaking graduates and students to act as interpreters, guides, translators and so forth. And for every one of those acting openly, another one was being recruited for work behind the scenes—another 24,000, listening in to telephone calls, monitoring conversations, translating every article that is sent out. Oh, they know what is happening in this town all right.'

The trouble with drunken Swedish journalists is that you don't know whether to believe a word they say. Or perhaps, as Cholerton, the old *Daily Telegraph* correspondent here in the thirties used to put it, 'In this country you can believe everything except the facts.' Tomorrow is our last day.

17

The Flame Goes Out

The Olympic Games finally came to an end today. I got a kick
out of the track and field events, the swimming, the rowing and
the basketball, but ... I'm afraid the Nazis have succeeded with
their propaganda. First, they have run the Games on a lavish
scale never before experienced, and this has appealed to the
athletes. Second, they have put up a very good front for the
visitors ...

William Shirer, *Berlin Diary*, 16 August 1936

Sunday 3 August

The day started later for some than for others. I tiptoed into the
darkened room across the corridor to find Wooldridge in a very poor
way. In between groans he explained from his bed how he had spent
the previous afternoon in company with some Americans and a lot of
vodka, watching the boxing finals on television. These in themselves
had been quite funny. In the absence of the United States, which had
won five boxing gold medals and a silver at Montreal, the Soviet Union
had been rather hoping to clean up in these events. But they had not
reckoned with their fellow-Socialists and pupils, the Cubans. Nor,
alas, had Wooldridge, who had prepared to back Russian hopes for
'the greatest afternoon in the history of Soviet boxing' with a modest
pile of his remaining roubles. The Cubans (who have been taught
much of all they know about boxing by the Russians) ended up with
six gold medals, two silvers and two bronzes, a haul only equalled once
before in the entire history of the Games (by the United States at St
Louis in 1904, when there had been hardly any other countries
present). The Soviet boxers had been left with one gold and six silvers,
and Wooldridge with only a very dim recollection of how the rest of
the day had proceeded. I went off to fix him a large black coffee and
returned to find him flat out, his face somewhat incongruously

covered by the previous day's *Daily Mail*. This was incongruous because almost the whole of the front page had been given over to Wooldridge's own report of Coe's 1,500 Metres triumph on Friday, with a picture of Coe breasting the tape, and all I could see was the headline, in huge black letters—'ECSTASY'.

With nine hours to go before the closing ceremony (which has been put back to tonight—bang go my tickets for *Boris Godunov* at the Bolshoi), it was time to begin trying to sum up the whole of this past extraordinary fortnight.

Firstly, now all is over bar the shouting, what can one finally say of the boycott? What effect has it had on the sport? No one can deny that there have been great moments to rank with any Olympics— Salnikov's 1,500 Metres in fifteen minutes in the swimming; the pole vault; the Coe–Ovett duels; the double triumph of the ageless Ethiopian Miruts Yifter (no one knows how old he is—he admits to thirty-five, but must be older), who on Friday added the gold medal in the 5,000 Metres to his win last Sunday in the 10,000. The Soviet authorities are cock-a-hoop over the haul of records—seventy new Olympic records, thirty-four world records. But all sorts of doubts must remain over their implied claim that this makes the absence of the Americans, in particular, irrelevant. At the United States swimming championships in Irvine, California, yesterday, American swimmers improved on the winning times recorded here in Moscow in no less than ten events. On the Irvine times, the Americans would have collected ten gold, twelve silver and five bronze medals if they had been here, and such possibilities are bound in retrospect to cast a slight shadow over the worth of 'Moscow gold'.

Again, in a wider sense, there can be no doubt that even as far as the Soviets are concerned, the boycott has played an enormously important part in muffling the whole atmosphere in which the Games have been held: for example the almost total lack of the usual round of receptions and parties; the absence of Mr Brezhnev and many of the top brass after the opening ceremony; the downplaying of the absurdly one-sided medals tables, in which the Soviet Union won more gold medals (eighty) than all the other countries, bar East Germany, combined (seventy-eight).*

* See over for footnote.

* The final medals count was:

	Gold	Silver	Bronze	Total
Soviet Union	80	69	46	195
E. Germany	47	37	44	128
Bulgaria	8	16	17	41
Hungary	7	10	15	32
Poland	3	14	15	32
Romania	6	6	13	25
Britain	5	7	9	21
Cuba	8	7	5	20
Italy	8	3	4	15
France	6	5	3	14
Czechoslovakia	2	3	9	14
Sweden	3	3	6	12
Australia	2	2	5	9
Yugoslavia	2	3	4	9
Finland	3	1	4	8
Denmark	2	1	2	5
Brazil	3	0	2	5
Spain	1	3	2	6
N. Korea	0	3	2	5
Austria	1	2	1	4
Ethiopia	2	0	2	4
Mongolia	0	2	2	4
Mexico	0	1	3	4
Greece	1	0	2	3
Jamaica	0	0	3	3
Switzerland	2	0	0	2
Netherlands	0	1	1	2
Tanzania	0	2	0	2
Ireland	0	1	1	2
Belgium	1	0	0	1
India	1	0	0	1
Zimbabwe	1	0	0	1
Venezuela	0	1	0	1
Uganda	0	1	0	1
Guyana	0	0	1	1
Lebanon	0	0	1	1

For comparison, the top 18 places at Montreal in 1976 were as follows:

Soviet Union	47	43	35	125
E. Germany	40	25	25	90
*U.S.	34	35	25	94
*W. Germany	10	12	17	39
*Japan	9	6	10	25
Poland	8	6	11	25
Bulgaria	7	8	9	24
Cuba	6	4	3	13
Romania	4	9	14	27
Hungary	4	5	12	21
Finland	4	2	0	6
Sweden	4	1	0	5
Britain	3	5	5	13
Italy	2	7	4	13
Yugoslavia	2	3	3	8
France	2	2	5	9
Czechoslovakia	2	2	4	8
*N. Zealand	2	1	1	4

*Not represented in Moscow

194

On the other hand, quite apart from the total practical failure of the boycott to influence Soviet determination to plough on with their increasingly murderous and indecisive attempt to subjugate the Afghans, there is no way that a jot of its laudably intended message has registered with the Soviet people. Anyone who thought the boycott could have such an effect has no conception of what a cut-off, insulated society this is, how totally differently the world looks when one is sitting in the middle of the Soviet Union, informed and guided as to what is going on solely by the endlessly reassuring tones of Radio Moscow. In political terms, from here, the Olympic boycott has simply looked tiny, peripheral—a failed Carter election stunt.

Obviously the astonishing feat of organization behind these Games, in everything from communications to transport—in all the ways it was feared the Soviet authorities would fall down—must be counted as a plus for the Soviet Government, and in many respects the parallels with Hitler's triumph in 1936 are inescapable. Those Games too were superbly organized, better than any before them. The Nazis made a tremendous effort, not just to lay on special food supplies (Berlin in the depression years was normally short of butter, meat, vegetables), but to show themselves to the world as reasonable, peace-loving people. Anyone who thinks that Berlin 1936 was a great militaristic display ought to read accounts of it. Alas, there is no book, but there are plenty of snippets in diaries and newspaper files. The emphasis in Berlin, just as here in Moscow, was all on 'peace' and 'friendship' ('a great demonstration of peace' it was officially called). There was not a tank and scarcely a bayonet to be seen. The soldiers were all 'gymnasts'.

But the parallels with 1936 are still closer. The one thing everyone knows about the Berlin Games is that ultimately, in some mysterious way, Hitler did not quite pull it off—that in particular there was the sharp sting in the tail of his racist triumph provided by Jesse Owens (who, curiously enough, died only a couple of months before the Moscow Games opened). In the ancient biblical phrase, 'God was not mocked' in 1936, nor has God been mocked here in Moscow. There was just too much at stake, too much falsity in what the Soviet Government hoped to put over to the world about their glorious Socialist society, too much to hide, for the thing not to come unstuck somewhere, and if the boycott was a part of that nemesis, I think that the real thing which has gone wrong with these Games is something much deeper and more subtle.

Part of the clue as to what that is lies in what even the most hardened men of the world among the sportswriters have had to admit has been the regimented joylessness of these Games, the instant repressive response to anything spontaneous or 'unplanned'. There has been plenty of manufactured, planned 'joy' and 'high spirits', as in the opening ceremony. But not only can nothing happen in this society that is unplanned in *theory*; it has not been allowed to happen in practice either, and the deadening message of that has run inescapably through the past fortnight, as a reflection on the extraordinary kind of society this is.

Another part of the clue lies in the astonishing discrepancy, as it has appeared again to many journalists here, between the system which prevails in the Soviet Union and the Russian people, who have seemed so warm, so ready to laugh, so contrary to their system in every way. As I am tempted to put it, in the shorthand of popular journalism, the reaction of most of my colleagues has been 'loved them, hated it'—'it' being the system, 'them' being the Russians themselves. Now this is really something so extraordinary that it demands reflection. How, without being merely sentimental, can one make this distinction between system and people? Because, after all, it is *their* system, they created it, it is still Russians who run this country. How can it be that, individually, they seem so nice, so human—and yet the system that they live under, seems so monstrous, so inhuman, so alien to them?

One might begin to answer such a question with two things I can see with my own eyes as I sit at a little table in the cafeteria down the passage from my room in the Rossiya. Out of the window, across the river, are the smokestacks of the old power station, with its Leninist slogan—'Communism equals the power of the Soviets plus the electrification of the whole country'. There is one side of the Russian enigma—the obsession with the masculine symbols of power and order. That more than anything is what strikes one about this society, this regime, this city—the apotheosis of power and order, to a degree which to a Westerner is almost incomprehensible.

On the other hand, on the table in front of me is a little glass full of wild flowers—what in the West we would call weeds, including a spray of rosebay willowherb. No one who had access to a florist or a garden would dream of putting rosebay willowherb in a vase—it droops almost immediately. But whoever picked these flowers did not have access to such luxuries. Nevertheless they made the effort. Like so many little things about this country it is simple, touching, almost child-like. Someone has tried to make a little human gesture of a kind which in the sophisticated, cynical, luxurious West most people would not dream of.

One of the most popular phrases in the Russia of the late nineteenth-century was the question *'Chto delat'*?—'What must be done?' It was taken from the title of a turgid, romantic 'revolutionary' novel by an author called Chernyshevsky, published in 1865. The reason why his title caught on was that it seemed to voice the question which everyone in Russia was asking. The whole of Russian society seemed to be falling apart, into chaos, misery, decay and apathy. There was an increasing sense that some great cataclysm was approaching. Tolstoy wrote a book with the title *What Must Be Done?* in 1886, while the most famous use of the phrase, of course, was Lenin's, when he took it as the title for the most significant of all his writings, the pamphlet on revolutionary tactics of 1902. And Lenin's answer to the question was quite simply—power, organization and order; the power that would only accrue to a tiny, ruthless, properly organized revolutionary party, the order that only such a party could impose on the shambles that was Russia.

In 1899, a quite different answer had been given by another Russian writer, Vasily Rusanov:

> 'What is to be done?' asked an impatient St Petersburg youth. What a silly question, what is to be done? If it's summer there are berries to pick and jam to make. And if it's winter, there is tea to be drunk with this lovely jam.

Here, in its most superficial, whimsical form, is the way the other half of the Russian temperament answers the question—the feckless, warm, irresponsible, child-like part, if you like, the part which rebels against the masculine principles of power and order, structure and discipline—but it is also the part which in its deeper expression, in the name of the great feminine qualities of feeling and intuition, marks out the Russians as one of the most extraordinary peoples in the world.

Actually, it is with these softer qualities of feeling and intuition that the Russians are most deeply, naturally at home. Not only do these qualities run strongly through the great Russian novels; it is precisely these qualities which have given those novels such pre-eminence ever since they were written—the unerring instinct of Tolstoy, Dostoievsky, Turgenev, for every tiniest nuance of feeling, for the inner world, for the intuitive spiritual dimension of life. It is that which gives the Russians, more than perhaps any other people on earth, that intangible thing we call 'soul'.

Yet it is a great law of life that human beings are never so vulnerable, so driven, as when they fall into the grip of those psychic functions which are least developed, least integrated in them. And that is perhaps what has happened to the Russians: that they have been, as it were, 'possessed' by those stern, rigid, masculine elements in the human psyche with which they are perhaps naturally least at home, the physical drive to power, the organizing principle of the mind. This may be the real tragedy of Russia, even the tragedy of Mr Brezhnev and his colleagues themselves, as they sit stupefied by yet another parade of huge rockets, another recital of meaningless statistics. Publicly, all emotion, all intuition, all individual, warm, inner life has been ruthlessly repressed—like Lenin fighting his impulse to pat the head of the composer whose music has so moved him—and all that is left is this dead pseudo-religion of power and order.

And yet, and yet—the real tragedy of Communism is that it so desperately tries to pretend, through its glorification of power and organization and the collective, that it *can* inspire the loftiest feelings, *can* speak of human dignity, *can* breathe the language of the soul. And it cannot do this because it denies those very parts of the human personality from which such things derive. As I tried to sum it up in my final despatch:

> More than anything else, these Games have been dead, they have been soulless, From a country which officially abolished the human soul in 1917, that is what shows. They try to fake it, often with incredible skill—but that is what is missing from everything this system touches. What it cannot touch is the unconquerable soul of people themselves.
>
> That is why, of all the host of impressions and memories which crowd in from the last fortnight, one I shall never forget is that of an Estonian—very serious, very deep. I asked him for a last thought to reflect on and he replied merely: 'There are many things outwardly which you can do nothing about. That is why you must look within.'
>
> That is the ultimate failure of the whole Communist idealogy—that there is in every human being something which no system, however, harsh, however powerful, can touch. Yet it

is from here that everything which makes us most fully and truly human springs.

In these Olympic Games, more than ever before, the rulers of this strange Soviet empire have tried to persuade the world that their system can touch those depths. And the real glory of the joyless, eerie Moscow Games of 1980 is how, in all sorts of subtle, unexpected ways, that claim has so totally been given the lie.

I decided not to go down to the Lenin Stadium for the closing ceremony, but to watch it, as Russian viewers would be seeing it, on television.

The broadcast began with a picture of Red Square and the Kremlin, then a panorama of Moscow, with its skyscrapers and tower blocks—to solemn martial music, followed by the Kremlin chimes playing the Internationale. Then, for the last time, the camera zoomed from the top of the Lenin Hills down into the great bowl of the stadium lying below, beneath its four huge banks of arc-lights.

Everything unfolded strictly according to the detailed timetable I had in my hand:

> 7.30 pm, 170 fanfare players enter the arena. At the same time the emblem of the 'Olympiad 80' is displayed by the Artistic Background. The fanfare is sounded. 400 dressing flag bearers enter to the sounds of the march music of R. Schedrin. They take position in groups of 100 men each, in the corners of the football field. 7.33 pm 1080 sportsmen holding ribbons, hoops, pendants and 300 young men and women, among who 150 are dressed in Russian national costume, are on the arena . . .

The competitors marched on to the field, accompanied by hundreds more flag-bearers. The scene was almost more impressive on television than it had been to see it live at the opening ceremony.

Finally the tiny figure of Lord Killanin gave the vast hushed arena his closing address. It was only a few sentences, culminating in the traditional invitation to 'the youth of all countries to assemble four years from now at Los Angeles'—but, just for a few words, he departed from his prepared text. 'I implore the sportsmen of the world to unite in peace before the holocaust decends.' It was a chilling moment (the Soviet television commentator, presumably translating from a pre-arranged text, completely passed it over). A few minutes later the Olympic flame began to die away, above the stadium, and as it went out I was seized by an irrational fear. I felt that, so long as that flame had been alight, we had somehow been all right—but now we were all suddenly back in darkness and uncertainty again. Anything could happen.

Not that there was any darkness on the field in front of us, for now, as the competitors left the arena, there began a display in its own way even more striking than that of the opening ceremony, not least because it was happening at night. Again the arena filled with wave upon wave of gymnasts, acrobats, Latvian milk maids, Circassian sword dancers—more than 12,000 of them in all—while the 5,000 soldier-gymnasts making up the Artistic Background performed their familiar miracles of precision and colour. At one particularly dramatic moment, as if to make a point after all the talk of there having been no children at the opening ceremony, the Soviet television cameras zoomed in on a particularly beautiful little blond boy in the audience, and stayed there until no one could have missed him.

At 8.45 the massed orchestras struck up a haunting 'pop song' specially written for the occasion—'Dosvideniya Moskva', 'Goodbye Moscow'—and 900 dancers brought on a huge, twenty-five-foot high model of Misha the Bear, which they carried round the arena. As if by magic, the dancers stepped back and the enormous bear gently floated upwards into the darkness, The Artistic Background was also show-ing a multi-coloured Misha, which now let down a series of gigantic multi-coloured 'tears' from its left eye. At that moment the television screen filled again with that beautiful blond child, waving goodbye to Misha, and the thought was inescapable: not only did they *know* that child was there. They *put* him there!

A few minutes later, after a further mass-waltz, flawless down to the last skirt-flounce, a series of spectacular firework showers exploded into the heavens above the Lenin Stadium, and the 1980 Olympic Games was over.

At previous Olympics, this would have been the cue for athletes, spectators and officials to flood down into the arena to mingle in a last great celebration, with impromptu dancing and music going on far into the night: not, however, in the Lenin Stadium.

Later in the foyer of the Rossiya I saw an extremely angry Dutch-man shouting at two rough-looking figures slouched in chairs in the middle of the floor, 'Why have you been following us?' He was determined to make a scene, summoning embarrassed members of the hotel staff to explain that the two men had been following him and three Dutch colleagues quite blatantly all evening, all the way down to the stadium, all the way back, and now right into the Rossiya. 'What the hell is going on?' The awkward looking staff melted away. The two men just continued to sit there.

The main dining-room was packed. The food was cold. A few journalists began to play the grand piano which stood on a dais in the centre of the long room. Others danced. The waitresses looked amazed. It was a last desperate bid by the West to whip up a little atmosphere, a little fun, a little spontaneity. It worked, for about twenty minutes.

I went to say goodbye to one or two of my Russian friends. They had worked unbelievably long hours during the previous three weeks, and most of them were going off—as part of the inevitable 'group'—for a holiday on the Black Sea a few days later. One girl had tears in her eyes as we said goodbye. She told me that a few nights previously she had run into an old *babushka* in the street. The old woman had said 'the great war is coming. In ten years time we shall be back to Adam and Eve.'

The next day our last few hours in Moscow had a dream-like quality. Most people had already departed, the Rossiya seemed strangely empty. I spent most of the morning collecting enough roubles to pay my telephone bill, travelling out to the suburbs to the only bank in the city where it is possible to pick up money cabled from abroad. My taxi driver said that he had taken no interest in the Olympics, although he had watched one football game on television. Just before I left my room for the last time I got a call from my Western journalist friend who had promised to fix up an interview with Alexander Posna, the senior commentator with Radio Moscow. Posna would be pleased to see me. 'Can he come to the Rossiya?' I asked. 'Our plane leaves in a couple of hours.' A few minutes later my friend rang back: 'Sorry, Posna says he cannot get into the Rossiya, it is only open to accredited foreign journalists.'

I climbed into a taxi with Wooldridge and Neil Wilson, both exhausted. As we travelled out to Sheremetyevo, I looked out, probably for the last time, on those now familiar streets and squares. My companions were asleep. After fifteen miles or so we passed on the left the huge monument of three iron 'tank traps' which marks the nearest point to which the Germans penetrated in 1941.

We arrived at the new German-built air terminal to find more journalists walking around like ghosts, all 'determined to catch that plane if it was the last thing' they did. We wandered round the *Beriozka* souvenir shop, which offered exactly the same souvenirs you can see anywhere in the Soviet Union—painted wooden bowls, carved ivory from the north, *matryoshki* wooden dolls, embroidered Ukrainian blouses, records (not of Rostropovich). I bought a couple of souvenir lighters, bearing the tower block symbol of the Games, thinking that at least I might take away a little Soviet petrol, only to find that they were labelled 'Made in France'.

We went up to the restaurant for a last glass of Georgian champagne and a plate of caviar. A tall, blonde girl from the *Sun* told us how she had spent a night on the train from Moscow to Leningrad because she had discovered that Muscovite lovers who cannot find anywhere else to go sometimes take the sleeper to Leningrad and back just to get a bit of privacy. She had called her piece 'The Loveski Express'.

We boarded our British Airways Trident. In the first-class in front were an extremely weary-looking Lord Killanin, Lord Exeter and Sir Denis Follows. The rear section was almost entirely filled with journalists. We began taxiing forward in the rain, and then as the plane left the runway, a remarkable thing happened. With one accord, the sixty-odd journalists in front of me—most of whom had come out to Russia three weeks before in a mood of nothing more than eager anticipation—let out a resounding cheer, and broke into a storm of applause.

I spent a good deal of the flight talking to an ITN reporter, Martyn Lewis. During the past fortnight he had inhabited a wholly different part of Moscow's Olympic archipelago from us journalists, staying with thousands of television and radio people out in the Hotel Kosmos. He said that things out there had been getting back to normal with amazing speed that morning. The guards in the television centre at Ostankino were already carrying guns again. The posters of 'Peace' and 'Friendship' had already come down. And the Kosmos had run out of orange juice—a close-run thing!

In fact it was a good illustration of the isolation from each other in which we had all been living that only now did I learn how Lewis had been at the centre of one of the biggest 'controversies' of the Games.

He had been approached by an Afghan wrestler, Ghulam Sedia Zargar, who had said that he and some of his Afghan team mates wanted to defect. Martyn had reported this on ITN, without actually naming Zargar (although the wrestler had asked for his name to be made public). The Afghans had then summoned a press conference, with their entire eighteen-man team and Soviet officials present, to deny the claim. They obviously knew which team-member was responsible because Zargar was escorted in separately from the rest, by plain clothes guards. At this point Lewis had felt free to name Zargar, as the wrestler himself had earlier requested (saying that his best hope of protection was that the world should know his name). Back in Britain and the States no one bothered to enquire as to why Lewis had thought it proper to name the man—but a huge uproar had broken out.

Lewis had been lashed for 'irresponsibility'. *Time* spoke of a 'journalistic lapse'. *The Times* even devoted a whole editorial to the affair—knowing nothing of the true background to the story. It was a tiny illustration of how totally different events in Moscow looked from outside the Soviet Union.

As the captain announced that we had left Soviet air space there was another loud cheer from the journalists.

Martyn told me another story about the strange country we had just left. A year or two ago a group of relatives of very senior Soviet officials had made a private visit to Britain. Among them was Mr Brezhnev's daughter. On arrival in London the first thing everyone in the group wanted to do was to visit Marks and Spencer's in Oxford Street—except Miss Brezhnev. Her colleagues assumed that her reason for not wanting to accompany them was that she was afraid of being identified by the capitalist press. But she explained that she did not need to visit Marks and Spencer, because there was a shop back home where she could buy everything that was on sale there. Her colleagues were amazed because they had assumed that they were the 'Inner Party', as privileged as it was possible to be in the Soviet Union. They had not realized until now that there was a still higher step on the ladder of privilege—a store which even *they* did not know about. The story (originating from a Russian) may be apocryphal, but the really interesting thing about it is even the possibility that the highest mark of material privilege in the Soviet Union might consist simply of being able to buy the sort of goods which everyone in Britain can find in Marks and Spencer's.

As we touched down at Heathrow, the journalists broke into a third round of applause. We staggered off the plane, through an empty customs hall. I gazed almost with gratitude at an illuminated advertisement for some American earthmoving equipment, simply because it was not talking of 'Peace and Friendship' or quoting Mr Brezhnev. Frank Keating and David Miller were being met by their wives, I by my sister. We all went off for our first drink in the 'free world'. Swept up on a great surge of nervous energy, I talked for another six hours that night about the experience we had been through, almost without drawing breath.

But why had we been cheering?

PART THREE

The Road from Moscow

August–December 1980

By gigantic efforts the men of the Kremlin have just about managed to show that they could stage an efficient, if soulless circus. They are now faced with a much more intractable problem—how to give their people bread—and this they cannot do without abandoning everything their system stands for. In that stark fact lies the real importance of the drama which in recent months has entered an entirely new phase, not just in Poland, but throughout the Communist world.

The *Spectator*, 30 August 1980

18

From the Lenin Stadium to the Lenin Shipyard

You can always see at once whether anyone talking of Russia has really lived there: it is a kind of freemasonry, entirely independent both of class and views.

Bernard Pares, *Russia* (1940)

There is something psychologically very strange about coming out of the Soviet Union back to the West. I am not saying that it affects everyone in the same way. But certainly a great many previous travellers had experienced similar feelings to those of us who sent up that involuntary cheer as our aircraft took off from the rainswept runway at Sheremetyevo on 4 August 1980. In fact I asked the air hostess whether she had ever known such a round of applause before: she replied, 'Oh yes, it's happened quite a few times.'

When I returned home I looked up the final paragraph of Laurens van der Post's *Journey into Russia*:

As I sat down in my seat in the British Comet ... I looked up to see the English faces of the crew calmly doing their work about me. I thought I had never seen happier and more resolved expressions ... suddenly I too felt myself to be so much lighter that I was almost giddy with lack of ballast. Until that moment I had not known what a weight on my spirit had been the Soviet system.*

It is not until you leave Russia that you realize how subliminally oppressive the whole experience of living there has been. Even so, if a diver is brought too quickly back to the surface, he notoriously suffers

---

* It is not just leaving the Soviet Union which has this effect. I remember once feeling the same sort of relief as I crossed the border from Hungary into Yugoslavia, and saying without thinking to a Yugoslav border guard, 'It's good to be back in the free world.' To do him justice, he laughed.

from the bends. And certainly I found that, for several weeks after stepping out of our 'compression chamber', I had considerable difficulty in adjusting again to life in the Western world.

After the wide open, litter-free spaces of Moscow, London seemed strangely small-scale and scruffy in those first few days back in England. As I began to acclimatize to all those familiar little things we take for granted in the West, I continually found myself wondering—why *had* we been cheering on that aircraft? Obviously it was a great relief to make telephone calls again without the near-certainty that they were being listened into; to be able to buy English newspapers without having to queue up at seven-thirty in the morning for the handful allowed in by the censors; to be able to walk into any corner shop and find a greater variety of goods than are publicly available anywhere in the Soviet Union.

But there were shocks too. It was a shock to see Western newspaper headlines again: 'HAVE YOU GOT THE LOVELIEST LEGS IN BRITAIN?' 'COUNCIL LEFTIES IN LOVE TANGLE', 'STEPPING INTO THE EIGHTIES—OUR QUEEN MUM', 'HEIRESS IN PLANE CRASH SEES FAMILY DROWN', 'JAIL THREAT TO TV BOSSES'. It was a shock to be reintroduced to the unbelievable vacuity of television commercials, the pornography on the news stands. It was deeply depressing to come back to Western coverage of the pitiful spectacle unfolding across the Atlantic as, amid the tired razzmatazz of the Party conventions, and the charges and counter-charges of the 'Billygate affair', the plastic pygmy-figures of Carter and Reagan prepared to battle it out for the leadership of the 'free world'.

After the epic grandeur of Russia so much that was going on in the West seemed diminished, petty, unimportant. I had written before on returning from East to West about how glib and complacent we tend to be in drawing comparisons between life in the West and that in the Communist world. Coming back from the Soviet Union this time I felt it more strongly than ever. The reasons why many Russians are so likeable and impressive do not just lie in the Russian character; they also lie in the hugely different experience of everyday life which our two societies have been through in the past thirty years.

We are accustomed to thinking of our decades of affluence and consumer abundance as an undisputed good, which the poor Russians would only like to get more of, if they could—and, as we can see from their much-publicized fascination with jeans and rock 'n roll and Marks and Spencer, that is partly true. But what we forget is the other side. In many ways, in their drab world of constant queues and shortages (and by our standards sheer poverty), life has gone on being as hard for them as it was for the people of Britain in the years of post-war austerity. And one of the consequences of that is that the peoples of the East have not been affected by so much that has trivialized and debilitated life in the West.

When Solzhenitsyn delivered his celebrated critical verdict on the West at Harvard in 1978 he put it even more strongly. He said that many things had surprised and shocked him when he first came face to face with the Western way of life, from the superficiality and conformity of our mass-media to 'the sense of strain which imprints so many Western faces' through our constant chasing after material goods. But what struck him most forcibly of all was the contrast between 'the weakness of human beings in the West—while in the East they are becoming firmer and stronger'. In the six decades since the Revolution, he concluded:

> We have been through a spiritual training far in advance of Western experience. Life's complexity and mortal weight have produced stronger, deeper, more interesting characters than those generated by standardised Western well-being.

A few weeks after my return I was present at a memorial service in London for a well-known literary and theatrical figure. Sad to say, a comparison of most of the unhappy, weak, self-indulgent faces present with those of the Moscow intelligentsia at the Spivakov concert I had attended in the Tchaikowsky Conservatory bore out only too clearly what Solzhenitsyn meant.

There was no getting away from it—for all its horrors, life in the East these days is simply a much more *serious* affair than it has become in the West. I even found myself once or twice in those August days yearning for life back in the 'compression chamber'. Almost nostalgically, I would find myself tuning in to the soothing tones of Radio Moscow for a link with Russian voices, Russian music, the grand simplicity of the Soviet world-view. One night I had heard on the BBC World Service that a particularly bloody battle was raging north of Kabul, between Soviet tanks and thousands of Afghan tribesmen. I switched over to Radio Moscow to hear how they were reporting that day's events in Afghanistan, just in time to hear a despatch from an *Izvestia* correspondent in the Afghan capital:

> Let us go for a walk through Kabul in the cool of the evening. All in the city is calm and still . . .

He went on to describe nothing more violent or upsetting than the wonderful five-year plan which had just got under way to rebuild the city. 'Already many old one-storey houses have been demolished . . . and 150,000 people have been moved into new twelve-storey houses.' Oh, it's soothing all right—so long as you do not actually have to live under it, all the time.

One of my wilder fantasies when I returned from Moscow was to express the wish that thousands more Westerners could have been present at the Olympic Games—partly because it might have introduced more of an air of festivity and joyousness into that grim, austere city, and partly because it might have brought home to some of them just how awful life in a Communist country can be. Just how foolish it was to conceive such thoughts was confirmed by various cuttings I was sent by friends and readers showing how some of my fellow-visitors to the Olympics had reported their impressions when they returned home.

There were, for instance, the Hoyles of Hadleigh in Suffolk, who had won a trip to the Olympics in a competition organized by the Ipswich Co-op, and whose views on the Soviet Union were recorded by the *East Anglian Daily Times* on 12 August. Peter and Wendy Hoyle (photographed surrounded by their souvenirs—he bearded, she bespectacled) were ecstatic about Moscow. They found the Russian people 'courteous, helpful, friendly and not intent on war' ('It was wonderful,' said Wendy, 'to get away to somewhere where nobody talked about war or nuclear weapons'). During their nine-day stay they had come across 'no indoctrination'. Far from the food shortages they had heard about, 'there was plenty, almost too much, food' in Moscow. Mr Hoyle saw so little of 'a massive police presence' that in the whole time he was there he 'came across only one policeman, who was checking tickets and large bags at the stadium' (I wouldn't mind betting he was a large, cosy man in blue who greeted them with the words 'Evenin' all'). 'Moscow is a great place for walking,' Mr Hoyle went on, 'we were free to come and go as we liked.' He was 'not aware of the mass evacuation of Moscow reported in the British press'. Altogether the only thing the couple found to concern them at all was that there seemed to be a slight 'shortage of newspapers'. 'Even the official newspaper *Pravda* was so scarce that it was pinned to notice boards for people to read.'

The Hoyles were not alone in finding the USSR something of a paradise. In the *British Medical Journal* of 30 August, Dr Michael Small, a consultant neurologist from Birmingham, waxed equally lyrical about Moscow's 'cleanliness', the 'entrancing ballet', the 'large and well-dressed windows of GUM', the sentries outside Lenin's tomb 'immaculate and motionless ... changed every hour with a slickness worthy of our own Brigade of Guards'. What above all he had not expected to find in Russia was 'the freedom, the normality of ordinary people', and he ended by tartly suggesting that 'reports in some British papers seemed to have come from a different Olympic Games.'

I gazed at such strangely dehumanized reactions in amazement.* Was the most horrifying symptom of what has happened to us in the West in recent years perhaps that people can no longer see the human reality of life under a totalitarian regime even when it is staring them in the face? In fact the one thing which weighed on me more and more heavily in those weeks after my return was how little really *any* of us in the West can seemingly grasp what life under a Communist regime is like, except for that tiny minority who have directly experienced it. I was struck by how obviously the considerable number of letters I received from readers in response to my various articles on the Olympics fell into two quite distinct categories. On the one hand were all those which I could see at once were from people who had no real experience of life in a Communist country. Whether they were hostile or favourable to what I had written did not matter: their authors seemed to have been looking at the Olympics and the Soviet Union

---

* I preferred the reaction of the father of a Greek friend of mine. In 1944–5 his factories in Greece were destroyed by Communist guerrillas, and he became a fervent anti-Communist. A few years ago, 'purely for business reasons', he signed a lucrative contract with the Soviet Government to repair ships. As a reward the Soviet authorities flew him to Moscow for the Olympics and treated him as a guest of honour. He returned vastly impressed, saying that 'only a totalitarian country has a hope of running the Olympic Games properly these days.' He may be right, except that it is curious to note that the foreign visitors most impressed by the Nazi organization of the 1936 Games (according to Shirer's *Berlin Diary*) were 'big businessmen'.

down the wrong end of a very long telescope. On the other hand was a handful of letters which were entirely different in tone. One was from a Russian-born journalist, another from an Estonian doctor, a third from a Czech woman who had been in Auschwitz and had left Czechoslovakia after the Communist takeover in 1948. They were different because they could see life on the other side of that great gulf which divides the world—a gulf that is psychological as much as political—in three dimensions, not just in terms of black-and-white caricatures. They understood—but was there any way other Westerners, without their experience, could even begin to understand? Then, something happened which was to throw into relief the strange nature of the system which rules over that dark 'other half' of the world, so vividly that it seemed to consign all the 'propaganda triumph' of the Olympics to the status of a mere historical footnote.

One of the more striking impressions I had formed in Moscow was that, in a way of which I had no suspicion before I arrived, the whole Soviet system seemed to be heading for some profound, unprecedented crisis. Shortly after my arrival, a resident Western correspondent had startled me, as we looked up at the walls of the Kremlin, by saying that he did not think this system could last 'more than another ten years'. At the time I was completely disbelieving, because I was only just beginning to recover from my initial awe at how incredibly solid, massive and unshakable the system seemed to be. But gradually as I began to pick up some of the many clues which were around, for anyone with eyes to see and ears to hear, I found myself thinking back to what he had said—and even though, surrounded by all the splendid cocoon of the Olympic bubble, it was still hard to accept his forecast literally, it did seem that something very strange was going on in the Soviet empire.

The two really important clues—though they were closely linked—were firstly the peculiarly dire and worsening state of the Soviet economy; and secondly the mood of desperation, which everyone agreed was like nothing the Soviet Union had known before. Only the most fragmentary evidence of this had been reaching the outside world, although the strikes which in May paralysed the giant car plants at Togliatti and Gorki, the most serious the Soviet Union had experienced in sixty years, were increasingly recognized as having been events of unusual significance. And certainly such stray scraps of information as reached the outside world in the weeks after the Olympics indicated that things were likely to get worse rather than better: for example, that floods and other factors were threatening a third disastrous grain harvest in succession (the previous year's harvest of 179 million tons had fallen nearly 30 per cent short of the target figure of 235 million tons), or that in July meat production on Soviet state and collective farms had fallen from its already very low level by another 14.7 per cent.*

It was probably a keen awareness of the added social strains this growing economic crisis was likely to impose on the Russian people which, more than anything, had been responsible for the Soviet authorities' decision the previous November to weigh in with what, in the months leading up to the Olympics, had looked more and more like an attempt at a 'final showdown' with the dissidents. No sooner had the Olympic flame been extinguished and the last poster proclaiming 'Peace' and 'Friendship' been taken down in the streets of Moscow, than in various parts of the city the trials resumed of the prominent dissidents who had been cut down in such a swathe by the pre-Olympic wave of arrests. On 25 August, forty-six-year-old Orthodox priest Father Gleb Yakunin appeared before a tiny courtroom, packed with 'some thirty young men in ill-fitting suits', charged with 'attempting to undermine the Soviet state' for his work as a member of the group monitoring observation of the Helsinki human rights provisions. Three days later he was sentenced to five years' imprisonment and five years' 'internal exile'. The following day, 29 August, a little group including Andrei Sakharov's wife Yelena Bonner huddled in a sharp early-autumn wind outside another Moscow courthouse while Tatiana Velikanova, the forty-seven-year-old mathematician who, like Father Yakunin, had been a prominent member of the 'Helsinki group', was sentenced to four years in a 'strict regime' labour camp and five years' internal exile. Members of Miss Velikanova's family who had been allowed into the courtroom for what Tass described as an 'open trial' said that they had been the only 'non-hostile' spectators present. When sentence was pronounced, the audience of KGB-men and specially selected workers had shouted 'not enough'. The only comment of Miss Velikanova herself had been, 'The farce is over.'

These were the biggest dissident trials in the Soviet Union since

* Figure from Central Statistical Board of USSR, reported by Reuters', 20 August 1980.

those of Professor Orlov, Dr Scharansky and Alexander Ginsburg in 1978, and meant that of the original twenty members of the 'Helsinki group' only five were not now in prison or exile.* But by the time the sentences were reported, the unrest the Soviet authorities so feared at the growing crisis wracking their empire had already blown up into a drama so astonishing that, day after day, it was covering the front pages of the newspapers of the West.

Around the ending of the Olympics there had appeared to be something of a lull in events in Poland. But on 8 August, the dustmen of Warsaw came out on strike, followed three days later by the city's bus and taxi drivers. Six weeks after the trouble had begun, it was already clear that this was becoming the most widespread and prolonged bout of industrial unrest in any Communist country since World War Two. The more immediate grounds for protest were still food shortages and the Government's attempt to raise meat prices; although behind that lay the appalling weakness and inefficiency of the entire Polish economy which, after ten years of grandiose 'reforms', such as a limited attempt to collectivize the country's peasant agriculture and the spending of huge sums on useless 'prestige projects' such as the vast Ursus tractor plant near Warsaw, had reached a state of near-collapse unequalled in the Soviet empire (except possibly by that of the Soviet Union itself). Poland had only kept going at all by massive borrowing from the West (some £8,000 million in the previous few years). But the real reason for the sheer scale of the unrest in Poland in the summer of 1980 ran deeper still: it was nothing less than the almost desperate weariness of the Polish people with the whole system under which they had suffered for thirty years.

On 14 August the crisis took a dramatic new turn. There were reports from the Baltic seaport of Gdansk that thousands of militant shipyard workers had taken over the great Lenin Shipyard, the largest in the country. That night, for the first time in six weeks, Warsaw Radio admitted that strikes had been taking place in the country.

On 15 August, the shipyard workers called for talks with the Polish

* Information on the trials of Father Yakunin and Miss Velikanova taken from Nigel Wade's reports in the *Daily Telegraph*, 26–30 August 1980. Further trials and arrests in different parts of the Soviet Union were reported in the weeks which followed. It was also reported that Professor Yuri Orlov had been sentenced to 'solitary confinement' in a strict regime labour camp in the Perm region for the second time in a year, even though his health was 'seriously deteriorating'.

prime minister, Mr Babiuch. Instead he appeared on television and said that there could be no easing of the meat shortage, and that strikes would solve nothing. On the same day Mr Gierek, leader of the Polish United Workers (or Communist) Party, flew back from two weeks' holiday in the Soviet Union, and over the next fortnight there unfolded the most extraordinary 'ping pong match' which any totalitarian Socialist country had ever seen.

On 16 August the number of workers on strike in Gdansk and surrounding towns was estimated to have reached 50,000. The Polish authorities cut telephone links with the port. On 17 August the strikers, led by a committee headed by a thirty-seven-year-old electrician, Lech Walesa, put forward a list of sixteen demands, including the right to hold free elections to their own trade unions; a partial end to censorship; limited freedom of speech and assembly; better food supplies; the freeing of political detainees; the abolition of special privileges for Party officials; and the publication of their demands in the press.

On 18 August, Mr Gierek responded by himself going on television to say that there could be no change in Poland's policies. On 19 August, the workers of the Baltic coast replied by stepping up their strikes throughout the Baltic region. On 20 August, the Government hit back by arresting eighteen leading Polish dissidents, including Jacek Kuron, head of the so-called Self Defence Committee (KOR), who had been providing a stream of information about the strikes and stoppages, both to other Poles and to foreign journalists who were now flooding into Poland by every available plane. On the same night, the Soviet Union itself began jamming Russian-language broadcasts from the West for the first time since 1973.

On 21 August the Polish Government issued veiled warnings that if events got any further out of hand they could lead to Soviet intervention. On 22 August, as uncertainty grew, Chancellor Schmidt of West Germany cancelled an important, long-awaited meeting with the East German Communist leader Erich Honecker. On 23 August, the First Deputy Prime Minister of Poland, Mieczyslaw Jagdielski, travelled to Gdansk for a first abortive round of talks with the strikers in the Lenin shipyards. On 24 August Mr Gierek announced a major reshuffle of the Polish Politburo, including the sacking of Mr Babiuch, and promised some form of free trade union elections. On 25 August the Government met the strikers' demands for the restoration of telephone links with Gdansk.

The Road from Moscow (August–December 1980)

By now the whole of the Western world was becoming familiar with the amazing scenes which were unfolding in the Lenin Shipyard—the grave, moustachioed figure of Lech Walesa; the serried ranks of kneeling Polish workers celebrating Mass beneath huge pictures of 'their' Polish Pope, John-Paul II; the crucifix above the table in the large hall where Walesa and his strike-committee were in almost permanent session, freely available at any time to journalists or to any of the 10,000-odd workers who were now in permanent occupation of the shipyards. But it was only now that, for the first time, the Soviet Union broke its silence on what was happening, as Tass described the events in Poland as 'an attempt by certain imperialist circles impudently to interfere in the internal affairs of the sovereign Socialist state'.

On 26 August Mr Jagdielski returned to Gdansk for more talks with the strikers, which continued until the 28th, as the whole Baltic coast, including the city of Szczezin, lay paralysed. On 29 August the Polish Government issued an official statement denying that Mr Gierek was about to resign. On 30 August the Government negotiating teams in Gdansk and Szczezin gave way to the strikers' demands. On 31 August, a twenty-one-point agreement was published, signed by Lech Walesa and Mr Jagdielski, providing for free trade unions, the right to strike, the easing of censorship, the release of political prisoners, better food supplies and everything the strikers had originally asked for (including the broadcasting of Mass on Poland's state television service). The signing ceremony itself was carried live on Polish television, the first time Polish viewers had been able to see Mr Walesa. As he was carried shoulder high through the Lenin shipyards, amid a cheering crowd of 15,000 supporters, Walesa told them 'we are the co-masters of this land.'

The Western press was beside itself with excitement. 'TRIUMPH FOR STRIKE POLES' proclaimed the *Daily Telegraph*. 'FREE TRADE UNIONS—VICTORY FOR POLES' said the *Sunday Telegraph*. 'POLISH STRIKERS WIN CHANGES IN COMMUNIST SYSTEM' ran the front-page of *The Times*, while its main editorial was solemnly headed 'The Decline of an Empire'—meaning the Soviet empire.

In Moscow, *Pravda* merely informed its readers that the recent difficulties in Poland, instigated by 'subversive centres abroad', seemed to have been settled.

The story was not yet over.

19

Remember Kronstadt

What happens when the proletariat is sick to death of the
dictatorship which acts in its name?

Robert Payne, *The Life and Death of Trotsky*

Once upon a time there was a Communist country in which the people
became increasingly restive at the miseries and oppression which they
had to endure. There were terrible food shortages. The economy was
so inefficient as to be on the verge of complete breakdown. The
workers felt particularly cheated that the trade unions and other
organizations which were meant to represent their interests were
merely puppet organs of the central Party dictatorship.

Eventually, though trouble had first expressed itself in a wave of
strikes elsewhere, unrest came to a head in a great seaport on the
shores of the Baltic. In a series of massive but peaceful meetings, some
16,000 dockyard workers and seamen drew up a list of fifteen
demands to the central government. These included free elections, by
secret ballot, to create truly representative workers' organizations; an
end to censorship; the liberation of those arrested for 'political'
offences; better food supplies; the abolition of special privileges for
Communist Party officials; and finally that their demands should be
made public through the press.

At first the Party leaders were nonplussed as to how to react.
Nothing like this had ever been seen before. Perhaps the workers
should be given free trade unions, some Politburo members suggested.
Back in Moscow, *Pravda* fulminated that the trouble had all been got
up by 'foreign subversives'. But for a while the striking workers on the
Baltic seemed to be carrying all before them. It was viewed as the
greatest challenge the Communist system had ever had to face: a direct
confrontation between that system and the very people in whose name
it had been brought into being.

What happened next, of course, is a matter of history—because the events I have been describing took place not in Poland, but in the Soviet Union. The date was not 1980, but 1921. The Baltic seaport in question was not Gdansk, but Kronstadt. And what happened when, under the inspiration of Trotsky, the Soviet leadership finally pulled itself together, was that it decided that the Kronstadt 'rebellion' should be put down without mercy and by a massive display of force (even though Trotsky himself, only a year or two earlier, had described those same Kronstadt sailors and workmen as 'the flower of the Revolution', for the crucial part they had played in bringing the Bolsheviks to power). The Red Army was sent into Kronstadt, with the secret police behind them; thousands of 'rebels' were massacred in the fighting which ensued; many more were summarily 'executed' as soon as they surrendered; and apart from a handful who managed to escape across the Baltic to Finland, almost all the survivors were taken off to Petrograd and murdered in the months which followed.

In the first heady days of what the Western press was calling 'the Polish triumph' in September 1980, it was salutary to recall the tragedy of Kronstadt, if only because it was a reminder of just how far back in the history of the Soviet system this pattern of events had been established. To the question, 'What happens when the proletariat is sick to death of the dictatorship which acts in its name?' the answer had come down the decades as unvaryingly and remorselessly as the responses of a litany: in East Berlin in 1953; in Poznan and Budapest in 1956; in Novocherkassk, where Khruschev had sent in the tanks to crush workers protesting against food price rises in 1962; in Prague in 1968; in Gdansk and Szczezin in 1970. It was as well to preserve a clear head about just what had been at stake during those heroic, unbelievable weeks in Poland, and a keen sense of realism as to how those events might eventually turn out.

Of course the Poles themselves were only too well aware what was at stake. As the leader of KOR, Jacek Kuron, put it when he was released by the Polish security police on 1 September (under the terms of the previous day's Gdansk agreement) in what became perhaps the most haunting phrase of the whole episode:

> We must work to increase the area of freedom and to diminish the area of totalitarianism—but not to exceed the limits set by Soviet tanks.

Disbelief may have continued in the West at the news of Mr Gierek's resignation as leader of the Polish Communist Party in the small hours of the morning on 6 September, and his replacement by Stanislaw Kania; at the broadcasting for the first time ever in any Communist country, the following day, of a religious service; at the spectacle of millions of Poles resigning *en masse* over the following weeks from their official state 'trade unions', to join Lech Walesa's new 'free trade union' Solidarity.

But as those autumn months went by, with reports of vast troop movements on the Polish frontiers, with constant rumours and reports from Moscow of how beadily the masters of the Kremlin were observing all that was happening (while Western newspapers continued to run such headlines as 'Brave New Poland' or 'Face of Eastern Europe Has Been Changed'*), the Poles were aware of what an extraordinary tightrope they were walking, because they knew only too well what living under a totalitarian regime really means. Whether or not they specifically remembered Kronstadt, they knew just how centrally rooted in the whole nature of the Communist system the basic conflict which had once again come to the surface in their country was.

Reading through the 'fifteen demands' made by the Kronstadt 'rebels' in 1921, it is almost uncanny to see how closely they were echoed in the 'sixteen demands' made by the strikers of Gdansk nearly sixty years later. And right at the heart of both sets of demands lay really just one. When the Kronstadt sailors demanded 'free Soviets, elected by secret ballot', just as when the Gdansk shipyard workers demanded 'free trade unions, elected by secret ballot', what they were really asking for was an end to the central principle on which the entire system of totalitarian Socialism rests; the principle, already firmly established by Lenin just three years after the Revolution, that in a Socialist country power flows in only one direction—from the centre downwards.

There was only one question even more important to Lenin than '*Chto delat'*?' and that was '*Kto? Kogo?*' ('Who? Whom?'). The correct answer, as Lenin never had any doubt, was 'the Party—the people', 'we—they'. And ultimately nothing in the world must be allowed to stand in the way of that principle, even if it means sacrificing the lives of thousands, or millions of people. The essence of totalitarian Socialism is quite simple: it is that nothing—no economic

---

* *The Sunday Telegraph* 2 November, *The Times* 4 November.

enterprise, no social organization, no work of art, no idea—shall exist except at the behest of, and to serve the purposes of, the Party (unless it be something either so harmless—or so useful, like the remains of private agriculture—that it can be permitted, under licence, to survive).

In the case of Poland, there was no way that the setting up of a 'free trade union movement' could be regarded as either harmless or useful. It was one thing to grant tactical concessions, under duress, on the tacit assumption that they could eventually be withdrawn again, as the opportunity arose. It was quite another to admit into the Polish state a second centre of real power—or even a third, if the Polish Roman Catholic Church is included. But of course the very mention of the Polish Church underlines the fact that, in Communist terms, the Polish situation posed unusual problems, not least the quite exceptional depth and strength of Polish nationalism. In terms of all power flowing from the centre downwards, the ultimate answer to the question 'Who? Whom?' in the instance of Poland was not 'the Party—the people', but 'the Soviet Union—the Poles'. And of this truth, despite all the initial euphoria in the West, the one group who never had any doubt, right from the start, were the Poles themselves.

It is one of the most remarkable facts about the twentieth century that there is no Communist country in the world where the government has been voted into power by a process of democratic choice. The nearest any country has come to this was in Czechoslovakia in 1948, where the Communists received just over a third of the votes in that country's last 'free election'; but even then it required a Soviet-backed *coup* and the threat of force to establish the Communists in power. There are six Soviet 'satellite' countries in Eastern Europe—Poland, East Germany, Czechoslovakia, Hungary, Romania, Bulgaria. In each of them the Communist government was established by use or threat of force. The Soviet Union itself is made up of fifteen nations; in fourteen of them the Soviet Government seized power by use or threat of force, while in the fifteenth, Russia, when the Bolsheviks seized power by *coup d'état* in 1917, the numbers crucially involved in that act probably amounted to not more than a few thousand men.

And yet the extraordinary thing is that these amazing operations have been carried out in the name of 'Democracy' and 'the People'. The largest empire the world has ever known, involving the enforced subjugation of more than a hundred different nations and nationalities,* has been set up in the name of 'bringing an end to imperialism'. For sixty years this vision has been publicly proclaimed, while all the evidence has suggested again and again (as today in Afghanistan) that the whole thing is just a gigantic piece of painted cardboard; that beneath the terrible weight of the apparatus of force which established it and which has kept it in being, are millions of people—nations and individuals alike—crying out inwardly that it is all untrue.

What made the challenge posed by the Poles to the Communist system in the summer and autumn of 1980 unique was not just the strength of Polish nationalist feeling, although this was obviously of enormous importance. The widespread belief that if the Soviet Union and its puppet allies were to invade Poland it would not just be a repetition of Prague 1968, but that the whole nation would fight back, created a tactical dilemma for the Soviet Union of a type it had never really faced before.

What made the situation in 1980 unprecedented was that the Poles were only articulating and making visible, with extraordinary courage, a new mood of desperation which in different ways was seizing almost the whole of the Soviet empire. If the Poles wanted enough to eat, how much more was that true of all except a few privileged minorities in the Soviet Union itself. The reason why the crisis confronting the Soviet empire was like none it had ever faced before was that it had never previously been confronted with such a combination of economic and ideological crisis. After sixty years, the Communist system was at last being brought face to face with one of its most fundamental contradictions—which is the built-in inability of its mode of economic organization to satisfy the peculiar claims of its ideology.

We have become used in the West to believing that our standards of living should continually be rising—and we are finding it a painful experience to adjust to the idea that it may no longer be possible. We are also familiar at least with the notion (even if we do not always honour it in practice) that no economic theory is infallible.

But in the Socialist world, the belief that, through total Socialist planning, it is possible to bring about a continual improvement in material standards of life is not just a theory. It is a fundamental article

* The Soviet Union alone is officially described as containing 'a hundred nations or peoples', most of them too small to justify setting up their own Republic.

of belief, a central pillar of the religion on which the whole system is based. When the Poles, let alone the people of Russia itself, demand something more than the pitiful supplies of meat and potatoes and bread than they are used to—at a time when those supplies have actually been quite seriously diminishing—there is no way they can be given what they want except by changing the whole system. And that is the one thing the Soviet empire and those who run it cannot do. They cannot change the system. Yet the system does not work, and at last, after sixty years, they know it.

How on earth did they get into this *impasse*?

20

The End of the Road

Nations are the wealth of mankind, its generalized personalities.
The least among them has its own special colours, and harbours
within itself a special facet of God's design.

Alexander Solzhenitsyn, Nobel Lecture, 1970

There is something about Russia which makes most of us
foreigners who live here spend most of our idle hours discussing
the country's ills, proposing remedies and speculating about
prospects for recovery. In a sense, this is patronizing. However
it also demonstrates Russia's unique ability to stimulate
foreigners' interest, even love. Perhaps because of the
universality of its great literature and art, perhaps because of its
size, strength and a particular kind of purity, Russia represents
the human condition and struggle of the human spirit more
vividly than our own countries. We are fascinated by what we
see here, we want to be part of the struggle. We personally—often
involuntarily—identify with this people's difficulties and fate.
This is not patronizing, but a testimony to Russia's greatness.

George Feifer, *Message from Moscow*

No nation on earth has presented such an enigma as Russia—both to
outsiders and to its own people.

One of the most thought-provoking books ever written about
Russia was by a Frenchman, the Marquis de Custine. Like many
'ideological pilgrims' of the twentieth century, he set off for Russia
because he was dissatisfied with the political systems of the West,
hoping to find in the great empire to the East an ideal model of
government. He was quite transfixed with horror at what he found
when he arrived: secret policemen everywhere; a grim uniformity of
architecture; censorship; huge parades; deification of the country's

leaders; the constant re-writing of history to suit the regime's purposes; a people enslaved by a tyranny beyond Western imagining.

He was particularly hypnotized by the symbolism of the Kremlin at the heart of the whole empire—this 'citadel of spectres', as he called it, this 'prison of peoples':

> The fear of an all-powerful man is the most terrible fear in the world; so one does not approach the Kremlin without shuddering ... in vain each little tower has its individual character and its particular use; all have the same significance—armed terror!
>
> To live in the Kremlin is not to live; it is to protect oneself; oppression creates revolt; revolt necessitates precautions; precautions increase the danger; and of this long series of actions and reactions is born a monster, despotism, which has built itself a house in Moscow—the Kremlin!

Finally, after several months alternately appalled and fascinated by this hell, he escaped back to the West. 'Never will I forget what I felt,' he said, as he crossed the Russian border back to freedom:

> A bird escaped from its cage, or coming out from under a vacuum bell, would be less joyous. I can speak, I can write what I think, I am free ... finally, I breathe!

Many pages of the Marquis de Custine's description of Russia read like the reactions of a particularly disillusioned Westerner at the height of the Stalin terror—but the year when the Marquis made his visit (which firmly converted him to a belief in Western ways of government) was 1839.

Many people, for various reasons, find de Custine's account of Russia hard to take. They point out, not without cause, all the aspects of Russian life, even in 1839, which the Marquis seemed not to have noticed: in particular that flowering of the Western liberal spirit which had already produced Pushkin and Lermontov, and which was to lead not many years later to a host of reforms, from the emancipation of the serfs to the abolition of the death penalty. There were few indications in his account that Russia was just embarking on that great effervescence of creativity that was to produce some of the greatest literature and music in the history of mankind. And it is a great mistake, as many such as Solzhenitsyn have been at pains to point out, to overestimate the degree of oppression, censorship and general tyranny which prevailed in Russia in the sixty years before the Revolution. Not only did Tolstoy, Dostoievsky, Chernyshevsky and many others actually have their books published in Russia (the censorship had become, by the standards of at least sixty countries in the world today, remarkably mild). Even when Lenin himself was sent off to the horrors of exile in Siberia for conspiring to overthrow the government, he was accompanied by his wife and provided by the authorities with a house, a sheep a week and the services of a housemaid.

Nevertheless there is no reason to doubt that de Custine faithfully reported on all that he saw and felt in Russia in the reign of Tsar Nicholas I. And the only fair conclusion one can come to is that, however one-sidedly, he was describing certain aspects of life in that country which seem somehow endemic to the very character of the nation, something which goes back a great deal further than just the last sixty years—through the despotisms of Catherine and Peter and Ivan the Terrible into the mists of Muscovite time.

I was once reading, at much the same time, two books about the experiences of two particular countries other than Russia under Communism. One was *Chinese Shadows*, the deeply moving description by Simon Leys of the destruction of traditional Chinese culture under the 'Cultural Revolution'. The other was *Cambodia Year Zero* by François Ponchaud, the first full-length account of the still almost unimaginable catastrophe which fell over that country in the years after the take-over by the Khmer Rouge in 1975. Both authors were steeped in the history of the country they were writing about. And both made a fascinatingly similar point. Leys was struck by how much of Chinese life under Communism seems to echo the very worst of Chinese society in the distant past—the rigid social stratification, the mystique thrown around the country's rulers, the deadweight of a vast, top-heavy bureaucracy. Ponchaud, in trying to account for the unbelievable cruelty of the Khmer Rouge, in a nation long known for its people's gentleness and delicacy, recalled how, centuries before, the original Khmers had in fact displayed a not dissimilar streak of murderous barbarity. And the conclusion I came to on reading these passages was that their line of thought may possibly point towards one of the most puzzling things about Communism.

It was no accident that the ideology later known as Socialism or Communism first began to appear in Europe about 200 years ago, at the time when the Age of the Enlightenment was giving way to the age of the Industrial Revolution and Romanticism. Men were losing their old cosmic religious view of human existence, and of the bonds which held each society together as a whole. The individualism born of the Renaissance increasingly seemed to be producing nothing but greed, exploitation and the tortured, egotistical soul-searching of the romantics. It was at this point that a new transcendent ideology began to emerge, to meet men's perennial hunger for some great universal cause and system, higher than just the petty human ego. The new Communism met that need, by holding out once again the vision of a great transpersonal cause, a unifying faith, the hope that all mankind could be one. It was this which gave Communism its enormous psychological power and appeal, because it was tapping some of the deepest spiritual instincts in man.

But Communism was not transcendent in the way Christianity and other traditional religions had been. It pushed on even further in the secular, materialist direction in which Western civilization was travelling. It did not derive its strength from the old appeal to the individual, inward soul. It projected everything outwards into the collective cause. It was here, as part of the collective, the group, the class, as part of *history*, that the individual could alone find significance. The whole secret of Communism is precisely that it rejects the inner kingdom of the individual, that centre where alone truth may be discerned, that centre from which alone a perception of individual moral responsibility derives.

Communism regards 'absolute truth' as an illusion. It only recognizes 'the truth of a situation'. Everything is relative, to the needs of the Cause. Under Communism there is no such thing as people's responsibility for their own inner kingdom. They must abdicate all moral responsibility to that great power beyond them, which alone can decide what is true, what is right, what must be done—the Party, the State. That is where the 'centre' is, outside, and only there.

This, I believe, is why when any nation falls under the dark, beguiling grip of Communism, what emerges among other things is a caricature of that nation's own worst collective characteristics—because the individual moral responsibility which alone can temper such characteristics has been removed. That is why Soviet Russia, like East Germany or other Communist countries, displays—in addition to those qualities which all Communist states share—so many of the least attractive characteristics with which it has been associated in the past: the official paranoia, the distrust of foreigners, the hypocrisy, the bullying of those weaker, the desire to emulate and impress those stronger. If England were to fall under Communism, I suspect that we should see a fine demonstration of many of our own worst national qualities.

But there is another, enormously important side to Communism, and in a way it is the message I was reaching towards during those unforgettable weeks when I was in the Soviet Union.

One of the themes which has run through this book is how much more *serious* a business life is in the East than it has become in the West. We have paid a terrible inner price in the West for our decades of material abundance, our obsession with the media and the playthings of affluence. Never more than today, as President Reagan succeeds to President Carter, and as the West slides into the worst recession for fifty years, has the Western way of life, in many respects, looked less attractive, less able to measure up, in Solzhenitsyn's words, to 'the mortal weight and complexity' of human existence.

There were many signs in 1980 that both the great world-systems—Socialism in the East and 'consumer capitalism' in the West—were entering a period of unprecedented crisis. And if we look back over the past ten or fifteen years and ask which of these two systems has produced the more remarkable individual human beings, there can be little doubt about the answer.

It is one of the great paradoxes of our time that it should have been Communism, by the very way it polarizes the most fundamental issues of human existence, which has produced so many men and women of real human stature. We only know of a few—Andrei Sakharov, Alexander Solzhenitsyn, Karol Wojtyla—but behind them into the darkness stretch untold thousands more. It is Communism, the faith which denies human individuality, which has produced the individuals—because it crushes down so hard on its millions of enslaved victims that, although a great many are crushed, some are simply forced into finding that irreducible human core within themselves in order to survive. It was from one such man, Vladimir Bukovsky, that I took the words printed at the beginning of this book and which have been its guiding thought throughout:

the lack of bitter experience of people in the West makes them incapable of imagining tragedy.

The ultimate lie of the Socialist system—and it is one shared by a great many people in the West who would not in any sense call themselves Socialists—is that the only components in the human personality which matter are body and mind, and that man's ultimate sense of identity derives from his membership of the group. The answer to that lie is not to be found in nuclear weapons. It is not to be found in winning victories in sports stadiums and proclaiming that 'sport is above politics'. It lies in each human heart and each human soul. And I have no doubt on which side of the great gulf which today divides mankind, people have learned through bitter experience to see that truth more clearly, and what it means to be fully human with a more courageous and unswerving eye.

When I returned from the Soviet Union, I was sent a book by an Estonian woman, now in exile in England. In the front she wrote:

> Look hard at others' eyes
> No one sees his own.
> Life's seal can be unsealed
> Its hidden knowledge known.

Index

(Olympic competitors are distinguished by a C., followed by their country. Particular Olympic events have all been placed together under Olympic Games: sporting events.)

Afghanistan, 15, 16, 26, 27; invasion of, 29, 30–4, 37, 38, 46, 78, 108, 110, 112, 169, 171, 174, 180, 185, 190–1, 203, 209–10

Aida, 135

Ali, Muhammad, 36

Amalrik, Andrei, 185

Andropov, Yuri, 75

Angola, 25

Arab nations (pull out of Games), 33

Arafat, Yasser, 73

Arbat, 49, 60–1

Armenia, 170n

Arrest, method of in USSR, 82, 113

'Artistic Background', 77, 80, 200

Ashkenazy, Vladimir, 184

Athens Olympics (1896), 134

Azerbajan, 170n

Babiuch, E., 214–15

Baltic States, 160, 164–5, 169–70; *see also* Estonia

Baring, Maurice (*What I Saw in Russia*), 15, 69, 156

Baryshnikov, Mikhail, 184

BBC World Service, 49, 73, 174, 185, 209

Beethoven, L. van, 79, 125, 181

Beriozka shops, 86, 90n, 91, 176, 202

Berlin Diary (W. Shirer), 192, 211n

Berlin Olympics (1936), 31–3, 162, 192, 195, 211n

Besford, Pat, 48, 49, 139

'Billygate' affair, 109, 208

Binyon, Michael, 102, 114, 140

Blue Guide (to Moscow and Leningrad), 13, 49

Bolshoi, 59, 90, 102, 135, 185

Bonner, Yelena, 39, 174, 213

Borisov, Vladimir, 40, 45, 166n

Boycott of Moscow Olympics, 27, 29, 30–41, 73, 78, 100; effects of, 103–5; Soviet attitudes to, 111–12, 185, 193–5

Brasher, Chris, 139–40, 183

Brezhnev, Leonid, 21–2, 24, 25, 26, 61, 68, 75, 77, 79, 81, 97, 102, 104, 114, 120–1, 125, 130, 155, 163, 165, 174, 193, 198, 203, 204

British Embassy, 82–3, 102–4

British Medical Journal, 211

British Olympic Association, 31, 33, 37–8, 185

Brodsky, Joseph, 185

Bruce Lockhart, R. H. (*Memoirs of a British Agent*), 104

Bryant, John, 14, 31, 45, 54, 149

Bukharin, Nikolai, 67, 124, 135

Bukovsky, Vladimir, 9, 25, 34–5, 47–8, 102, 227

Buses (for Olympics), 51, 57, 83, 85–6, 133, 181

Byelorussia, 169n

Cambodia Year Zero (François Ponchaud), 225
Campbell, Ian (C. Australia), 173
Carrington, Lord, 39
Carter, President Jimmy, 26, 29, 31, 34, 36–7, 109, 112, 195, 208, 227
Carter, Jimmy (C. GB), 171
Catherine the Great, 46, 225
'Chaika lane', 75, 81
Chataway, Chris, 139
Cheating, allegations of Soviet, 26, 136, 172–3, 176–7
CHEKA, 60, 152; *see also* KGB
Chernyshevsky, Nikolai, 197, 225
Children, absence of from Moscow, 97–8
Children's World (toy store), 97
Chinese Shadows (Simon Leys), 225
Churchill, Winston, 46
Closing ceremony, 199–200
Coe, Peter, 95, 143, 149–50, 182
Coe, Sebastian (C. GB), 16, 95, 136, 141, 143–4, 148, 149–50, 155, 177, 182–3, 185, 193
Collective farms, 86–7, 90, 128–9
Collectivization of agriculture: Soviet, 128–9; Estonian, 160; Polish, 214
Comaneci, Nadia (C. Romania), 96, 136, 173
Communism, nature of, 225–8 and *passim*
Cosmonauts, 25, 79, 124, 132
Coubertin, Baron Le, 51, 153
Cram, Steve (C. GB), 182
Crawford, Haseley (C. Trinidad), 145
Cripples, absence of from Moscow, 98, 190
Cubans, 78, 145–7, 192, 194
Cultural Festival, Olympic, 87–8
Custine, Marquis de, 223–5
Czechoslovakia, invasion of (1968), 30, 218

Daily Mail, 14, 31–3, 38, 50, 85, 95, 101–2, 108, 135, 140, 142, 143, 149, 193

Daily Mirror, 24, 139
Daily Telegraph, 48, 216
Daniel, Yuli, 184, 190
Davies, Sharron (C. GB), 150
Delegations, 58, 67, 118
Deportations (from Estonia), 160
Détente, 21, 25–6
Detskiy Mir (Children's World), 97
Dinamo (KGB Sports Club), 152–3
Disillusionment with system in USSR, 116–17, 130
Dissidents, 28–9, 31, 34–5, 39–40, 102, 213–14, 227–8
Dityatin, Alexander (C. USSR), 177
Dostoievsky, Feodor, 63, 187–8, 198, 225
Doust, Dudley, 99, 139
Dr Zhivago (Boris Pasternak), 179, 186, 188–90
Dudko, Father Dmitri, 34, 39–40
Dzerzhinsky, F. E., 60, 124, 152

East Anglian Daily Times, 210–11
East Berlin, 218
Edinburgh, Duke of, 103
English, David, 14, 31
Estonia, 157ff, 170n
Ethiopia, 32, 156

Family, Soviet attitudes to, 154–5
Feifer, George, 106, 116–17, 223
Financial Times, 74
Finland, 66, 156, 158, 163–5
'Floor ladies', 53, 142, 180
Fodor, Eugene (guide book), 43, 99
Follows, Sir Denis, 31, 33, 37, 202
Food, produced by private enterprise in USSR, 128
Food poisoning, 133, 143
Food shortages (under Socialist system), 28, 29, 41, 58, 66, 70, 92, 116–17, 213, 217–18
Ford, President Gerald, 25
Foreign visitors to Moscow, 75, 99, 210–11
France, 33, 100, 172
Fresco, Monty, 95, 138, 142

Index

Gagarin, Yuri, 124
Galich, Alexander, 184
Gdansk, 214–16, 218–19
Gierek, E., 214–15, 218–19
Gilels, Emil, 87
Ginsburg, Alexander, 27, 31, 214
Ginsburg, Evgenia, 130
Golovin, Valeriy, 108–10, 118, 157, 185–6, 190
Goncharov, G. P., 28, 34
Goodhew, Duncan (C. GB), 99–100, 150
Gorki (city), 35, 51, 115, 116, 212
Gorky, Maxim, 47, 125
Gorky Street, 51, 60
'Great Patriotic War', 97, 130, 188
Grigorenko, General Pyotr, 102
Guardian, 24
GULAG (prison-camp system, run by KGB), 153, 189
GUM (department store), 55, 62–3, 91, 102, 142, 211

Haritonenko ('sugar king'), 103–4
Harris, Norman, 139
Helsinki Agreement (1975), 27, 28, 165
'Helsinki Monitoring Group', 27, 28, 34, 213, 214
Helsinki Olympics (1952), 22, 151, 154
Hildreth, Peter, 14, 118, 122–3, 139, 143
Hitler, Adolf, 33, 111, 153, 195
'House of Trade Unions' (formerly Club of Nobility), 66–7
Houvion, Philippe (C. France), 172
Hoyles of Hadleigh, 210–11
Hoyte-Smith, Joslyn (C. GB), 146
Hubble, Philip (C. GB), 92
Hulls, Sidney, 139
Hungary: invasion of (1956), 31, 164, 218; author's visits to, 121, 147, 207n

Identity cards, 52, 57
Inflation (in USSR), 116
Informers, 112

Intelligentsia (Moscow), 184, 209
International Olympic Committee, 21–4, 27, 32–3
Interpreters, 85, 107–9, 157
Israel, 23
Ivan the Terrible, 63, 96, 137, 225
Izvestia, 114; see also *Pravda*

Jack, Ian, 14, 73, 102, 118, 139, 157, 175

Kachanov, Valeriy (C. USSR), 149
Kalinin Prospekt, 61
Kania, Stanislaw, 219
Keating, Frank, 14, 50, 81, 138–9, 143, 204
Keeble, Sir Curtis, 103
KGB, 34, 40, 47, 60, 71, 75, 95, 106, 112–13, 116, 122, 141, 142, 152–3, 174, 190–1, 200–1, 211, 213; see also Police
Khatchaturian, Aram, 80n
Khruschev, Nikita, 57, 69, 77, 130, 135, 167, 175, 218
Kiev, 27, 172
Killanin, Lord, 23n, 24, 32, 66–7, 77, 79, 109, 202
Kirov, Nikolai (C. USSR), 146, 148
Kirov, Sergei, 123
Komsomol see Young Communist organizations
Koniev, Marshal, 124
Korbut, Olga, 154, 176
Kosygin, Alexei, 130
Kozakiewicz, Wladyslaw (C. Poland), 172
Krause, Barbara (C. E. Germany), 96
Kremlin, 21, 52, 55–7, 63, 65, 67, 69; de Custine on, 224
Kronstadt 'rising' (1921), 217–18
Krupskaya, 62
Krylatskoye, 23
Kto? Kogo?, 219–20
Kung, Andres, 163n, 163–7 *passim*
Kuron, Jacek, 215, 218
Kustodiev, 68
Kutuzovsky Prospekt, 75–6

Laidoner, Col., 159, 160
Lake Placid (Winter Olympics, 1980), 36
Latvia, 47; *see also* Baltic States
Lefertovo, 102
Lenin, V. I., 52, 61–2, 72, 86–7, 88, 97, 155, 157, 161, 197, 219, 225; Museum, 61–2; Mausoleum, 63, 118–30 *passim*, 211; cult of, 120ff
Lenin Shipyard, 214–16
Lenin Stadium, 25, 28, 71, 72, 77–81, 95, 102, 145ff, 173, 199–200
Leningrad, 27, 75
Leonard, Silvio (C. Cuba), 145, 146–7
Leonidov, 64
Lermontov, Mikhail, 55, 187, 224
Levin, Bernard, 83
Lewis, Martyn, 202–4
Leys, Simon (*Chinese Shadows*), 225
Los Angeles, 24
Louis, Spiridon, 134
Lubyanka, 60, 67
Lunacharsky, 123

Maclean, Sir Fitzroy (*Eastern Approaches*), 67, 135
Marks and Spencer, 98, 203–4, 209
Marx, Karl, 59, 60, 120–1
Marx Prospekt, 60
Mayakovsky, Vladimir, 51, 77
Medals won in Olympics, 1980, 92–3, 100, 105, 136, 177, 192, 193; final medals table, and comparison with Montreal, 194n; *see also* Olympic Games: sporting events, for specific results
Melbourne Olympics (1956), 31, 139
Melentev, Alexander (C. USSR), 93
Mennea, Pietro (C. Italy), 145
Message from Moscow, 106, 223
Metro, 69–70
Metropole Hotel, 59
Mexico Olympics (1968), 23

Miller, David, 14, 139, 143, 204
Minsk, 27, 154, 172
Misha Bears (Olympic 'Mascot'), 34, 51, 58, 80, 99, 200
Moldavia, 169n, 185
Montreal Olympics (1976), 22, 25–6, 147, 149, 153, 192; medals table, 194n
Morizov, Pavel, 154
Morning Star, 108–9, 182
Moscow, city of, 22, 28, 50–2, 55–65, 66–73 and *passim*
Munich Olympics (1972), 23, 94, 152, 177
Munster Express, 162
Museums: Lenin, 61–2; History and Reconstruction of Moscow, 96–7; Pushkin, 175

Neizvestny, E., 184
News of the World, 34–5
Nezhdanovoye, 49, 60, 155–6
Nicholas I, 21, 225
Nixon, President Richard, 21–2, 24
NKVD, 47, 60, 67, 123, 135
Novocherkassk, 218
Novodevichy, 77
Novy Arbat, 61, 69
Nureyev, Rudolf, 184

Oakes, Gary (C. GB), 148, 150
Observer, 37
O'Connor, Terry, 50
Oerter, Al, 146
OGPU, 46, 60
Okudzhava, Bulit, 49
Olympic Games, 1980: opening ceremony, 76–80; closing ceremony, 199–200
sporting events:
athletics: 100 Metres, 136, 143, 145; final, 146–7; 800 Metres, 136, 143, 146–8; final, 147–8; 1,500 Metres, 177–8; final, 182; 5,000 Metres, 178, 193; 10,000 Metres, final, 156; Decathlon, 141, 143, 147, 148–9; Triple Jump, 146;

Women's 400 Metres, 146; 400
  Metres Hurdles, 148; Pole
  Vault, 172; Hammer Throw,
  176–7; Marathon, 178, 183
swimming: Men's 200
  Metres Butterfly, 92; Women's
  4×100 Metres, 92; Women's
  100 Metres Freestyle, 96;
  Men's 100 Metres
  Breaststroke, 99–100; 1,500
  Metres Freestyle, 100, 193
Modern Pentathlon, 49, 92;
  Free Pistol Shooting, 84–5, 93;
  Cycling, 136; Yachting, Flying
  Dutchman Class, 162, 166–7;
  Football, 172–3; Women's
  Field Hockey, 177; Boxing,
  192
Olympic Village, 71–2, 171, 178
Onishchenko, Boris, 26, 34
Ordzhonikidze, Sergei, 123
Orlov, Prof. Yuri, 27, 170, 214n
Orwell, George, 15, 65, 106, 119
Ostankino, 28, 202
Ovett, Steve (C. GB), 16, 136, 141,
  143–4, 148, 149, 155, 177, 182
Owen, David, 27
Owens, Jesse, 33, 195

Palace of Congresses, 135–6
Pares, Bernard, 207
Pasternak, Boris, 179, 186–90
  passim
Pasternak-Slater, Michael, 146
Päts, Konstantin, 159, 160, 165
Pattison, Rodney, 166
Paul, Nick, 133–5
Paustovsky, Konstantin, 64
'Peace Decree' (1918), 157, 169
Peredelkino, 181, 185–90
Peter the Great, 101, 225
Pimen, Patriarch, 178
Pimenov, Yuri, 68
Pirita, 166
Plisetskaya, Maya, 80n, 87
Poland, 15, 41, 73, 115, 174,
  214–16, 218–22 *passim*
Polenov, Vasily, 69

Police, 52–3, 59, 71–2, 72n, 76,
  113, 122, 172, 202, 210, 223; *see
  also* KGB and Security
Political prisoners, 34, 170; 'none in
  Russia', 191, 214
Pollution (in Soviet Estonia), 161,
  164–5
Ponchaud, François (*Cambodia
  Year Zero*), 225
Ponomaroyova, Nina, 154n
Popov, O., 87
Popov, Vladimir, 101, 131–4, 172,
  176, 177–8
Posters, Olympic, 51, 59, 61, 76,
  202
'Potemkin Village', 46–8, 76,
  85–92, 108, 162
Pozna, Alexander, 112, 201
Pravda, 49, 58, 216, 217
Pre-Olympic 'clean-up', 34–5, 40n
Press Centre, 57–8, 95, 101, 131,
  181
Privilege in Soviet Union, 117, 154,
  203
Pugacheva, Alla, 87
Pushkin, Alexander, 70, 175, 187,
  224

Quarrie, Don (C. Jamaica), 145

Radek, Karl, 124
Radio Moscow, 73, 90, 107, 109,
  112, 114, 174, 195, 201, 209–10
Reagan, President Ronald, 208, 227
Records (World and Olympic):
  importance attached to by Soviet
  authorities, 96, 104–5, 193;
  broken in 1980 US swimming
  championships, 193
Red Army, *see* Afghanistan,
  Czechoslovakia, Hungary,
  Poland, etc.
Reddaway, Peter, 40n
Red Square, 55–7, 63, 69, 91, 95,
  122, 190
Reed, John, 123, 169
Remont (repairs), 59, 90
Restaurants, tourist, 99

Revolution (1917), 61, 68, 126–9, 187–8 and *passim*
Ritchie Calder, Lord, 175
Rodda, John, 138–9
Rolls Royce, Lenin's, 61–2
Romanians, 96, 136
Rossiya Hotel, 51, 52–4, 55, 66, 72, 76, 85, 137, 174, 176, 190–1, 196, 201
Rostropovich, Mstislav, 181, 184, 202
Rusanov, Vasily, 197
Russell, Bertrand, 125, 167
Russian character and customs, 100–1, 107–10, 180, 208–9, 223–8; as individuals, 107, 187–90; psychology, 110–12, 156, 187–9, 196–9
Russians, The (Hedrick Smith), 13, 51, 82n, 129n, 155
Russian/Soviet empire, 110–11, 169–70, 220–2

Sadovoye Koltso, 57
Saint Basil's Cathedral, 52, 63
Sakharov, Andrei, 25, 35, 39, 51, 174, 213, 227
Salnikov, Vladimir (C. USSR), 100, 193
Saneyev, Victor (C. USSR), 146
Satter, David, 74–6, 81, 98
Scharansky, Anatoly, 27, 214
Schedrin, Rodion, 80, 87, 199
Security, 52–3, 81–3, 86, 95, 96, 99
Sedykh, Yuri (C. USSR), 176–7
Seifert, Richard, 101
Serbsky Institute for Psychiatry, 102
Serov, Valentin, 69
Shaposhnikova, Nataliya (C. USSR), 95
Shaw, Bernard, 47
Sheremetyevo, 28, 50, 83, 100, 201–2
Shirer, William, 192, 211n
Shneidman, N. Norman, 94, 131, 145, 151ff, 171, 173

Shops, 51, 59, 70, 90, 91, 116
Shortages, 114–17 and *passim*
Shostakovich, Dmitri, 80n, 184
Sinclair, Rear-Admiral, 159, 166
Sinyavsky, André, 184, 190
Slusarski, Tadeusz (C. Poland), 172
Small, Dr Michael, 211
Smith, Hedrick, *see Russians, The*
Snowden, Mrs Philip, 89, 92
Socialism: drabness of life under, 119 and *passim*; quasi-religious nature of, 120–2, 226–7
'Socialist Realism', 68
Solidarity, 219
Solzhenitsyn, Alexander, 25, 34, 61, 70, 109, 115, 185, 209, 223, 224, 227
Soviet attitudes to sport, 23, 150ff, 171–4
Soviet Constitution (1977), 26, 127
Soviet economy, 116–17, 128–9, 130, 212, 221–2
Soviet empire, *see* Russian/Soviet empire
Soviet record in Olympics (before 1980), 23, 26, 94
'Soviets', destroyed by Lenin, 126, 219
Soviet spectators, attitude of, 23, 136, 172
Soviet Union: facing unprecedented crisis, 114–18, 212–13, 214–16, 227; Republics comprising, 169–70n
Spectator, 143, 205
Spivakov, Vladimir, 181, 184, 209
Spontaneity, Soviet intolerance of, 146, 149, 172, 196
Squares (Moscow): Dzerzhinsky, 60, 97; 50th Anniversary of October, 55, 61; Mayakovsky, 51; Nogin, 96; Red, 55–7; Revolution, 55
Stalin, Josef, 46–7, 51, 57, 59, 64; rebuilding of Moscow, 51–2, 65, 68, 130; skyscrapers, 52, 64–5; death, 66–7, 83, 97, 123–5, 130, 160, 184, 187–8, 224; show

trials, 67, 134–5, 187; purges, 123–4, 130, 184
Straub, Jurgen (C. E. Germany), 182
Strikes in USSR (1980), 115–16, 212
Sun, 202
Sunday Telegraph, 118, 216, 219
Sunday Times 99, 116–17
Sverdlov, Yakov, 59, 124

Taganka Theatre, 88, 179
Tallinn, 27, 28, 35, 157ff
Tancred, Peter, 38
Tartu, 158, 164, 165, 170n
Taylor, Frank, 139
Tchaikowsky Conservatory, 91, 181, 183–4
Ten Days That Shook The World, 123, 169
Thatcher, Mrs Margaret, 25, 26, 31–3, 39, 100, 185
Thompson, Daley (C. GB), 141, 147, 148–9, 150, 154, 155
Times, The, 24, 40n, 102, 208, 216, 219
Togliatti, 115–16, 212
Tolstoy, Leo, 57, 63, 187–8, 192, 198, 225
Totalitarianism: nature of, 106, 112–14; Orwell on, 119, 125–8, 217–22
Tower blocks, 50, 51, 52, 61, 64–5, 71–2, 77, 202
Toys, 97
Transport (for Olympics), 57, 133, 181
Tretyakov art gallery, 67–9
Trotsky, Leon, 124, 217–18
Turgenev, Ivan, 63, 187, 188, 198
Twenty-Second Communist Party Congress, 135

Ukraine, 169n, 170, 175–6
Ulanova, 64
Union Jack, 82–3, 100, 183
United States, 23; pulls out of Olympics, 37; *see also* Carter, President Jimmy

Vaughan, Henry, 30
Velikanova, Tatiana, 28, 34, 213, 214n
Vietnam, 25, 32, 108, 132
Viren, Lasse (C. Finland), 156
Visitors to Russia: privileged, 89, 90, 157–8; relief on leaving, 207–9, 224
Vnukovo airport, 21, 28, 157–8
Volgograd Pravda, 133
Volkov, V. (C. USSR), 172
Vyshinsky, Andrei, 67, 135
Vysotsky, Vladimir, 179–80, 185

Wade, Nigel, 140, 214n
Walesa, Lech, 215–16, 219
Walsh, Matthew and Priscilla, 162
Warren, Dave, 147
Webb, Sidney and Beatrice, 46
Wells, Allan, 136, 145, 146–7, 149, 154
Wells, H. G., 120, 125
Wells, Margo, 149
West: Russian attitudes towards, 98, 108–110, 112; triviality of, in comparison with life in Socialist world, 108–10, 208–9, 227; difficulty in comprehending Soviet Union, 112–13, 131–4, 210–12 and *passim*
West Germany, 34, 38
What Must Be Done?: Lenin, 125, 197; Tolstoy, 197; Chernyshevsky, 197; Rusanov, 197
Wilkins, David (C. Ireland), 166–7
Wilkinson, James (C. Ireland), 166–7
Wilson, Edmund, 66
Wilson, Harold, 25
Wilson, Neil, 138, 201
Wojtyla, Karol (Pope John-Paul II), 216, 227
Wood, Andrew, 103
Wooldridge, Ian, 14, 31, 53–4, 66, 73, 83, 90, 101–2, 138, 142, 173–4, 176, 185, 192–3, 201
World Student Games (1973), 23

Yagoda, Ghendrik, 67, 135
Yakunin, Father Gleb, 29, 34, 213,
    214n
Yevtushenko, Yevgeni, 87
Yifter, Miruts (C. Ethiopia), 156,
    177, 193
Young Communist organizations
    (Komsomol, Pioneer, Young
    October), 97, 108, 155

Zagorsk, 87, 90
Zhdanov, Andrei, 124
Zhukov, Georgi, 124
Zil (the 'l' is for 'Lenin',
    abbreviation of 'from Lenin car
    works'), 81
Zimbabwe, 168, 177–8
Zinoviev, Grigory, 124